Flavors

Flavors from Home

Refugees in Kentucky Share Their Stories and Comfort Foods

Aimee Zaring

UNIVERSITY PRESS OF KENTUCKY

Publication of this volume was made possible in part by financial support from Catholic Charities and Kentucky Refugee Ministries.

Scholarly publisher for the Commonwealth,
serving Bellarmine University, Berea College, Centre College of Kentucky, Eastern Kentucky University, The Filson Historical Society, Georgetown College, Kentucky Historical Society, Kentucky State University, Morehead State University, Murray State University, Northern Kentucky University, Transylvania University, University of Kentucky, University of Louisville, and Western Kentucky University.

Editorial and Sales Offices: The University Press of Kentucky
663 South Limestone Street, Lexington, Kentucky 40508-4008
www.kentuckypress.com

Map by Dick Gilbreath.

Except where noted, photos are by the author.

The Library of Congress has cataloged the hardcover edition as follows:

Zaring, Aimee.
  Flavors from home : refugees in Kentucky share their stories and comfort foods / Aimee Zaring.
     pages cm
  Includes bibliographical references and index.
  ISBN 978-0-8131-6091-7 (hardcover : alk. paper) — ISBN 978-0-8131-6093-1 (pdf) — ISBN 978-0-8131-6092-4 (epub)
  1. International cooking. 2. Cooking—Kentucky. 3. Immigrants—United States. 4. Refugees—United States. I. Title.
   TX725.A1Z37 2015
   641.59—dc23   2014047963
ISBN 978-0-8131-6959-0 (pbk. : alk. paper)

This book is printed on acid-free paper meeting the requirements of the American National Standard for Permanence in Paper for Printed Library Materials.

Manufactured in the United States of America.

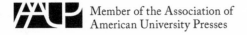   Member of the Association of
          American University Presses

To those without a home
To those making a home
To those who have found home
To my parents, who taught me what home is

When I walk into my kitchen today, I am not alone.
Whether we know it or not, none of us is.
We bring fathers and mothers and kitchen tables,
and every meal we have ever eaten.
Food is never just food. It's also a way of getting at something
else: who we are, who we have been, and who we want to be.

—Molly Wizenberg, *A Homemade Life*

Contents

Photographs follow page 132

Preface

Growing up in Louisville, Kentucky, in the 1970s and 1980s, I had few opportunities to interact with people from other cultures in my largely white, middle-class, suburban community. Sure, the city had its established immigrant neighborhoods—most notably, German and Irish—but I never saw the range of diversity that exists today: African women wrapped from head to toe in colorful *kangas* waiting for buses, Muslim mothers in *hijabs* dropping their children off at school, Bhutanese men strolling down the street wearing flat-topped *topis* on their heads. As a child, the only time I caught a glimpse of someone ostensibly "foreign" was on TV (for those old enough to remember, think Zsa Zsa Gábor and Ricardo Montalbán).

Despite this lack of early contact, or perhaps because of it, I have always had a genuine interest in cultures different from my own. So when I boarded a bus in the spring of 2008 to tour my hometown as part of a Leadership Louisville Center program, I was thrilled to share a seat with a dark-haired, friendly faced Bosnian native. Zeljana Javorek spoke so enthusiastically about her job as an English language trainer (ELT) manager at Catholic Charities Migration and Refugee Services that it reignited my old desire to work with people from other countries—in particular, to teach them English, the language I love, in the city and state I love even more. Zeljana invited me to visit her school, which I did. And the rest, as they say, is history.

At the schools where I have had the pleasure of teaching English to foreign-born students, we occasionally hosted potlucks, giving students the opportunity to share the exotic flavors and cuisines of their homelands: savory *sambusas* from Somalia; tender, succulent pulled pork and *frijoles negros* from Cuba; juicy, vegetable-stuffed *momos* from Bhutan. At these potlucks, it made no difference that we didn't all share the same language, customs, faith, economic status, education level, or skin color. We were simply a group of hungry, adventurous, appreciative souls, chewing and smiling from ear to ear like happy Buddhas. As Franz Kafka wrote,

"So long as you have food in your mouth, you have solved all questions for the time being."

These potlucks inspired this book. At first, I planned to collect only recipes, hoping to preserve them while they were still close to their native sources and before they became altered or Americanized. Soon, however, it became apparent that to present these dishes without telling the stories of the refugees who lovingly prepared them would be like forgetting the saffron in the Persian rice dish *tachin* or omitting the hot chili peppers in the Bhutanese stew *ema datshi*. What eventually emerged, and what the contributors of the recipes and I offer you now, is a collection of oral histories representing some of the diverse refugee populations that have resettled in the commonwealth of Kentucky in the last half century, as explored through their foodways.

Food and culinary traditions are like the *Cliffs Notes* to a culture. One dish can encapsulate the history, topography, climate, and even religious practices of a people and place. As my Burmese friend Mya Zaw says, "If you want to know about our culture, look to the food."

In visiting these refugees' homes and kitchens, listening to their courageous stories, and sharing meals with them, I began to rediscover and appreciate my own cultural heritage, my own personal narrative. As I saw my refugee friends redefining their lives and re-creating their homes during a time of major transition in my own life, I took heart that I, too, could—and would—do the same.

I hope these stories and recipes feed your body, mind, and spirit as much as they have mine. As my Iranian friends say before a meal, *Nooshe jan* (may your soul be nourished).

Introduction

Something curious happens when you talk to people from other countries about their native foods. I once told a Pakistani student in my English as a second language (ESL) class that I liked *boorani*, a layered eggplant and yogurt dish from her region of the world. Her eyes widened beneath the hood of her hijab as she gasped with delight, "How do you know about boorani?" I received a similar reaction while shopping at an ethnic grocery store one day for the ingredients I needed to test a recipe. An African customer at the counter, noting my purchases, raised his eyebrows in shock. "How do you know about cassava leaves?" he asked. "Are you married to an African?"

Nobel Peace Prize winner and former president of South Africa Nelson Mandela said, "If you talk to a man in a language he understands, that goes to his head. If you talk to him in his language, that goes to his heart." I have always believed that food—like a smile, a painting, a piece of music, or a dance—is a kind of universal language—a "heart" language. And I have found that to be true while working on this project.

Over the years, through my involvement with Kentucky's refugee resettlement agencies and as an ESL teacher, and particularly while writing this book, I have made many friends from countries as close to our shores as Cuba and as far away as Vietnam. I've had the honor and privilege of being invited into my new friends' homes. I've laughed with them, grieved with them, celebrated births and weddings with them. I've even cried tears of joy with them as they've been sworn in as US citizens. And I've eaten with them. And eaten. And eaten some more.

If death is the great equalizer, I'm convinced that food is the great unifier. Some of the stories told to me and recorded in this book (with their tellers' permission) might never have been shared if not for the social, pleasurable, nourishing, comforting, healing, and even sacred attributes of preparing and eating a meal together. The kitchen was our safe place, and

1

food was our common ground. What came out of these kitchen visits appears in these pages—forty-two recipes and twenty-three stories of courage, perseverance, and reinvention. *Flavors from Home* spotlights not only the foodways but also the day-to-day struggles, hopes, dreams, fears, and successes of the refugee communities that are changing the face—and flavors—of Kentucky.

COMING TO AMERICA

As of this writing, there are approximately 15.4 million refugees in the world, but on average, only about 1 percent of refugees are resettled into the two dozen or so industrialized nations that are willing to accept them, according to the United Nations High Commissioner for Refugees (UNHCR). The Refugee Act of 1980 defines a refugee as someone who is outside his or her country of nationality and is unable or unwilling to return to that country because of persecution or a well-founded fear of persecution based on race, religion, nationality, membership in a particular social group, or political opinion.

Actress and humanitarian Angelina Jolie has been quoted as saying, "In my experience, going home is the deepest wish of most refugees." But for many refugees, going home is not an option. Economic migrants choose to move to another country to improve their lives, and they can return home if they choose. Refugees, in contrast, are either forced to flee or driven from their homelands and generally cannot return safely.

In the United States, refugees are resettled in hundreds of cities and communities. In the early years of refugee resettlement, the largest percentage of refugees came from Indochina and the former Soviet Union. In the last couple of decades, however, refugees have been arriving from all over the world, especially war-torn areas of Africa, Europe, Central and South Asia, and the Middle East.

The commonwealth of Kentucky is home to several official refugee resettlement agencies that work closely with the US Department of State and the US Committee for Refugees and Immigrants (USCRI). At this time, Catholic Charities Migration and Refugee Services (MRS), Kentucky Refugee Ministries (KRM), and the International Center of Kentucky are the major players in the state's refugee resettlement efforts, and they are mentioned frequently throughout this book. These agencies currently resettle an average of 2,500 refugees a year, with approximately 70 percent of them going to metropolitan Louisville, according to the Kentucky Office for Refugees (KOR).

Exactly how many refugees are currently living in Kentucky is hard to ascertain. Official records weren't kept until the early 1990s, and they don't include refugees who haven't registered with or received assistance from a resettlement agency. Many of these uncounted refugees are "secondary migrants"—that is, refugees who relocate from their initial resettlement site in the United States to another location. But it is safe to say that in the past two decades, Kentucky agencies have resettled tens of thousands of refugees representing more than forty different nationalities and ethnic groups. (See the appendix, "Fast Facts about Refugees.")

Refugees are asked to adapt to American ways from the moment they are accepted for resettlement in the United States. They come to America with little more than the clothes on their backs, often knowing little to no English, and they are expected to be well on their way to self-sufficiency within months of their arrival. But one thing they don't have to adapt to, especially with the widespread availability of international ingredients, is American foodways. In fact, the majority of refugees I know still cook only their native foods at home. As Naomi Duguid writes in *Burma: Rivers of Flavor*, for many refugees, "food is the last refuge."

KITCHEN AS REFUGE

When refugees prepare their native dishes in their American kitchens, it's like a lifeline to their home countries, a way for them to find solace in an unfamiliar land, retain their customs, reconnect with their personal past and heritage, and preserve a sense of identity. For new refugees in particular, the kitchen is also a place where they can produce a sense of normalcy and stability in an otherwise strange and sometimes scary new world. It is a place where they can serve rather than be served, a place where they can express themselves and exercise some degree of control in a land where they often feel powerless and unheard.

To give you an idea of how important native foods are to new refugees, Bosnian native Mirzet Mustafić, who resettled in Kentucky in 1994, drove more than 100 miles to Lexington once a month to shop at a store that carried eastern European items for the growing Bosnian refugee community in Bowling Green. That said, I found that refugees who have been in the United States the longest, such as Mirzet and Irene Finley from Hungary (1957), do not prepare their native dishes as often as they used to. It will be interesting to see if new refugees' culinary habits follow the same pattern.

"I *Was* a Refugee"

The first time I spoke to one of my contributors, Rwandan native and restaurateur Nicolas Kiza, I asked if he was a refugee, a prerequisite for inclusion in the book. He said yes and then corrected himself: "I mean I *was* a refugee." That's an important distinction. For simplicity's sake, I often use the word *refugee* to refer to the contributors of this book and all immigrants who come to the United States as refugees, victims of human trafficking, asylum seekers, and others with a similar status. However, "refugee" is a temporary status. Refugees are required by law to apply for a green card (permanent residence) after being in the country for one full year, and most of the refugees I know can't wait for the day they become US citizens and can declare America their new home country.

I narrowed the focus of this book to refugees because the refugee experience is unique and because I found few books that featured stories about refugees and the cuisines of their home countries. Next, I looked for people with powerful stories (which describes just about every refugee I know) who enjoy cooking their native foods and were willing to share both their stories and their recipes.

The majority of refugees featured in *Flavors from Home* are from Louisville, reflecting Kentucky's refugee demographics; however, for greater inclusiveness and to more fully capture the diversity of refugees' experiences in the Bluegrass State, I visited other cities with significant refugee populations, including Bowling Green, Lexington, Owensboro, and areas in northern Kentucky. Including a representative from every refugee population or every country wasn't feasible, but I made a concerted effort to feature those countries from which the greatest number of refugees have resettled in Kentucky: Bhutan, Bosnia, Burma (now Myanmar), Cuba, Iraq, and Somalia. The four Burmese refugees included in this book reflect the diversity in Myanmar, a country with approximately 135 different ethnic groups. I also included refugees from some of the smallest and most persecuted minority ethnic groups, including a Burmese Rohingya and a Somali Bantu.

Choosing to concentrate on that which unites us rather than divides us, I included little information about politics, war, and other conflicts, unless it was critical to a contributor's story, provided a historical backdrop, or clarified situations or events. In these stories, you will follow individuals through the jungles of Burma and through the jungles of the Democratic Republic of the Congo—one fighting for his life and the other running for his. You will meet one of the original Vietnamese "boat people" who spent more than thirty days at sea and later became one of Louisville's most successful restaurateurs. You will meet highly educated men and women—doctors, lawyers, engineers—who once had thriving careers in their homelands but have struggled to find employment in America or have had to accept low-income jobs well beneath their education and skill levels. You will meet some who are disenchanted with their lives in the United States and others who would bleed red, white, and blue if they could. Some have been able to achieve the American Dream—raising families, buying cars and homes, and even opening their own businesses after years of sweat, sacrifice, and determination.

Some of these refugees have started their own restaurants or catering companies and are having a direct impact on our regional foodways: Huong "CoCo" Tran (Roots and Heart & Soy), the Akrami family (Ata's Catering and Shiraz Mediterranean Grill), Dr. Mahn Myint Saing (Simply Thai), and Nicolas Kiza (Kalisimbi Bar and Grill). Many more refugees are working behind the scenes as cooks or other support staff. William Thang has worked in food preparation for restaurants and a grocery store and aspires to open his own restaurant featuring his native Burmese cuisine. Azerbaijani Elmira Tonian once served food from a street cart in

Ukraine just to survive; she now uses that cooking expertise and her own creative flair to make original dishes for her friend's catering company. That friend, Arina Saforova, co-owns an ethnic market to make her native foods more accessible to immigrants and Americans alike.

Some refugees are growing their own vegetables in community gardens and selling their produce at farmers' markets and restaurants as part of the farm-to-table movement and to supplement their households' income. Still others share samples of their native cuisines through community festivals and events or simply among their families, friends, neighbors, and coworkers. Because money is scarce for many new refugees, food sometimes serves as currency, offered in exchange for other goods and services or as a means of repayment.

Make It Your Own

America has always been a land of immigrants, and what we consider "American" cuisine is a reflection of that melting pot. Louisville chef and Korean American Edward Lee writes in *Smoke and Pickles: Recipes and Stories from a New Southern Kitchen*, "There is a rich diversity in our cuisine—this thing that, for lack of a better term, we call American Cuisine—that is defined by our never-ending search for reinvention." Just as refugees are reinventing their lives and homes in the United States, they are also contributing to the endless reinvention that is American cuisine.

Foods that are considered "southern" today were influenced by Native Americans, Spanish explorers, European immigrants (including the Scots-Irish, many of whom settled in Kentucky's Appalachian region), and African and Caribbean slaves. Waves of immigrants from more diverse regions of the world, especially after the Vietnam War, continued to influence regional American cuisine. Based on my own observations, the foodways among Kentucky's refugees today tend to mirror the African American "soul food" tradition of making the most with the ingredients on hand and finding inventive ways to create filling, homemade dishes from scratch.

Each chapter in this collection is followed by one or more recipes from the refugee featured in that section. The only stipulation I gave the cooks was to select recipes that represent their homelands in some way—preferably a dish that comforts them and makes them feel closer to home. By giving them this flexibility, I hoped to gain broader insight into their cultures—and them—through their personal selections.

What dishes would emerge? Main entrees. One-dish meals. Fresh vegetables, grains, and legumes. Bean soups and rice- or potato-based dishes. Dumplings, breads, and plantains. Hmmm. Not so different from the traditional starch-laden comfort foods of the South—and prepared with the same great care. Appetizers and desserts are scarce in these pages; both are considered luxuries in many of the represented countries, whether due to food scarcity in general or the scarcity or cost of ingredients such as fruits, eggs, and sugar. Every country has its "sweets," but for many of the contributors, desserts weren't their go-to comfort food.

One thing remained consistent: almost every contributor resisted providing an actual recipe. Translating the ingredients and methods was difficult for many, especially those with poor English skills, but more important, most contributors simply hadn't learned to cook this way and didn't want to stifle others' creativity in the kitchen. They preferred to teach me the way they themselves had learned to cook—and still do: by memory, instinct, taste, observation, imagination. These are the tools of their trade.

"Aimee, you have to make it your own!" my Iranian friend Arash Taarifi would admonish me whenever I tried to pin down an ingredient or a measurement. Though frustrating at the time, these words eventually became my rallying cry, and now I find myself using recipes and exact measurements less and less in my own cooking.

Whenever possible, I used the recipe's name in the contributor's native language, along with an English translation. If the cook didn't know the name of a recipe or none existed, we made one up that accurately reflected the dish. In the introduction to each recipe, I note any unusual ingredients and where to locate them, helpful tips in preparing the dish, and suggestions for adapting the recipes to American tastes and kitchens. Sidebars sprinkled throughout the chapters provide further information about cultural topics and ingredients.

Recipes were tested more than once in test kitchens by myself and by volunteers. All the contributors reviewed their recipes (and stories) for accuracy. Yet, as we all know, things can get lost in translation. Bear in mind, too, that many factors play a part in the success of a recipe, including stovetop and oven temperatures, cooking equipment and methods, quality of ingredients, and, of course, the cook's experience and knowledge.

Some of the ingredients in these recipes should be handled with care. For example, turmeric, curry, and saffron can stain skin and fabrics. In addition, some hot chili pepper varieties can cause allergic reactions, skin irritation, or a temporary burning sensation.

Rather than relying heavily on food styling or staging, and for the sake of cultural preservation and authenticity, every effort was made to photograph contributors in their natural environments, and the dishes are shown on the cooks' own serving pieces.

A NOTE ABOUT CHAPTER ORDER

One of the first questions I asked each refugee was, "When did you come to the United States?" I did this partly to put them at ease because I knew it would be an easy question to answer. Almost everyone, without hesitation, could tell me the exact date he or she had arrived. One contributor could even pinpoint the exact hour of his arrival. Their date of arrival is something they will never forget—a type of death, but also a rebirth.

Thus, the stories are ordered by date. This helped spotlight trends in Kentucky refugee populations over the past fifty years, as well as how the communities and refugee resettlement agencies have responded and adapted to these immigrant influxes. Of course, you don't have to read the chapters in sequence. You might prefer to read all the stories from the same country or region, allowing the details and anecdotes of one to enhance and shed light on another. Feel free to create your own journey, or, as my good friend Arash Taarifi would say, "Make it your own!"

Part of the proceeds from this book will help support the efforts of Catholic Charities Migration and Refugee Services and Kentucky Refugee Ministries.

1

Hungary

Irene Finley, October 23, 1957

"I just realized . . . how will we know each other?" Irene Finley asks over the phone in her honey-thick Hungarian accent.

Irene and I have never met, but I feel like I already know her. A friend told her about my project, and the next thing I knew, I had a handwritten recipe for chicken paprikás and a tape entitled "Irene's Testimony."

It is a clear-skied spring morning. The fresh air and blooming flowers are as comforting as the rocking chairs lining Cracker Barrel's front entrance. I easily find Irene in the restaurant's gift shop, a brown-eyed blonde wearing a Mickey Mouse T-shirt, just as she described. Irene's husband Frank, a retired vocational teacher, is joining us. When our breakfast plates arrive, piled high with made-to-order eggs, pancakes, grits, and biscuits and gravy, Irene and Frank bow their heads to pray over their food, and I see how central faith is in the couple's life. In fact, ever since experiencing a spiritual reawakening in the early years of her marriage, Irene takes every opportunity—from formal speaking engagements at schools and churches to casual conversations with people she has just met—to share the story of how God delivered her family safely out of Hungary decades ago.

On October 23, 1956, a group of peaceful student-led protesters marched through the Hungarian capital of Budapest, protesting the government's Soviet-backed policies. Although the revolution of 1956 ultimately failed, it paved the way for the democratization that would later come to Hungary and other eastern bloc nations.

"Anything could have happened to us, but God had a purpose for my life."
—Irene Finley

Irene was only eleven years old at the time, but she recalls those volatile months following the revolt with astounding clarity. She remembers the scarcity of food and standing in line for bread with her older sister; her parents' overnight decision to take their children and flee with only the clothes on their backs, a small parcel of food, and a small stash of money hidden inside their gloves; walking more than forty miles in the deep snow and bitter January cold as they made a narrow escape to Yugoslavia under the cover of night.

Back in the 1950s, the capital city of Hungary, a country roughly the size of Indiana, was far from the hub of tourism and commerce it is today. Irene grew up on the "Pest" side of Budapest, east of the Danube River and across from the hilly "Buda" side. It was filled with factories and apartment housing for blue-collar workers. Irene's mother was a seamstress, and her father worked in a factory as a shoe designer. The family lived in a two-room apartment and sometimes rented out the kitchen just to make ends meet. They did a lot of canning, which supplemented their food supply throughout the year. They also ate horse meat (though many horse lovers might bristle at the idea), which was a cheap alternative to other meats and a good source of nutrients.

At the time, few people had automobiles, and there was no TV. The main religion was Roman Catholic, but people weren't allowed to preach the gospel publicly or mention Jesus. Even though her parents weren't religious, Irene remembers that she always had a hunger for the Lord, often running off and sneaking into churches as a child. She believes, in fact, that God's hand was on her family when they joined the exodus of about 200,000 refugees leaving Hungary. What if they had been stopped by one of the Russian guards checking tickets on the train out of Budapest? What if the family who invited them in for a meal during their long trek to the Yugoslavian border had turned them over to the enemy? And what if the barbed wire fence at the border hadn't already been cut, allowing just enough space for a body to squeeze through? Irene would think years later that it was as if God had gone before them, like the parting of the Red Sea, and all they had to do was walk through.

"We could have been shot," Irene says. "Anything could have happened to us, but God had a purpose for my life."

Irene and her family arrived at Ellis Island on October 23, 1957—exactly one year from the start of the Hungarian Revolution. After ten months of living on Cream of Wheat, cheese, and rice in three different refugee camps, they spent their first Thanksgiving in New York, and the feast they sampled (except for the turkey, which they had never had and were afraid to eat) must have tasted like manna.

New York lived up to Irene's expectations of America—a rich, stylish, progressive country. However, the family didn't stay in the Big Apple for long. At the time, official refugee resettlement organizations did not exist. Refugees had to find sponsors—relatives living in the States, or a church or some other organization willing to help them until they could get on their feet. Irene had an aunt and uncle living in eastern Kentucky.

If Irene had any preconceived image of the South, it was of plantations and southern belles in hoop skirts. Imagine her surprise when she found herself on a train wending through the mountains and hollers of Appalachia toward McRoberts, a small coal-mining community near Hazard.

"It is really a dramatic shock when you come from one culture and go to another culture and just totally have to change your way to be like the other country," Irene says.

There is a good reason why there are few refugees in eastern Kentucky. Immigrants and refugees typically, and understandably, go where the jobs are. In Appalachia, jobs are hard to come by, even for the locals. Irene's father had no other choice but to leave town and learn a new trade. He went to Virginia and apprenticed in shoe repair.

Irene was placed in a first-grade class even though she should have been in eighth grade. But within six months she had learned a great deal of English. She loved her teacher and her school, where the students read the Bible every morning and recited the Pledge of Allegiance. She was fortunate that she never experienced discrimination. Rather, people thought she was unusual and interesting because she was from another country. What was unfamiliar to Irene, however, was the sight of African Americans. She had never seen a black person in Hungary. She was scared of them at first but soon realized that they were no more foreign than she was.

After completing his apprenticeship, Irene's father sent applications all over the country and finally landed a job at Bacons, in Louisville's St. Matthews neighborhood. In the early 1960s he opened his own shop in Clarksville, Indiana. Years later the family moved back to

Louisville, where Irene's father ran a shoe repair shop at the corner of Shelby and Gray Streets. Even though he never learned English well, Irene's father achieved the American Dream: a house and a new car that he purchased without borrowing a dime, and a successful business and career.

Irene and Frank, married for almost fifty years and with three children, are like a comedy duo as they tell the story of how they met, interrupting each other's version to make corrections.

"I couldn't stand him," says the spunky Hungarian. "The only thing I liked about him is that he had pretty blue eyes and he talked to my girl-friend." (Frank's friend was apparently ignoring Irene's girlfriend, his date for the evening.) Frank teases that he knew Irene would come around eventually.

After they married, Irene worked in clerical jobs for a few years before choosing to stay home and raise their children. After the children had grown, she went back to work as a manager at the Dairy Queen in Mount Washington, where she and Frank still live. It's a quiet neighborhood; their home, situated on a spacious lot, is lovingly decorated and filled with warm memories from Irene's past: a Hungarian doll collection, an eastern European–inspired bathroom, and framed pictures of Budapest. Irene remained at Dairy Queen for eighteen years, often sharing her story of escape and survival with coworkers and customers.

When I ask Irene, who has been here longer than any refugee I know, if she has any advice for newly arrived refugees, she gives the same winning recipe she followed herself: "Persevere. Learn the language. Work wherever you can get started. Work your way up. Everything is possible if you work hard." But above all, Irene credits her faith for her success in this country. "We, as a nation, should be praying for our leaders and thanking God that we live in a country where we have freedom of religion," Irene says. She cautions that what occurred in Hungary could just as easily happen here. "We need to intercede and be aware of what's happening around the world instead of being apathetic and allowing things to go on until they reach a point of no return."

The Power of Paprika

Paprika is one of the most consumed spices in the world. It is versatile and goes well with beef, poultry, fish, vegetables, and sauces; it can be used as a garnish or to add color to a dish. The spice is made when *Capsicum annuum*, a pepper plant from the nightshade family that is native to the Americas, is dried and ground into a fine powder. It is believed that Columbus brought the paprika pepper plant to Spain from the Antilles. The spice is now commonly associated with cuisines in Hungary, Turkey, Spain, Portugal, Greece, Romania, Croatia, Serbia, Bulgaria, and Morocco.

Many types and flavor grades of paprika exist, ranging from sweet to hot. Hungary and Spain produce the most well known paprikas. The "regular" paprika commonly found in grocery stores is usually a blend of varieties and has a relatively neutral flavor. This is a good choice for garnishing or adding color to a dish.

Sweet paprika has a rich, pungent, bell pepper taste and lacks heat. It's a good multipurpose paprika and is an essential ingredient in Hungarian goulash and chicken paprikás. Hot paprika is made from dried chili peppers and is similar in taste to cayenne, but less spicy. Spanish paprika (or pimentón) tends to be a little more robust in aroma than Hungarian paprika, with a smoky, woodsy, or "cooked" flavor. Smoked paprika can be either sweet or hot, but it should be used sparingly because of its intense flavor.

Paprika peppers are loaded with capsaicin (the heat element in chilies), which has anti-inflammatory and antioxidant properties. Capsaicin has been known to help improve blood circulation and digestion, as well as fight common infections.

Irene's Chicken Paprikás

Chicken paprikás (PAP-ree-cahsh) is classic Hungarian comfort food. The creamy red paprika sauce is a trademark of Hungarian cuisine. This dish is traditionally served with *nokedli* (no-KED-lee), a small eastern European egg noodle (similar to the German spaetzle).

Irene inherited a love of cooking from her mother and grandmother, who taught her how to cook when she was a young girl. Though she serves mainly American food now, on special occasions or when she is entertaining guests, she will cook Hungarian food. A common request is her chicken paprikás, one of her personal favorites.

Hungarians generally use a combination of dark and white chicken meat in their paprikás, but for a healthier version, substitute boneless, skinless chicken breasts or chicken tenders (reduce the cooking time for tenders).

Serves 4 to 6
Ready in about 45 minutes

> 5 tablespoons vegetable oil
> ½ cup chopped onion
> 2½ teaspoons sweet paprika (preferably Hungarian)
> Ground cayenne pepper to taste (optional)
> 1 teaspoon salt
> 1 teaspoon black pepper
> 1 whole chicken, separated into legs, thighs, wings, etc. (or 4 to 6 boneless, skinless chicken breasts or 10 to 12 chicken tenders)
> 1 (8-ounce) container sour cream (preferably regular)
> ¼ cup all-purpose flour
> ½ cup 2 percent milk

Heat oil in a Dutch oven or large saucepan. Over medium heat, sauté onion until translucent. Add paprika, cayenne pepper, salt, and black pepper. Stir to combine. Add chicken and just enough water to cover.

Bring to a boil, then turn down to medium-low heat. Cook with the lid partially covering the pan until the chicken becomes tender, about 30 minutes or less. (For chicken tenders, adjust the cooking time to 15 to 18 minutes.) Stir occasionally. Make sure not to overcook the chicken. When the chicken is done, remove it from the pot and set aside. Reserve the liquid and keep it warm over low heat. Cover the chicken with aluminum foil to keep it warm.

In a small bowl, combine sour cream, flour, and milk. Stir or whisk briskly, until smooth.

Raise the heat to medium and whisk this sour cream mixture into the liquid in the Dutch oven. Stir until it thickens to a gravy consistency. Add chicken and combine.

Serve over homemade dumplings (see Irene's Nokedli recipe), store-bought dumplings, or spaetzle (Irene prefers the Maggi brand of spaetzle). If desired, garnish with a sprinkle of sweet paprika or cayenne pepper. Irene likes to serve this dish with a side salad.

Irene's Hungarian Goulash

In Hungary, goulash is also referred to as shepherd's stew. One theory is that the dish originated in the ninth century, when Hungarian shepherds would add hot water to dried meats and vegetables to make soup. Goulash can be served plain, like a stew, or with the small Hungarian egg noodle nokedli.

In this recipe, Irene incorporates potatoes, which add heartiness to the dish and help thicken the sauce. Although in many goulash recipes the sauce is poured over the dumplings in the last stage, Irene says that Hungarians almost always combine the dumplings in the final mix.

Serves 4 to 6
Ready in about 1½ to 2 hours

> 2 tablespoons olive oil
> 1 large yellow onion, chopped
> 4 to 5 cloves garlic, peeled and chopped or minced
> 2 tablespoons sweet paprika (preferably Hungarian)
> 1 teaspoon dried crushed chili pepper, 1 whole chopped jalapeño,
>   or ½ teaspoon ground cayenne pepper (optional)
> 1½ pounds stew meat, cut into ½-inch cubes
> ½ tablespoon salt
> ½ tablespoon black pepper

4 large carrots, peeled and cut into 1-inch pieces, or 1 (16-ounce) bag mini-carrots

3 potatoes, peeled and chopped into 1-inch chunks

In a large pot, heat olive oil. Sauté onion and garlic in oil over medium heat, stirring occasionally, until the onions are translucent. Take care not to burn the garlic. Add paprika, crushed chili pepper to taste, meat, salt, and black pepper. Brown the meat on medium-low heat. Add just enough water to cover the meat. Taste the liquid and add more salt, pepper, and other seasonings if desired. Bring to a boil, then lower heat to medium-low.

Add carrots and cook with the meat, with the lid partially covering the pot, for about 20 minutes. Add potatoes and more water, if necessary—just enough to cover the meat, potatoes, and carrots.

Continue to cook slowly for about 30 minutes over medium-low heat, partially covered, until the vegetables and meat are tender. (The sauce should reduce by about half. Adding the dumplings later also thickens the sauce slightly.)

While the meat is cooking, prepare dumplings (see Irene's Nokedli recipe) or spaetzle.

When the meat is cooked through, add the cooked dumplings or spaetzle to the goulash. Stir until well combined. Serve warm with a side salad.

Irene's Nokedli (Hungarian Dumplings)

Nokedli are popular in eastern Europe. They are traditionally served with goulash or chicken paprikás but can also be served as a side dish with butter and topped with parsley.

I know what you're thinking: make dumplings from scratch? But these chewy little dumplings are fairly easy to make and can be whipped up in a flash. Some recipes use a noodle grater (or spaetzle maker) to form the dumplings, but Irene's version doesn't—good news for those who don't own one of these gadgets.

Nokedli can be made in advance, but only about an hour ahead of time, Irene advises. She also suggests adding some butter or a bit of gravy from goulash or paprikás to keep the dumplings moist while rewarming them in the microwave. (Use the warming feature or a low wattage for a short period, increasing the time as necessary.)

Pressed for time? Many stores carry frozen or dried dumplings or spaetzle (Irene likes the Maggi brand).

Serves 4 to 6
Ready in less than 30 minutes

8¼ cups water (divided)
½ tablespoon salt
4 large eggs
1½ cups all-purpose flour (more as needed)

Bring 8 cups of water to a boil in a medium saucepan (make sure the pan is deeper than wide). Add salt.

Meanwhile, beat 4 eggs in a medium bowl. Add ¼ cup of tepid water. With a fork (not a whisk), slowly add the flour and stir until the mixture becomes sticky and difficult to stir, but don't beat it completely smooth. (It might be necessary to add more flour to achieve the proper consistency.)

Drop ½-teaspoon portions of dough into the boiling water. (Every time the spoon is dipped into the hot water, it helps remove the sticky dough from the spoon.) The curve of the teaspoon give the dough a slight crescent shape as it's dropped into the water (but the shape isn't critical). When the dumplings and water start rising almost to overflowing, quickly turn the heat down to low.

Cook for approximately 10 minutes, or until the dumplings begin to float to the top. Test for doneness by cutting into a dumpling. The center should be firm, not mushy or doughy.

Carefully transfer the dumplings to a colander and drain. Rinse with warm water (to keep them from cooling).

Irene Finley, 1957

If you're serving Hungarian goulash, add the dumplings to the stew mixture just before serving.

Jó étvágyat
(Hungarian for *bon appétit*)

2

Vietnam

Huong "CoCo" Tran, August 2, 1975

Huong "CoCo" Tran says, "Ask me anything. I don't mind." Her words are as warm and generous as the smile that follows, and soon I will learn just how much they reflect her mission in life: to give back.

CoCo and I are seated on backless stools at a high-top table in her vegetarian restaurant, Heart & Soy, in Louisville's eccentric Highlands neighborhood. We are surrounded by lively persimmon walls and colorful photos of soybeans, soy milk, and tofu. If anyone knows tofu, it's CoCo. Behind the main dining space is a smaller glassed-in room containing a gleaming stainless steel tofu machine—according to CoCo, the first in Kentucky. It is, however, just one of CoCo's many firsts.

A natural trailblazer, CoCo has introduced Louisville to a host of international culinary delights. In 1981 she opened her first restaurant, The Egg Roll Machine, the first Chinese fast-food restaurant in Louisville. In 1984 she gave the city its first modern Vietnamese and French cuisine restaurant, Café Mimosa. After becoming a vegetarian, coinciding with her conversion to Buddhism, CoCo opened Zen Garden in 2000, the city's first Asian vegetarian restaurant. Zen Tea House followed in 2008, another new concept for Louisville. Heart & Soy and its adjoining sister restaurant, Roots, are CoCo's latest ventures. Both are vegetarian restaurants dedicated to "mindful, compassionate cooking." Heart & Soy showcases Asian "street food," while Roots features international fare with CoCo's unique twists on her native Vietnamese cuisine.

"I love to create. I love to bring the new idea to this town." —Huong "CoCo" Tran
(Photo by Julie Johnston)

"I love it," CoCo says, smiling and shaking her head emphatically. "I love to create. I love to bring the new idea to this town."

People have taken note. In 1990 CoCo was recognized in *Louisville Magazine* as one of the city's leading businesswomen. In addition to receiving positive reviews in the local and national press, Roots and Heart & Soy have consistently received the *LEO [Louisville Eccentric Observer] Weekly* Readers' Choice Best Vegetarian Food Award. CoCo has even cooked for dignitaries, including the Dalai Lama's staff when His Holiness came to town in 2013.

Once when an interviewer asked CoCo how old she was (she was forty-four at the time), she responded, "I'm fourteen. I came here fourteen years ago, and I start from scratch. I had to learn how to talk, how to eat. . . . I was like a newborn baby. I start over."

CoCo's childhood was relatively normal and happy in Vietnam's south-central coast province of Quang Ngai—a well-known Vietcong stronghold during the Vietnam War and the setting of Tim O'Brien's classic short story "The Things They Carried." Her father was a businessman and a prominent supporter of democracy. When the political climate changed, creating instability in her hometown, she moved to the family's city home in Saigon, where she lived from 1965 to 1975.

During this period, her mother died in a plane crash. CoCo, only eighteen at the time, helped her older sister raise their younger brothers and sisters. CoCo also assisted in her sister's restaurant, Café Mimosa (the same name she later gave to her own restaurant in Louisville). However, CoCo wasn't allowed to cook at the restaurant, and her sister used to shoo her out of the kitchen. CoCo admits that cooking wasn't her forte. Everything she knew about cooking she had learned by watching her mother and sister and the servants in her parents' household. What happened when she did cook? "I burned the rice. I cook terrible," she says.

CoCo made up for her lack of cooking skills with her keen senses. "I taste. I smell. I look. That's the way I cook. That's the way I learned." She sampled dishes at other restaurants and reported back to her sister. "I know what's good and what's not."

Let's Talk Tofu

Tofu is made by coagulating soy milk (made from soybeans) and pressing the resulting curds into blocks. Tofu is believed to have originated in ancient China 2,000 years ago, and it has been a staple in Asian cuisine for hundreds of years. In recent decades it has grown in popularity in Western countries, often standing in for meat in vegetarian cooking. On its own, tofu is bland, but it easily absorbs marinade flavors and can be used in a variety of dishes—from soups to desserts.

Each week, roughly 1,000 pounds of tofu are produced at Roots and Heart & Soy. The soybeans, which come from London, Ohio, are some of the freshest and purest available in the area, according to CoCo. Her fresh, organic, non-GMO (genetically modified organism), and MSG-free tofu is available for sale at Heart & Soy.

Many varieties of tofu exist (regular, silken, firm, extra firm, etc.), so be sure to use the type specified in a recipe. Tofu is sold at most groceries and can generally be found near the produce section in a refrigerated unit.

When she wasn't helping at the restaurant, CoCo worked as a pharmaceutical representative, a job that required travel. She was visiting her childhood home in Quang Ngai when her life—and the lives of her countrymen—took a drastic turn. On April 30, 1975, Communist troops from North Vietnam and the Provisional Revolutionary Government of South Vietnam invaded and overtook Saigon, ending the war and a century of Western influence. CoCo found herself in the midst of a mob scene as she tried to make her way to a ferry and return to Saigon. Her older sister, who was unable to leave at the time, asked CoCo to escort her adopted eleven-year-old daughter to freedom and safety. CoCo still recalls, even thirty-odd years later, the horrific accident that occurred just hours after the child was entrusted to her care. With thousands of people fighting their way onto the ferry, CoCo and the young girl were pushed into the water as they boarded. CoCo surfaced. The child never did. CoCo spent the rest of the day and night frantically searching for the little girl. Eventually she had to return to Saigon—alone and defeated. (She never forgot the child and spent the next three decades trying to lo-

The tofu machine at Heart & Soy produces about 1,000 pounds of fresh tofu every week.

cate her. Finally, in 2008, she found her niece alive and well in Vietnam with two children of her own.)

Because of CoCo's father's politics, the family knew they were no longer safe in Vietnam. On May 2 CoCo and members of her extended family—twelve adults and six children—left Saigon with only some cash and some gold and an extra change of clothing. The only thing they knew for sure was that they would pay any price for freedom.

The family members staggered their individual departures to avoid arousing suspicion and reconnected near Long Hai beach, where American ships were supposed to be waiting to pick up refugees. No ships were in sight. The family negotiated with a fisherman, paying him to transport them on his small, poorly supplied fishing boat toward international waters. CoCo remembers how dark it was that first night at sea and how terrified she was, not knowing where they would end up or whether they would even survive another day. Finally, in the distance, they spotted a merchant ship. Just when they thought their luck had turned, the captain of the Taiwanese merchant ship demanded the exorbitant sum of $9,000 for food and transportation. They gave him everything they had and traveled from port to port, alongside cows and buffalo. They stopped at Thailand, Hong Kong, and Okinawa, but each port refused them entry. At the time, no official refugee program existed to support the people who were fleeing Vietnam. Without relatives or sponsors at these port cities, no country was willing to take in CoCo's family.

Meanwhile, CoCo's younger brother, Tran Thien Tran, was in America working tirelessly to find a way to help his stranded kin out on the open seas. He was living in Kentucky, attending the University of Louisville's J. B. Speed School of Engineering. The family's hope was that Tran could find them local sponsors so they could join him in the States. After thirty-six days at sea, the Trans finally got word that Taiwan would admit them, on the condition that they not stay on the island for an extended period. Back in the States, sponsoring groups from local churches and the University of Louisville, along with a few individual households, rallied to assist the Tran family.

A grainy photo from the *Louisville Times* shows a tearful CoCo giving her brother a long-awaited hug at Standiford Field airport. It is hard to reconcile this woman with the confident, relaxed, successful restaurateur sitting across from me now and smiling broadly, brown eyes shining behind maroon-rimmed glasses—the American Dream personified.

Soon after CoCo arrived in Louisville, her sponsor announced that she was taking CoCo downtown for lunch. CoCo's first dining-out experience in the United States was McDonald's. She had never had a hamburger or any kind of fast food in Vietnam. The sponsor ordered for her. "I open my eyes and ears," CoCo says. "I watch her order." CoCo thought to herself, *I can do like this with Vietnamese food. I can cook. I can sell.* But it would take six years for this idea to become a reality. In the interim, she worked at Derby Cone, packing ice cream cones and earning $2.01 an hour, standing for long stretches in a sweltering factory.

"My tears and sweat come together," CoCo says, remembering those early years in a foreign land. "I feel so bad how poor I am."

CoCo and her family managed to save enough money for a down payment on their first home. But instead of this being a joyful event, CoCo cried because she had never been in debt before. She felt poor and ashamed.

One day CoCo's boss at Derby Cone overheard her talking about her desire to open a fast-food Chinese restaurant. He jumped on the idea, imagining a big chain like Kentucky Fried Chicken. "I had little dream," CoCo says. "He had big dream." Her boss signed a three-year lease for a small space on Bardstown Road and placed CoCo in charge of the restaurant. CoCo initially included some Vietnamese dishes on the menu, but when she found that "Louisville wasn't ready," she switched to all Chinese food. Like so many start-up enterprises, the restaurant's first year was a bust, and her partner pulled out. However, CoCo convinced him to let her buy his share with a low-interest loan. She worked even harder, seven days a week. Once when she was sick, she used the space under the sink as a makeshift bed.

Three years later, CoCo's hard work began to pay off. The Eggroll Machine had done so well that CoCo opened another restaurant, Café Mimosa (formerly located at the site where CoCo and I now sit). CoCo named her newest restaurant Roots because she felt like she was returning home. But where in the world did the name CoCo come from? CoCo laughs and explains that her staff gave her this familial nickname, derived from *cô* (aunt in Vietnamese).

Although she never married or had children, CoCo has almost two dozen nieces and nephews. And between them and her businesses, CoCo jokes, "I think that's enough."

If Louisville has anyone to thank for its vegetarian restaurant scene, it may be a Buddhist monk. CoCo met him in 1998 in California, and he talked to her about the environment, health, and compassion. After that life-altering conversation, CoCo became a vegetarian. And once she changed her diet, the severe asthma and allergies she had battled for years cleared

Roots and Heart & Soy are dedicated to "mindful, compassionate cooking." (Photo by Julie Johnston)

up. Her immunity and overall health improved. She began to cook healthier. "That's why I want to pass it on to everybody and to bring the good health to family and to other people," she says.

In 1998 CoCo sold Café Mimosa to one of her staff because serving meat no longer aligned with her personal convictions. Those convictions presented another dilemma when two of her nephews, brothers Michael and Stephen Ton (the former a trained chef and the latter a businessman and restaurant manager), asked for her help in starting their own restaurant. She didn't want to cook with meat or fish and didn't want to help others do it either. So she made a deal with her nephews. She would help them find a location and introduce them to people she knew. The rest was up to them. Their restaurant, Basa (a type of catfish found in Vietnam and Thailand), opened in 2007. Specializing in Vietnamese cuisine with a modern French flair, it quickly made a splash and was even a finalist for the James Beard Best New Restaurant Award in 2008. CoCo is very proud of her nephews.

"It's very tough," she says of running a restaurant. "You have to love what you do. If you know what you want to do, hang in there. Be patient. You can't do it if only half your heart is in it."

CoCo has now lived in the United States longer than she lived in Vietnam. "The first twenty-five years I do what I need to do to survive," she says. "Last twelve years, I just want to do whatever I can for other people. I never forget when I first came to this country, they helped me."

One way CoCo gives back to her community and to her loyal customers is by offering a free meal at Roots and Heart & Soy the Wednesday before Thanksgiving. Donations are voluntary and benefit local charities.

"I never say thank you enough to be in this country and be in this town. Every day I want to say thank you. I tell you true, this is the best country. I am very strong because I have freedom."

CoCo's Green Curry Soup

Although yellow curry soups are more common in Vietnam, CoCo created this green curry recipe and serves it at Roots to distinguish it from the yellow version offered on her Heart & Soy menu.

This has become one of my favorite go-to soups. Flavorful, healthy, and easy to prepare, it's perfect for any season.

Green curry paste, commonly sold in small cans, can be found in most Asian markets and in the ethnic sections of some American markets. One tablespoon of green curry paste yields a mild level of heat. Start off with a small amount, taste, and add more if desired. For extra nutrition and a punch of green color, CoCo likes to put some spinach leaves in a blender and add them to the soup in the final stages of cooking.

Edamame are young, green soybeans. They can be found fresh and frozen at Asian, ethnic, and some organic markets such as Whole Foods. This recipe uses just the bean removed from the pod (shelled).

Lemongrass is an aromatic herb commonly used in Southeast Asian cooking. It is available fresh and sometimes frozen at Asian and some well-stocked American markets. The root end and the green leaf ends can be discarded, as well as the outer layer or two of the stalk. For this recipe, the stalk can be thinly sliced, put into a food processor, and finely ground.

The potatoes can be left unpeeled for additional nutrients and to save time.

Serves 6 to 8
Ready in about 1 to 1½ hours

> Vegetable or olive oil for frying tofu and coating pan
> 2 pounds firm tofu (about 2 16-ounce packages)
> 1 yellow onion, diced
> 2 teaspoons fresh ginger, peeled and minced
> 1 to 5 tablespoons green curry paste
> 2 to 3 carrots, peeled and cubed
> 1 potato, peeled and cubed
> 1 sweet potato, peeled and cubed
> 1 cup frozen or canned corn, drained
> 1 cup edamame soybeans (shelled)
> ½ stalk celery, diced
> 2 teaspoons ground lemongrass (preferably fresh)
> 2 (32-ounce) cartons vegetable stock
> Salt and pepper
> 2 (13.5-ounce) cans unsweetened coconut milk (for best results, use regular not light)
> Fresh basil and cilantro, chopped (optional)

Coat the bottom of a large fry pan with oil and heat over medium-high heat. (For best results, use a nonstick pan and make sure it is very hot.) Drain tofu of excess moisture. Cut tofu blocks widthwise into about 7 or 8 (½-inch-thick) slices. Fry the tofu slices until lightly brown on both sides, 5 to 10 minutes per side. Flip only once for best results. Remove and drain on paper towels and cut into bite-size pieces (about ½-inch cubes). Set aside.

Heat oil in a large (8-quart) stockpot over medium heat. Sauté diced onion until fragrant and translucent. Add ginger and curry paste. Stir and cook 2 minutes. Add tofu, carrots, potato, sweet potato, corn, edamame, celery, lemongrass, and enough vegetable stock to cover the vegetables. Stir and season to taste with salt and pepper. Bring to a boil. Lower heat. Stir the coconut milk in the can, and then add it to the soup. Cover and simmer on medium-low heat for 20 to 25 minutes or until all the vegetables are tender, stirring occasionally.

Garnish with basil and cilantro and serve with toasted French bread.

CoCo's Soft Spring Rolls and Peanut Sauce

This recipe is one of CoCo's personal favorites—and now one of mine. Spring rolls are a traditional and ubiquitous appetizer in Vietnam. Serve them at your next party and impress your friends, but keep in mind that spring rolls dry out quickly and are meant to be eaten right away. They also make a light, delicious, healthy meal.

Rice paper, vegetarian mock (meatless) ham, and rice noodles can be found at Asian markets and in some American groceries' ethnic sections. The veggie ham can be omitted, but if so, increase the amount of tofu (to roughly 1½ to 2 pounds).

Make sure to use rice paper, not spring roll wrappers, for this recipe. Rice paper, made from rice and water, is stiffer and comes in various sizes and shapes. This recipe is based on a 9-inch-diameter rice paper sheet. CoCo suggests using a cutting board or plastic wrap when assembling the spring rolls, to avoid sticking and tearing. For more efficient assembly, have all the filling ingredients washed, prepped, and lined up in order.

The peanut sauce recipe included here is not the one CoCo uses in her restaurant, which omits the peanut butter because of customers' possible food allergies. However, this is a delicious, easy alternative. Leftovers can be used as a dipping sauce with steamed vegetables.

Serves 8 to 10 (makes about 25 to 30 spring rolls)
Ready in about 1¾ hours (including prep time for the peanut sauce)

Spring Rolls

1 (8-ounce) package thin rice noodles (or rice vermicelli)
Olive oil for sautéing
2 carrots, shredded
1 to 2 celery stalks, cut in half lengthwise and on the bias
1 small head white cabbage, shredded
Salt and pepper
1 pound firm tofu (1 16-ounce package)
½ pound vegetarian mock (meatless) ham (optional)
1 (12-ounce) package rice paper (9-inch diameter)
Fresh mint or basil leaves

Peanut Sauce

1¼ to 2 cups hoisin sauce
1 cup creamy peanut butter
1 to 2 teaspoons cayenne pepper or hot pepper sauce
½ to 1 cup hot water
Ground peanuts (optional)

To Prepare the Spring Roll Filling

Boil enough water for the amount of rice noodles being used (refer to package directions). Cook for 5 to 10 minutes or until the noodles are softened. Rinse with cool water, drain well, and set aside.

Heat enough oil to cover the bottom of a fry pan (preferably non-stick) over medium-high heat. Stir-fry carrots, celery, and cabbage until soft. Season to taste with salt and pepper. Transfer vegetables to a plate or storage container to cool until ready to use.

Clean out the same fry pan and heat enough oil to cover the bottom over medium-high heat. (Make sure the pan is very hot before frying.) Drain tofu of excess moisture. Cut tofu blocks widthwise into about 7 or 8 (½-inch-thick) slices. Fry the tofu slices until lightly brown on both sides, 5 to 10 minutes per side. Flip only once for best results. Remove and transfer to paper towels to remove excess oil, if desired.

If using vegetarian ham, slice and pan-fry like the tofu, adding more oil as needed. Transfer to paper towels to remove excess oil, if desired.

Cool all filling ingredients before assembling the spring rolls.

To Prepare the Peanut Sauce

In a medium bowl, combine hoisin sauce, peanut butter, and cayenne pepper to taste. (For a slightly sweeter sauce, add more peanut butter. For less sweetness, add more hoisin sauce and hot pepper.) Add hot water, a little at a time, until the ingredients are well mixed and the texture is smooth and creamy and of the preferred consistency. Serve cool or at room temperature. Garnish with ground peanuts just before serving. Store leftovers in the refrigerator.

To Assemble the Spring Rolls

Take one sheet of rice paper and quickly dip it into a large bowl of warm water (for about 2 to 3 seconds), making sure it is completely immersed. If you're using a shallow bowl, you may need to rotate the paper. (Do not leave the paper in the water too long, or it will break down too quickly and be harder to roll.) Remove the paper (it should still be slightly firm) and hold it over the bowl to let the excess water drip off. Place the paper on a clean counter, a sheet of plastic wrap, or a plastic cutting board. (The paper will continue to soften and become gelatinous as it absorbs water during assembly.)

Place 1 tablespoon of the cooled vegetable filling in the middle of the rice paper, spreading it out lengthwise (to approximately 3½ to 4 inches). Top the vegetables with about 1 tablespoon of tofu and ham (2 to 4 pieces), followed by 1 tablespoon of rice noodles and 2 mint or basil leaves. Do not overstuff to avoid tearing the paper.

Fold the end of the rice paper closest to you over the filling. Make sure the filling ingredients are tucked in, then fold in the sides. Slowly roll the rice paper away from you, keeping the ingredients tight and the edges straight, until the paper ends. Transfer to a serving plate, seam side down. Repeat the wrapping process until all the spring rolls and filling have been used.

Serve cold or at room temperature with peanut sauce. These are best served immediately or within an hour of making; otherwise, the rice paper will dry out. To keep them fresh, wrap each roll individually in plastic wrap, or store them in a single layer in a lightly oiled airtight container. Use plastic wrap to divide multiple layers so the rolls won't stick together and tear. Keep refrigerated.

CoCo's White Beans and Cabbage

This isn't a Vietnamese dish, but it's a good example of how CoCo blends Eastern and Western culinary influences. This dish appears on the Roots menu and can be served as a main entree or a side dish. For best results, don't substitute another cheese for Asiago.

Serves 4 to 6
Ready in about 30 minutes

2 tablespoons olive oil
2 cloves garlic, minced
1 shallot, chopped
1 (15-ounce) can great northern beans, drained
1½ heads white cabbage, shredded
Salt and pepper
5 to 6 ounces baby spinach
¼ cup grated Asiago cheese

Heat oil in a large sauté pan and add garlic and shallot. Cook until fragrant. Add beans and cabbage. Cook over medium heat until soft. Season with salt and pepper to taste. Add spinach and Asiago cheese. Stir over low heat, just long enough to warm and blend. (Do not let the spinach become limp.) Serve warm.

Ăn ngon nhé
(Vietnamese for *bon appétit*)

3

Iran

Azar and Ata Akrami, July 1979

Azar (AH-zar) Akrami tells me that her name means "fire" as we sit in the beautiful Iranian native's stylishly decorated East End Louisville home. Across the family room her tall, soft-spoken husband of fifty years, Ata (AH-tah), quips, "That makes me ash."

Fire. It warms our body, cooks our food, and fuels our soul. It seems a fitting element for Azar. We've only just met, but I can already sense a fiery, passionate spirit behind my hostess's soothing voice and bright blue eyes. And I will soon learn that this spirit infuses every ounce of her incomparable Persian cooking.

When I first contacted Azar and Ata's older son Ramin (Rah-MEAN) about featuring his popular restaurant Shiraz Mediterranean Grill in my book, he immediately deferred to his parents. They ran a catering business (Ata's Catering) out of their home for twenty-five years and are the inspiration behind Shiraz. Ramin also suggested that I feature one of his parents' secret family recipes rather than a dish from Shiraz's menu. According to Ramin, many of the most unusual, authentic Persian dishes don't translate well in the fast-paced restaurant business; they are too time-consuming.

Azar reiterates this point as she lays out a lavish spread of delectable Persian dishes on two adjoining countertops in the kitchen for our dinner party. "Persian food takes time," she says, "because everything is done from scratch."

The only dish I recognize is *shirazi* salad, a light cucumber and tomato salad that I've enjoyed many times at Shiraz. Ramin kindly pre-

Azar and Ata Akrami are the inspiration behind Shiraz Mediterranean Grill.

pares a plate for me like a father would for a child, introducing each dish: *khoshtehgharch* (stew of mushrooms), *katehrayhan* (sweet lemon basil rice), *khoreshtehloobia* (stew of green beans and potatoes), kabob *hosseinie* (kabob in a pot), *tachin* (rice and chicken), *torshiliteh* (pickled vegetables), *torshisier* (pickled garlic), and, last but not least, a basket full of fresh herbs and radishes—apparently, an essential part of any Persian feast.

Azar cooks like this almost every weekend. The gathering of friends and family is also a household trademark. "Iranians are known for their hospitality," Ramin says. The proof is all around me.

Joining us this evening are Azar and Ata's younger son Ashcon (who has been involved with Shiraz since 2007), their daughters-in-law, grandchildren, nieces, longtime friends from Iran, and other grown "children" the couple has unofficially adopted over the years. Food, laughter, and life fill the house.

My hosts notice I've been avoiding the sprigs of watercress on my plate. They insist I eat the herb between bites of each dish, especially the stems, which deliver more flavor than the leaves. I do as they instruct, feeling like a rabbit as I munch on a mouthful of greens. The watercress is surprisingly peppery, with sweet undertones.

Persian cuisine and Iranian cuisine are interchangeable terms for the traditional and modern styles of cooking related to Iran. Persian cooking uses an abundance of herbs, including parsley, basil, mint, tarragon, cilantro, and watercress. Ramin notes that herbs add a pleasant textural contrast while also complementing and enhancing flavors—not to mention the health benefits they provide.

"It's all about balance," says Ramin, who gets animated every time he talks about his native food. "Nothing about Iranian cuisine is overpowering."

Persian cuisine has influenced many of its neighboring countries' cuisines, including Turkey, Afghanistan, India, Greece, Armenia, Azerbaijan, Georgia, and Russia. Much of this culinary cross-pollination can be traced back to the exchange of herbs and spices, including the highly coveted saffron, along the ancient Aryan trade routes.

Azar is a purist when it comes to saffron, a staple ingredient in Persian cuisine. You must start with premium saffron, she says. She usually purchases hers online, directly from Iran. The saffron must come only from the stigma of the flower, and it must be ground into a very fine powder for the best flavor, aroma, and color.

Not all the dishes served at tonight's dinner are familiar to all Iranians, according to the family. Iranian cuisine is as regional as American. However, some ingredients, such as herbs, eggplant (known as the "potato of Iran"), rice, yogurt, dried fruits, nuts, lamb, chicken, and fish are ubiquitous throughout the country.

I ask my hosts why Shiraz, which features Persian food, is called a "Mediterranean Grill." Ramin explains that in addition to the similar cuisines in their region of the world, some Persian groceries and restaurants use broad terms such as Middle Eastern, Mediterranean, or International in their titles to appeal to a broader audience.

Iranians aren't big dessert eaters, but our meal concludes with a creamy banana pudding made by Ramin's wife Cheryl, a Louisville native and the designated baker in the family. Iranians almost always have tea at the end of their meals. Cheryl shows me how to properly drink Iranian tea—biting off a bit of a sugar cube, then taking a sip of tea and letting the sugar dissolve in the mouth with the tea's heat.

Throughout the evening, our conversation frequently digresses. One minute we are talking about the approximately 200 crocus flowers it takes to produce one gram of saffron, and the next we're discussing the Persian king Cyrus the Great, who wrote what is considered the world's first declaration of human rights. Invariably, our conversation always returns to the Baha'i faith. And why shouldn't it? It was the family's faith, after all, that brought them where they are today.

Ata and Azar and their two sons had a very comfortable, prosperous life in Tehran. Ata was a chief accountant for an international Iranian oil company, and Azar worked for a short time as a psychologist before staying home to raise her children. The couple had met at a Baha'i conference in Africa. Ironically, the faith that brought them together eventually separated them from their homeland and many of their loved ones.

Baha'is have a long history of persecution. During the Islamic Revolution of 1979, they were particularly vulnerable. Under the Ayatollah Khomeini's new constitution, Baha'ism was not acknowledged as a minority religion, and its adherents were forced to either renounce their beliefs or face severe penalties, including denial of employment, imprisonment, and even execution. All these adverse consequences were documented by such groups as the United Nations and Amnesty International.

Azar and Ata had already been making plans to leave the country when the revolution erupted. Azar explains one of the reasons behind that decision: "I knew that for me, I could not deny my faith, but if they asked me about one of my sons, I didn't know what I would do."

The family moved to the United States and put down roots in Louisville, where they had friends. The Akramis, who knew little English, weren't sure how they would make a living, but it was important that they earn their own keep. "Immigrants are prideful people," Ramin once told me. "They don't like to take handouts. They want to be self-sufficient."

Saffron: From Stigma to Spice

If there is any ingredient closely identified with Persian cuisine, it's saffron. Saffron is considered one of the most expensive spices by weight in the world, but a little high-grade saffron goes a long way.

Saffron is derived from the saffron crocus flower (*Crocus sativus*). Though related to the more common spring-flowering crocus, *Crocus sativus* is an autumn bloomer. The saffron crocus flower has three deep red stigmas that are harvested by hand at the peak of bloom. Harvesting usually involves the whole town. Gathering the flowers begins at daybreak, before the sun becomes too intense. The tedious work of removing each stigma is performed into the wee hours of the night. The stigmas are then dried to produce saffron threads (also called filaments, strands, or silks).

The taste of saffron has been described as bittersweet, hay-like, earthy, or even metallic. Saffron has a semisweet, woody scent. Color, taste, and smell depend on the region where the saffron was grown. Crocin, the strong water-soluble dye found within the stigmas, gives saffron its vibrant yellow-orange color.

Where saffron originated is a widely debated subject. Greece? Asia Minor? Persia? In any case, saffron has been used and valued for several millennia as a fragrance, spice, dye, and medicine.

In Persian cuisine, saffron is commonly infused in water and poured over rice during the last stages of cooking, as in the famous baked rice dish tachin. Saffron gives Spanish paella its color, and it is used extensively in Turkish, Indian, Arab, and European cuisines for seasoning and color.

Today, Greece, India, and Iran are the world's leading producers of saffron. Iran produces the most saffron worldwide, and Iranian saffron is regarded as premier for its flavor intensity.

Like any precious commodity, there are plenty of counterfeit versions around. You should buy saffron only from a reputable source. Many grades of saffron exist. The two most common are filaments, with the pale yellow style attached to the stigma, and pure stigmas (considered superior and therefore more expensive). Because of its high value, saffron is extremely important to the local economies where it is produced.

As the proverb goes, "Necessity is the mother of invention." So cooking, which had been an enjoyable pastime for Ata and Azar in Iran, soon became an economic necessity.

Azar always had a natural talent for cooking, but don't assume she learned how to cook from her mother. According to Azar, her mother's meals were overly healthy because her husband was a doctor. "No frying. No oil. The food was tasteless," Azar complains. Fortunately, both she and Ata learned some basics from Ata's mother.

When they moved to the States, Azar studied Persian cookbooks and added her own touches. Together, the couple enjoyed exploring and experimenting with their native dishes and sharing them with friends and family. Before long, word got out about their mouthwatering food, and they began to cook for small parties, charging only for the cost of the ingredients. Soon their passion turned into a catering business.

Young Ramin and Ashcon helped with the catering company and learned the ropes, but neither of them initially went into the food industry. They both graduated from the University of Louisville and followed different career trajectories: Ashcon pursued sales, and Ramin became an electrical engineer. Ramin even owned his own successful automation and information technology company based in South Carolina. For years, Ramin commuted between Louisville and South Carolina. "I was a weekend dad," he laments. He always dreamed of opening an Iranian restaurant, but he had to fight the old belief system ingrained in his head. "In Iran, a cook is a bad word," Ramin says. "If someone wants to offend you, they call you a cook, which is the equivalent of a dishwasher."

On one of his weekends home in Louisville, Ramin stopped at the Persian grocery store on lower Brownsboro Road and learned that a small, cheap rental space was available a few doors down. Could this finally be the opportunity to follow his true calling? With his parents' and his wife's blessing, and using most of the equipment from Ata's Catering, Ramin opened Shiraz Mediterranean Grill. Named after the city in southern Iran, Shiraz quickly became a success, mainly by word of mouth.

That's how I learned about Shiraz—through a friend. From the moment I picked up my order at the first 600-square-foot, carry-out-

"I just put a front to an old passion of mine: Mommy's cooking." —Ramin Akrami

only location and tasted the creamy hummus, perfectly crisped *lavash* bread, tangy tabbouleh, and juicy fire-grilled *joojeh* (chicken) kabob (the most popular item on the menu), I knew that Shiraz would be a hit with the community and a welcome addition to Louisville's ethnic eateries.

The restaurant, which serves "fast gourmet" food, opened in 2006 and now has four locations, one of which houses the commissary where the food for the other restaurants and catered events is prepared. A special cooking apparatus, called a *manghal* grill, gives Shiraz dishes their signature wood-fired taste.

Today, 80 to 90 percent of his business still comes from word of mouth, according to Ramin. With its affordable prices, generous portions, and fusion of exotic flavors, Shiraz has definitely "spiced" up Louisville's growing ethnic restaurant scene. But Ramin doesn't plan to stop at Louisville. He dreams of one day having a Shiraz in every major metropolitan city in the country. In fact, Ramin recently signed a contract to expand Shiraz into other cities in Kentucky, as well as into Indiana and Ohio. He is well on his way to turning his dream into a reality and expanding the Akrami legacy.

"Here in America," Ramin says, "you have the opportunity to do what you are good at, to follow your passion."

Shiraz, for all intents and purposes, is still a family-run business. Ata, who is now in his early eighties, works long hours and oversees operation of the commissary, which includes purchasing, preparation, and distribution.

Both Ata and Azar have been a constant source of wisdom, encouragement, and support to their sons. As Ramin likes to say, "I just put a front to an old passion of mine: Mommy's cooking."

Azar and Ata's Tachin
(Crispy Golden Rice and Chicken)

Tachin (tah-CHEEN) is a popular, decadent, and incredibly flavorful baked dish generally consisting of rice, saffron, chicken, and yogurt. It is usually served to large groups on special occasions, but the recipe can be divided in half for smaller gatherings. Tachin is a family favorite. In fact, one of Azar's granddaughters told me, "I could eat this for an early lunch, lunch, early dinner, dinner, and a late-night snack."

Don't let the many steps in this recipe intimidate you. The fusion of Persian flavors will whisk you and your guests away to an exotic land at your very own dinner table.

Persian spice (*advieh*) is a critical ingredient in this dish, producing an amazing aroma and flavor. A unique blend of cinnamon, cumin, cardamom, ginger, rosebud, and other spices, it can be found in most Iranian, Persian, Indian, or specialty stores, sometimes under different names, such as "Rice Seasoning."

Azar puts a special spin on this traditional dish by adding garlic to the yogurt sauce, which can also be used as a dipping sauce served on the side. To make a dipping sauce, increase the first 3 ingredients of the yogurt sauce by ¼ to ½ (depending on the number of guests). Reserve this extra amount for dipping and top with fresh chopped mint (optional). Store in the refrigerator until ready to serve.

If you're using large pieces of chicken, use fewer than the recipe calls for, so that all the pieces fit in one large pan. For a better presentation and easier selection of chicken pieces, Azar arranges the chicken around the rice instead of incorporating it with the rice, as is the more customary serving method.

According to Azar, it's best to use a high-quality, aged basmati rice because it provides a longer grain and absorbs liquid better. Likewise, Azar buys only premium saffron at a Persian store in Louisville or online, directly from Iran. Her trick for producing a fine powder is to grind the saffron in a coffee grinder (used only for this purpose). Grinding the saffron with a mortar and pestle also produces decent results.

If you're cutting the recipe in half, use a smaller glass-bottomed baking dish. After being packed down, the rice should fill the dish completely to ensure the proper consistency—that of a dense rice "cake."

For the health-conscious among us, it's tempting to reduce the amount of butter in this recipe, but don't: it's necessary for the *tahdig*—the bottom layer of rice—to brown properly (see "Getting to the Bottom of Tahdig" in chapter 18).

Serves about 8 (depending on the size and number of chicken pieces)
Ready in about 2 to 3 hours (not including soaking time for the rice)

Rice
6 cups high-quality, aged basmati rice
6 tablespoons salt

Yogurt Sauce
1 (16-ounce) carton plain, thick and creamy, good-quality yogurt
1 to 2 garlic cloves, minced
3 tablespoons fresh lemon juice
3 egg yolks
3 sticks butter, melted

Chicken and Sauce
2½ pounds chicken with skin and bones (about 10 small to
    medium pieces of mixed parts)

1 teaspoon Persian spice
1 teaspoon cumin
1 teaspoon black pepper
2 teaspoons garlic salt
Kosher salt (optional)
1 teaspoon freshly ground saffron (divided)
5 tablespoons fresh lemon juice

Pre-preparation

A minimum of 2 hours before preparing the dish (or the night before), place the basmati rice in a large mixing bowl and rinse 3 times in warm water to remove excess starch. Drain the water and fill the bowl with clean, lukewarm water (enough to cover the rice plus ½ inch). Add 6 tablespoons salt (or 1 tablespoon salt per cup of rice) to the water. Set aside and keep at room temperature.

While the rice is soaking, take 16 ounces plain yogurt and drain the excess liquid (through cheesecloth, a paper coffee filter, or a fine mesh strainer) over a bowl and store the yogurt in the refrigerator. (This is a very important step: too much liquid in the yogurt will produce soggy rice.)

To Prepare the Rice

Rinse and drain the soaked rice. Boil 12 cups water in a large stockpot. Add the rice to the boiling water. Boil for about 8 to 10 minutes, or until the rice begins to float and is soft in the center but still firm on the outside. Drain in a large colander and rinse with cold water (so the rice doesn't continue cooking). After the rice is thoroughly drained, set aside.

To Prepare the Yogurt Sauce

To the drained yogurt, add minced garlic and 3 tablespoons lemon juice and stir. Place the yogurt sauce in a large mixing bowl (big enough to hold 6 cups of rice). Add 3 egg yolks (or 1 yolk for every 2 cups of rice) and whisk. Add the slightly cooled melted butter and whisk briskly.

To Prepare the Rice and Yogurt Sauce Mixture

Preheat oven to 350° F.

Add the rice to the yogurt sauce and combine thoroughly. Transfer the rice mixture to an ungreased 9- by 13-inch glass rectangular baking dish. (It's important that the dish is clear so the tahdig can be monitored for doneness during the baking cycle). Use a spatula to pack the rice down tight (6 cups will completely fill a 9- by 13-inch pan), and then smooth the surface. Cover with aluminum foil (shiny side down). With a fork, poke the foil a dozen times to allow the rice to steam.

Place the rice mixture in a preheated oven and bake 1½ to 2 hours (adjusted, as needed, based on the amount of rice). Toward the end of the cooking time, periodically check the rice on the bottom of the dish. The rice is done when the sides and the bottom are a deep golden brown (but not burned) and crispy.

To Prepare the Chicken

After putting the rice in the oven, wash the chicken, pat it dry, and arrange the pieces in a large, shallow sauté pan with a lid (the pan should be large enough to accommodate the chicken pieces in a single layer). Sprinkle all the spices (but only ½ teaspoon saffron) over the chicken. Pour boiling water over the chicken, just enough to cover. Add 5 tablespoons lemon juice (or less for a slightly sweeter taste) to the liquid in the pan. Cover and cook over medium-high heat on a low boil for 40 minutes to 1 hour (adjust the time according to the number and size of chicken pieces). About halfway through cooking, taste the sauce and add extra seasonings, if desired. Make sure the chicken doesn't overcook or begin to fall apart, but otherwise leave it undisturbed. (The liquid should reduce by half or more.)

When the chicken is cooked through, cool it slightly and remove the skin and bones (except for the drumsticks). Return the chicken to the same pan and sprinkle the remaining ½ teaspoon saffron over it. Spoon the juice over the chicken. Cook on medium-low heat for another 10 minutes, then remove from heat.

To Serve the Tachin

When the rice is finished baking, take it out of the oven. Place a large serving platter on top of the baking dish, making sure it covers the dish completely. Using oven mitts and holding both sides of the baking dish and platter securely, carefully invert the baking dish onto the platter (you might want to recruit a helper for the flip). Slowly lift the baking dish off the rice and replace any loose pieces. Arrange the chicken pieces around the rice cake on the platter. Serve with garlic-yogurt dipping sauce (optional).

Nooshe jan
(Farsi for "May your soul be nourished")

4

Myanmar (Burma)—Karen

Dr. Mahn Myint Saing, December 20, 1990

Dr. Mahn Myint Saing and his wife Chaveewan (SHAH-vee-whan) have been dishing out authentic Thai cuisine at their Simply Thai restaurant in Louisville since 2006.

When I visit on a misty day in March, their eldest son Jade, general manager of the restaurant, is in Atlanta to watch the University of Louisville's men's basketball team play in the Final Four tournament. City pride is alive and well in this St. Matthews neighborhood restaurant, with food and drink specials to honor the occasion. Even Dr. Saing and Chaveewan (married for more than thirty-five years and known by their employees as "Pa" and "Ma") are wearing U of L sweatshirts. "We are Louisvillians," Dr. Saing proudly announces. "We weren't born here, but we were raised here."

Dr. Saing's riveting journey from Burmese jungle to Bluegrass State is reminiscent of the movie *Forrest Gump*, in which the title character's life takes so many extraordinary turns that it seems almost fantastical. But Dr. Saing's story is no work of fiction.

In the bar area of the recently expanded restaurant, where the walls are painted the yellow-gold of turmeric, Dr. Saing begins with a history lesson. Borrowing a piece of paper, he draws a map of his native country of Burma (now Myanmar) in Southeast Asia. He labels India and Bangladesh to the west, China to the north and northeast, Laos to the east, Thailand and Malaysia to the southeast, and, finally, his beloved home city of Rangoon (literally translated "end of strife" and now known as Yangon) at the southern tip of Burma.

The population of Burma comprises about 135 ethnic groups, each

"We are Louisvillians. We weren't born here, but we were raised here." —Dr. Mahn Myint Saing (with his wife Chaveewan)

with a distinct culture and language. However, there are 8 generally recognized ethnic groups, including Karen (kah-REHN) and Chin. The vast majority of Burmese refugees who have resettled in the United States since 2001 are Chin and Karen, according to a 2012 study by the Burmese American Community Institute (BACI). Burmese refugees are one of Kentucky's largest resettled populations, with particularly high concentrations in Bowling Green and Louisville.

Picking up his story, Dr. Saing fast-forwards through his childhood to age twenty-three, when he became a medical doctor and was responsible for covering a service area of 50,000 people—all by himself. He delivered babies, treated snakebites, and performed amputations. "Whatever come your way, you got to do it." Sometimes he saw 100 patients a day. "You know why that much?" he asks. "Because I don't care about money. If they don't have money, I give them money to buy protein."

It was partly due to Dr. Saing's generosity that he amassed such a loyal following over the years. But another factor was that, among his particular Karen group, male elders had a royal-like status. When the other elders in his family passed on and he was the only one left, his people turned to him as their leader in the fight against the military government (junta), whose human rights violations have been well documented by the United Nations and other organizations.

"The problem is with the army," Dr. Saing explains in simple terms. "They seize the power, never give any democracy to anybody. That's why we fight."

The civil war in Burma is one of the longest in history, dating back to about the time the country gained independence from the United Kingdom in 1948. The conflicts have centered around political, religious, and ethnic issues. Sometimes these conflicts persist even when the refugees have resettled elsewhere. I once had two Burmese students in my class who did not share the same language, ethnicity, or faith. Despite the fact that they came from the same country, they wouldn't even sit next to each other.

In addition to being a doctor, Dr. Saing was a martial arts instructor. When he went underground and formed his own battalion to fight the junta, many of his martial arts students came with him. At one point, he had as many as 1,000 followers who were willing to lay down their lives for him and their cause. For roughly eight years, Dr. Saing lived underground, fighting in the jungle. He sums up his many near-death experiences: "I was shot. I got stabbed. I got malaria and was unconscious for seven days." Miraculously, he lived, thanks to a whopping 40 ampoules of quinine.

But even during those warring years, there were a few moments of comic relief. Dr. Saing chuckles as he recounts the time he was sitting on a stone in the middle of a stream, taking a bath, when a young Karen girl came upon him and, observing his long hair and full beard, gasped, "Is it Jesus Christ?"

During that time, Dr. Saing traveled to Bangkok, where he and Chaveewan met through mutual friends. Chaveewan was employed in her mother's restaurant in the heart of the city, gaining hands-on experience working in a professional kitchen. Chaveewan had never even seen a Burmese person before she met Dr. Saing. But apparently, she was so smitten that she decided to follow him into the jungle. "We got thousands [of men] with guns," says Dr. Saing. "She's the only girl." So what did Dr. Saing do to protect his beloved? He surrounded her with thirty of his toughest bodyguards, led by his brother, with these instructions: "If someone even looks at her, kill them."

I ask Chaveewan, who has joined us now that the lunch crowd has dwindled, how long she stayed in the jungle. "Until I became pregnant with Jade," she half teases.

There was a brief period in the 1980s when things settled down enough politically for Dr. Saing to return to private practice. On August 8, 1988, however, a student-led uprising (known as 8888) against the junta called him back into action. This time, the army won. Dr. Saing's clinic and house were destroyed. "They are so ruthless," Dr. Saing laments. "They come and kill village[rs], including children, because the village support[s] me. So I think I should leave. I know that I can't win by fighting. It's no use."

Dr. Saing never had to stay in one of the nine main refugee camps in Thailand that dot the eastern Burmese border. As of 2013, more than 100,000 refugees still remained there—some for decades—after fleeing their homeland. He and Chaveewan took their family, including three young sons, and fled to the United States. In December 1990 they arrived in Louisville and were resettled through Catholic Charities. At the time, there were few if any other Burmese refugees in town. The heaviest influx of Burmese refugees to Kentucky occurred from about 2007 through 2010, according to statistics from the Kentucky Office for Refugees.

Like other refugee physicians, Dr. Saing couldn't practice medicine in the United States. He took whatever odd jobs he could get to support his family: car salesman, supervisor at Sears, sushi chef, even dialysis technician. Chaveewan, who had earned a bachelor's degree in business administration in Thailand, found employment at Thai Siam, the only

Burma or Myanmar: Which Is It?

That's the million-dollar question. The international community and the country's own people refer to it by both names.

In 1989 the military government changed the country's name from Burma (officially, the Union of Burma) to Myanmar (officially, the Republic of the Union of Myanmar). This came on the heels of the August 8, 1988, uprising against the military junta in which thousands were killed.

Proponents of the old name argue that the new name was instituted by an undemocratic military regime and that any name change should occur only when the people mandate it through a democratically elected government. Proponents of the name Myanmar say that since Burma was the country's name during the years of British rule, the new name is more in step with the country's break from its colonial past. With recent democratic reforms, Myanmar has increasingly become the more popular name throughout the world. But if you're speaking to someone from Myanmar (Burma), it's best to follow their lead or simply ask which name they prefer.

Most refugees I've met refer to their native country as Burma or, more likely, they specify their ethnic group, such as Karen or Chin. My Burmese friends tell me that they do so because they want to differentiate themselves from the Burmans (or Bamar) ethnic majority.

Thai restaurant in town, owned by an elderly Thai woman. After working there for a couple of years, Chaveewan gained enough confidence and experience to start her own restaurant, Bangkok Buffet, featuring Thai cuisine. After fifteen years of hard work and dedication, Chaveewan and Dr. Saing finally realized a long-held dream when they opened the doors of Simply Thai. After only a few short years, their growing customer base necessitated a move to a larger space across the street, the restaurant's current location.

Simply Thai has won the *LEO [Louisville Eccentric Observer] Weekly* Readers' Choice Award for best Thai restaurant several years in a row. It sets itself apart from other Asian restaurants by using only the freshest, most authentic ingredients and keeping its menu up to date. Dr. Saing and Chaveewan travel regularly to Thailand to sample the newest food trends

Simply Thai—the realization of a long-held dream.

and modify their menu accordingly. However, the one dish they will probably never tinker with is the most popular, pad thai, which uses a sweet soy sauce, sugar, and vinegar and is similar to the kind made in Burma.

Adding to the restaurant's authenticity are the cooks, all of whom are either Thai or Burmese and have experience with Thai cuisine. More important, all of them have been trained by Chaveewan, who also trained her husband, her sister and brother-in-law (owners of Louisville's Thai Café), and her sons, who have followed in their parents' culinary footsteps.

When I ask who is the better cook, Dr. Saing laughs. "Chaveewan is. She's my guru." Unlike in his native country, where he played the role of leader, here at Simply Thai Dr. Saing follows his wife's lead. "She knows every aspect of Thai cooking," he boasts. "The whole Thai community knows who cooks the best [Thai]. If they want to eat, they come here." Patrons also appreciate that they can custom-order their dishes according to their preferred heat level.

A second Simply Thai location opened in 2012 in Middletown, operated by the couple's middle and youngest sons. Although Dr. Saing, who is now semiretired, and Chaveewan hope to continue to grow their business, they don't want to get so big that the quality of their food suffers.

They also believe strongly in giving back to the community that has supported them all these years and in helping other refugees. Some of their pay-it-forward endeavors have included providing interpreting services, hiring refugees to work in their kitchens, and supplying food to Kentucky Refugee Ministries' annual Global Gourmet fund-raiser.

They might be Louisvillians, but Dr. Saing and Chaveewan have never forgotten where they came from. In 2011 Dr. Saing traveled to Thailand, where a hospital and a school had been built for the orphans of the 2004 tsunami. While there, he made upgrades to both facilities and treated patients. But in all these years, Dr. Saing has never returned to his own homeland. "I cannot," he says wistfully. "I am still the enemy of the state." But that doesn't stop some of his loyal followers from begging him to come back and lead them again. According to Dr. Saing, the best thing he or anyone can do for Burma is to pray for the country. "That is the most powerful thing."

When I leave Simply Thai carrying a doggie bag filled with the exotic aromas of *khao soi* and red curry, it strikes me that, through their marriage, Chaveewan and Dr. Saing have accomplished what Burma—and all nations—can only aspire to. "We are from different races," Dr. Saing says. "We speak different languages. We worship different gods. But we have total tolerance."

Dr. Saing and Chaveewan's Red Curry

Burmese and Thai cuisines are close relatives, but each has its own distinct style and classic ingredients. Thai cuisine is known for its extensive use of coconut milk, and this recipe is no exception.

Jade Saing, the couple's oldest son and manager of Simply Thai in Louisville, says that although this dish represents a staple Thai curry, it is also very popular in neighboring countries such as Burma and with foreigners. Red curry recipes vary widely, and this is Chaveewan's unique take on the dish.

Red curry paste is a common ingredient in many red curry recipes, but you won't find it here. That's because the combination of ingredients in this recipe creates a red curry flavor from scratch.

Palm sugar (extracted from the sap of a variety of palm trees) is commonly used in Thai cuisine, particularly in desserts but also in curry pastes and sauces. Southeast Asian recipes often call specifically for this type of sugar, but brown or turbinado sugar can be substituted. Palm sugar, which comes in many shades of brown and many degrees of smoky flavor, can be found in Asian or specialty stores.

Lemongrass is an aromatic herb commonly used in Southeast Asian cooking. It is available fresh and sometimes frozen at Asian markets and some well-stocked American markets. The root end, the green leaf ends, and the outer layer or two of stalk should be discarded. For this recipe, finely slice the stalk crosswise with a large knife or cleaver, then mince.

Galangal (guh-LANG-guh) is also common in Asian cuisine and is used in curry pastes, soups, and stir-fried dishes. Although it is a rhizome that resembles ginger, galangal has a distinct peppery taste with citrus notes. It can be found in Asian groceries. Some say you can substitute ginger in this recipe, but purists say no. You decide.

The Kaffir lime tree is native to Indonesia. The leaves, which are emerald green, double-lobed, and highly aromatic, are used in Asian dishes such as curries, soups, and salads. They can be found fresh, dried, or frozen in Asian or specialty stores. Some say that lime zest, lime juice, or fresh young lime or lemon leaves can be substituted, but none of these truly replaces the incomparable Kaffir leaf. Add a couple of Kaffir lime leaves to the sauce while it simmers to impart more flavor and aroma to this dish.

Chicken and bamboo shoots are the main solids in this recipe, so for additional textural variety and nutritional value, feel free to add other quick-cooking vegetables such as broccoli, zucchini, bok choy, or napa cabbage during the simmering phase.

Serves 4 to 5
Ready in about 1¾ hours (includes 1 hour for marinating the chicken)

    3 tablespoons fish sauce
    2 (13.5-ounce) cans coconut milk, unsweetened (divided)

3 tablespoons palm sugar (or brown sugar) (divided)

2 pounds boneless, skinless chicken breast, cut into thin, 1-inch
strips

4 tablespoons canola oil

2 tablespoons fresh garlic, minced

½ cup white onion, minced

2 tablespoons fresh lemongrass, minced

1 tablespoon fresh galangal (or ginger), minced

2 tablespoons chili powder

1 cup bamboo shoots (canned is fine)

4 to 5 fresh Kaffir lime leaves (optional)

1 teaspoon salt

In a large bowl, mix fish sauce, ½ cup coconut milk, and ½ table-spoon palm sugar. Combine well. Add chicken. Marinate in the refrigerator for 1 hour.

In a large saucepan, add oil, garlic, onion, lemongrass, galangal, and chili powder to taste. Cook on medium-high heat until oil appears on top of the mixture. Add the marinated chicken. Cook for 5 to 6 minutes. Add the remaining coconut milk, remaining palm sugar, bamboo shoots, any additional quick-cooking vegetables, a couple of Kaffir leaves (optional), and salt. Cover. Continue cooking for 15 minutes on medium-low heat, stirring occasionally.

Garnish with Kaffir lime leaves if desired. Serve with jasmine or brown rice or Thai rice noodles.

Dr. Saing and Chaveewan's Khao Soi (Noodles in Curry and Coconut Milk Broth)

It is believed that khao soi (cow-SOY) originated in Burma and then spread to Laos and northern Thailand, where it is a popular street food. One of the few Burmese-influenced dishes on the menu at Simply Thai, this soup-like dish can be served with vegetables or a variety of meats, including chicken, pork, or beef. Its curry-like sauce contains coconut milk.

Burmese cuisine can certainly have a "kick," but don't expect spicy heat from this recipe (although you can add more red curry paste or additional spices to suit your tastes). This dish is light and refreshing, perfect for spring or summer dining. It shows off the region's diverse flavors and is a great introduction to Southeast Asian food for the less adventurous.

If you prefer more sourness, add the juice of an entire lime. Although the cilantro is optional, it really makes the dish pop.

Serves 2 to 3
Ready in about 45 minutes

> 2 tablespoons oil (any kind)
> 3 garlic cloves, crushed
> 3 shallots, chopped
> 3 cups coconut milk
> 1 cup chicken broth
> 1 tablespoon red curry paste
> 1 teaspoon curry powder
> ½ pound boneless, skinless chicken breasts, cut into thin, 1-inch strips
> 2 tablespoons fish sauce
> 2 tablespoons sugar
> ½ teaspoon turmeric
> 1 tablespoon fresh lime juice
> 1 (6-ounce) package fresh wheat egg noodles (thin, not wide) or Thai rice noodles
> ¼ red onion, thinly sliced (optional)
> Cilantro (optional)

Heat oil in a large saucepan until hot. Add garlic and shallots. Stir for 1 minute. Add coconut milk, chicken broth, red curry paste to taste, curry powder, and chicken. Heat to boiling, then reduce heat and simmer for 20 to 25 minutes. Add fish sauce, sugar, turmeric, and lime juice. Stir to combine. Reduce heat to a warm setting.

In a medium saucepan, bring 3 cups of water to a boil. Stir in noo-

Dr. Mahn Myint Saing, 1990

dles. Cook for 3 to 4 minutes. Drain noodles and place in a large bowl. Pour the curry mixture over the noodles.

Serve in individual bowls with a lettuce spring mix on the side, topped with an optional garnish of red onions and cilantro.

Mein mein saa
(informal Burmese expression for "Enjoy a delicious meal")

5

Bosnia

Mirzet Mustafić, October 30, 1994

Mirzet (Mer-ZET) Mustafić claims that he knows just about every Bosnian in Bowling Green. If the dozen customers who greet him by name at the Mediterranean Food Store during our interview is any indication, I believe him.

The Bosnian-owned grocery, located southwest of Western Kentucky University, feels like it's been plucked from a cobbled street corner in eastern Europe and transplanted into the Bluegrass State. The store's shelves are lined with staples from Mirzet's motherland: Vegeta (a popular vegetable seasoning mix), fruit preserves, candy, canned sauces, and freshly baked breads.

Mirzet and I sit at a booth in the store's attached restaurant. He has dark hair, bright blue eyes, and a friendly, teddy bear face. Even though he has been in the United States for almost twenty years, his accent is thick and his English is limited. For Mirzet, it hasn't been critical to learn English. He and his family speak Bosnian at home, the factory jobs he has held require little English, and the sizable Bosnian community allows him to speak in his native tongue. One of Mirzet's first jobs in Bowling Green (the home of General Motors' Corvette) was making furniture—quite a change for the University of Sarajevo graduate who practiced law for fifteen years in the former Yugoslavia.

Bosnia and Herzegovina, as the region is now known, is a republic located in the Balkan Peninsula in southeastern Europe. Several factors contributed to the Bosnian War (1992–1995) that broke out between Bosnian Serbs and non-Serbs after the dissolution of Yugoslavia, a mul-

Mirzet Mustafić grilling ćevapi and lepina at Bowling Green's International Festival. (Photo by Abdulah Rastoder)

tiethnic region. In Mirzet's opinion, the 1991 meeting in Karađorđevo between Croatian president Franjo Tuđman and Serbian president Slobodan Milošević, without a Bosnian Muslim (Bosniak) representative present, increased the ethnic tensions and hostilities. The war claimed about 100,000 lives, according to the International Court of Justice in The Hague. The majority of those killed were Bosniaks.

Prior to the war, according to Mirzet, people of all ethnicities and religions got along. But the war changed everything. Mirzet remembers all too well the morning of April 8, 1992, when units from the Serbian paramilitary, Serbia's main army, and other forces entered his hometown of Zvornik on the eastern Bosnian border and took over. Zvornik was one of the first towns to experience ethnic cleansing during the war. Over the course of just two months, the "Zvornik massacre" resulted in the death of hundreds and the expulsion of tens of thousands of Muslims (the majority population at the time) and non-Serbs.

Mirzet's heritage is Muslim, but he claims he is not religious. "As you can see," he says, smiling and pointing to his Heineken beer.

To this day, few Muslims live in Zvornik, Mirzet says. At the time of this writing, there was a news report that several young Serbs had attacked a group of Muslims on their way to a mosque on the religious holiday of Eid. Clearly, old prejudices die hard.

Mirzet, his wife, and their two small children fled to Serbia, where extended family assisted them. The civic-minded Mirzet opened an office and hoped to continue his work as a lawyer. Unfortunately, he had to give up after eight months; he was losing money, and he had trouble communicating with his clients, most of whom were Hungarian.

Before the war ended, Mirzet and his wife Ljiljana, a physician and head of a transfusion department, made one of the most difficult decisions of their lives: they would not return to their home country. In the fall of 1994, through the assistance of the United Nations High Commissioner for Refugees (UNHCR), they arrived in the United States with only $200 to their names and a single hope in their hearts: to provide a better and brighter future for their children.

They were one of the first five Bosnian families to settle in Bowling Green, the third most populous city in Kentucky after Louisville and Lexington. The arrival of Bosnian refugees in Kentucky peaked from about 1997 through 2000, according to the Kentucky Office for Refugees (KOR). Based on the 1990 and 2010 censuses, Bowling Green's population rose by about 17,500 during that twenty-year period. Mirzet believes that Bosnian refugees and other immigrants accounted for a significant part of that population growth, and they have likely contributed to the city's economic growth as well.

The Bosnian community's influence on Bowling Green is perhaps most evident in its restaurants. Bowling Green is home to about ten Bosnian-owned restaurants and a few bakeries, according to Mirzet. But before any of these existed, and before the Mediterranean Food Store opened, Mirzet remembers a time when it was nearly impossible to get his native foods locally. For the first year or so after arriving in Bowling Green, Mirzet took orders from other Bosnian refugees and made monthly runs to a Lexington store that carried the ingredients they craved, such as Vegeta, pumpkin seeds, and lamb.

Mirzet summons his friend, the owner of the Mediterranean Food Store, over to our table. The two speak to each other in Bosnian, but I can tell that Mirzet is ordering something for us to eat. He then continues his story.

When he and his family arrived in Bowling Green, the small refugee resettlement agency that existed at the time (now the International Center of Kentucky) provided temporary housing and English classes, but it was clear to Mirzet that more assistance was needed. Mirzet opens a large binder on the table. "Can you see?" he asks—an expression he often uses when he wants to explain something, give an example, or highlight the importance of what is about to follow. The binder is a promotional and informational guide for the Bosnian Club, which Mirzet was instrumental in establishing. The nonprofit, nonreligious, and nonpolitical club was founded on May 4, 1996, with the ambitious mission to preserve Bosnian traditions, ways of life, sports, and education. Mirzet also hoped to increase the Bowling Green community's understanding of the Bosnian people, their customs, and the devastating circumstances that forced them to flee their cherished homeland. (As of 2013, KOR's database listed more than 5,000 resettled refugees from Bosnia and Herzegovina. However, this is just an estimate; the exact number of Bosnians living in the state is likely much higher.)

Cultural groups like the Bosnian Club exist throughout the state and the nation. They provide not only a critical support system for refugees and immigrants in their new land but also a link to their shared cultural heritage. Mirzet says the Bosnians are a tight-knit community, and when one of their own is sick, needs assistance, or has a problem, Bosnian Club members rally to collect money or hold a fund-raiser. The club now has more than 300 registered members.

International Center of Kentucky, Bowling Green Office

The International Center of Kentucky is headquartered in Bowling Green and has been active since 1979. In that time, it has resettled more than 10,000 refugees from around the globe. According to the KOR, since the mid-1990s, the greatest refugee populations have been from Bosnia and Burma (Myanmar), with significant influxes from Cuba and Iraq as well.

The center coordinates closely with the Department of State and the US Committee for Refugees and Immigrants to provide a strong support system and the necessary assistance to ensure refugees' successful assimilation. With limited resources from the state and federal governments, the center offers the following services to its clients: temporary housing, job placement, school enrollment, help applying for social services, ESL classes, driving instruction, after-school activities for children, and hygiene and other health lessons.

"The International Center of Kentucky remains the beacon of hope for refugees, asylees, and victims of human trafficking in the Bowling Green and Owensboro areas," says the current executive director, Albert Mbanfu. The center appreciates and welcomes support from individuals and organizations so that it can continue to provide its many programs and services.

Mirzet flips to another page in the binder that lists the Bosnian Club's many annual tournaments and activities, including soccer (Mirzet's favorite sport), fishing, volleyball, and chess. In addition, the club hosts contests for best smoked meat and best garden, a music night on New Year's Day, and an International Women's Day celebration on March 8—a unique holiday carried over from their country. As Mirzet flips through the pages of that binder, his pride for the club is apparent, as is his love for both his homeland and his adopted country. The Bosnian Club's emblem is a perfect symbol of that combination: it features a US flag on one side and a Bosnia and Herzegovina flag on the other.

A stout Bosnian who has been sitting at the bar suddenly saunters over to our table. He knows Mirzet, of course, apologizes for eavesdropping, and says to me, "If you want to hear a story, I could tell you some stories." Then, in the most mesmerizing blend of southern Kentucky and Bosnian accents, he spins a few yarns, and I am reminded, as a writer, how healing storytelling can be—particularly for refugees whose voices have been silenced for too long.

In 2010 Mirzet published his own story in his native language, *Oprosti Mi* (Forgive Me). He pulls out a copy of the book, which he has never translated into English (too cost prohibitive), and shows me black-and-white pictures of his parents, the street he used to live on, and the tool store owned by his paternal grandmother and grandfather. Mirzet wrote the book partly to educate American audiences about his cultural heritage and the atrocities that occurred during the Bosnian War, but also to share what it's like to travel thousands of miles from your homeland and start over.

Mirzet's eyes well up as he tries to explain the title's meaning. He says that old friends from his family's past came back after the war to deliver the same powerful message: Forgive me. For not doing more. For not doing enough. Or, in some cases, for not doing anything.

Our lunch suddenly appears. Placed before me is a bowl of *punjene paprike*, a dish consisting of meat-stuffed bell peppers in a seasoned tomato sauce, topped with a dollop of sour cream. Accompanying this is a plate of *ćevapi*—ten miniature sausages wrapped in a warm blanket of Balkan flatbread (*lepina*), served with sour cream and onions on the side. It looks delicious, but I can't imagine eating all of it.

Mirzet wants to contribute his personal ćevapi recipe to the book. In Bosnia he cooked ćevapi whenever he helped out at his brother's restaurant. He also made the small, savory sausages when he worked a second job in Bowling Green at a grill and sports bar. He now makes ćevapi every September for the International Festival in Bowling Green, and they have become one of his specialties. Though he leaves most of the home cooking to his wife, who makes a mix of Bosnian and American dishes, Mirzet likes to grill at least once a week.

Somehow I end up eating almost every bite of my peppers and ćevapi—they're that good. But before my visit is complete, Mirzet invites me to his home in a quiet neighborhood, just minutes from the restaurant, so he can give me some fresh produce from his garden. His spacious back-yard has a deck, a grill (naturally), a small greenhouse, and several rows of well-maintained vegetables, including cucumbers and a number of variet-ies of bell peppers. He selects for me the best of the ivory-colored peppers, which Bosnians commonly use in their punjene paprike, so I can experi-ment with the dish at home. (See Zeljana's Punjene Paprike in chapter 6.)

Today, Mirzet works as a machine operator (producing fabric soft-ener sheets), and his wife is a physician's assistant. Although they haven't been able to return to the professions they had in the former Yugoslavia, Mirzet and his wife are thankful for every job they've had in the Unit-ed States. They've managed to buy a nice house and put their children through school. Their children's successful completion of college and in-tegration into American society are a source of great pride for the couple. Their son Mirza, a Western Kentucky University graduate, is now in Bos-nia pursuing a career in politics. Daughter Majda, who studied business and graduated from the University of Kentucky, lives in Louisville and manages a paint store.

After all these years, Mirzet says he still misses his home and his friends and family back in the former Yugoslavia. He misses the healthier lifestyle of walking everywhere instead of relying on cars or public trans-portation, and he misses the strong bond between neighbors. He also be-lieves there should be more vacation time in America. Yet, he quickly points out, "Most things are better in the US."

Mirzet's Bosanski Ćevapi (Bosnian-Style Sausages)

"Bosnian meals and their preparations come with a heavy dose of Eu-ropean, Balkan, and mostly Bosnian traditions," Mirzet says. Ćevapi or *ćevapčići* (chuh-VOP-chee-chee) is from the Persian word *kebab*. It is a grilled minced-meat kebab commonly found in southeastern European countries. It is one of Serbia's and Bosnia and Herzegovina's national dishes. Traditionally, five to ten of these small sausages (ten is considered a full serving) are served in a lepina (a type of Bosnian flatbread) with on-ions and sour cream on the side.

Mirzet, who considers himself a "grill man," makes these every year for the Bosnian Club's booth at the International Festival in Bowling Green. Double or triple the recipe for larger gatherings, or halve it for smaller groups.

Using a combination of meat such as ground beef, ground lamb, and ground pork is encouraged. It does wonders for the overall flavor and texture of the sausages.

Ćevapi can be cooked on the stovetop, in the oven (at 400° F), or over a gas or indoor grill. However, these methods yield a much different flavor than Mirzet's preferred method—a charcoal grill using lump charcoal or "natural" hardwood charcoal.

Other types of oversized white rolls can be substituted for lepina. Choose one with a crunchy exterior and a soft interior, such as a ciabatta or kaiser roll. I brushed a kaiser roll with olive oil and toasted it on the grill. This worked well, and I recommend toasting whichever bread you use.

Vegeta is a common ingredient in Bosnian cuisine. It is a multivegetable seasoning mix that can be found in European or specialty markets or online. I think it's the magic ingredient in this dish, giving the sausages their unique flavor. For authentic results, try to hunt down some Vegeta rather than using a substitute (see "Veggies or Vegeta?" in chapter 6).

Serves 4 to 10 (makes about 40 to 50 small sausages)
Ready in about 1¼ hours (not including the 12–24 hour refrigeration time)

2 pounds ground beef (80 percent fat), or a combination of ground
   beef, lamb, and pork
1 tablespoon salt
1 tablespoon Vegeta (or other multipurpose vegetable seasoning
   mix)
1 tablespoon ground black pepper
1 tablespoon minced dry onion
½ tablespoon garlic powder
½ tablespoon baking soda
Sour cream (optional)
Chopped onions (optional)

In a large bowl, mix the meat, salt, Vegeta, black pepper, dry onion, garlic powder, and baking soda with clean hands for about 2 minutes (don't overwork the mixture). Cover with plastic wrap and refrigerate for 12 to 24 hours to allow the ingredients to meld and the meat to firm. Remove from the refrigerator and hand-mix the meat for a minute or so.

Line a large platter or baking dish with foil or wax paper to hold the ćevapi. Roll the meat into equal-sized logs, about 2½ inches long by ¾ inch wide (the size of a pudgy adult index finger). Wet your fingers periodically to keep the meat from sticking to them. If you're not cooking right away, place the sausages in the refrigerator until 1 hour before you're ready to grill.

Oil the grill with beef fat or other grease and preheat on medium-low. For best flavor, grill over charcoal, wood, or lump charcoal (aka "natural" hardwood charcoal).

Grill the ćevapi, turning them periodically, until they are well browned on all sides and cooked through in the middle. Cooking time varies, but it should take approximately 10 minutes. Drain the sausages on paper towels, if desired.

Serve 5 to 10 sausages inside a lepina or other comparable bread, such as a ciabatta or kaiser roll, with fresh chopped onions and sour cream on the side.

Mirzet's Bosanski Lepina (Bosnian Flatbread)

Lepina (also known as *somun*) is an egg-free flatbread that is thicker than pita but has the same hollow, puffy center (reminiscent of an English muffin). It is a popular bread in the Balkans, both at home and as a street food. This flatbread is commonly served with ćevapi, but it can also be served with jam or jelly and used for sandwiches.

This recipe calls for the dough to rise only twice, but a third rising of 30 minutes or so will produce a slightly lighter, airier texture. Try serving this bread fresh out of the oven with garlic and rosemary oil or hummus.

Mirzet, who learned this recipe from his mother, admits that it can be difficult to master. If you lack the time or the inclination to experiment with this bread, any oversized roll with a crunchy exterior and a soft interior makes a suitable substitute, such as ciabatta or kaiser rolls. Lepina is also available at European bakeries and groceries.

Makes 5 to 6 individual breads
Ready in about 1½ hours (depending on how long it takes for the dough to rise)

½ ounce fast-rise yeast (or 2 ¼-ounce packets)
1 tablespoon sugar
7 cups all-purpose flour
¾ cup warm water
2 tablespoons salt
2 cups warm milk (more or less as necessary)

In a large bowl, mix yeast, sugar, 1 tablespoon flour, and warm (not hot) water. Allow to stand for about 5 minutes, until the yeast softens and begins to foam.

Over a small bowl, sift the remaining flour. Add the flour and salt to the yeast mixture, and add as much of the warm milk as necessary to make a soft dough. Knead by hand for a few minutes.

Cover the dough with a towel and let it sit for 1 hour in a warm place. An ideal temperature is between 80 and 95° F (the interior of an oven works well). The dough should double, or almost double, in size. The longer the dough is allowed to rise, the bigger the air pockets. After the dough has risen, generously dust your hands and a flat working surface with flour and knead the dough for about 5 minutes. The dough should absorb more flour at this point and become stiffer. Knead for another 5 minutes.

Heat oven to 450° F.

Divide the dough into 5 or 6 equal-sized balls. Flatten them slightly with the palm of your hand. Roll each ball (either by hand or with a rolling pin) into a ½-inch-thick circle (no thinner), and cover with a kitchen towel. Allow to sit for 10 minutes.

Brush each circle of dough with water. Using the back of a knife (the nonsharp side), make a crisscross pattern on the top of each lepina.

Place the lepina on a baking stone or baking sheet lined with lightly greased aluminum foil (if the dough is well floured, greasing the foil may not be necessary). Bake until the bread turns slightly brown, about 15 minutes. (If the bread starts to brown too quickly, cover the top loosely with foil until the inside is done.)

Prijatno!
(Bosnian for "Have a nice meal!")

6

Bosnia

Zeljana Javorek, September 9, 1999

Zeljana (Jhel-YAH-nah) Javorek has a special place in my heart. If it weren't for her, I might never have begun working with refugees, which means, come to think of it, that I never would have written this book.

The way Zeljana and I met is a classic example of being at the right place at the right time. But it's more than that. We both seized the opportunity presented to us—a guiding motto in Zeljana's life.

"You have to be able to sell yourself," Zeljana once told me, referring to refugees who are starting new lives in America. "Give people an opportunity to get to know you. Build a network around yourself in order to succeed."

Zeljana was doing just that when I met her in the spring of 2008. I happened to sit beside the friendly Bosnian native during a bus tour of our city, Louisville. Zeljana spoke with passion about her job as an English language trainer (ELT) manager with Catholic Charities Migration and Refugee Services, and she invited me to visit her school and help out as a volunteer, which I did. But I lost track of Zeljana after I stopped volunteering at Catholic Charities and took a part-time job teaching English to elderly refugees. Writing this book gave me the opportunity to reconnect with Zeljana and learn more about her story. I was especially curious to know how the Bosnian refugee, who knew little English when she arrived in the United States, had advanced to where she is now—administering an entire English as a second language (ESL) program with an average of 650 students per year.

"I think we've all been given certain gifts to make this world a better place and to help make one another's burdens a little lighter." —Zeljana Javorek

Zeljana grew up in the central Bosnian city of Zenica, about a ninety-minute drive from the capital city of Sarajevo. The old Yugoslavia, before the Bosnian War began in 1992, is best described in her own words:

When I close my eyes with a great nostalgia I see my four-story apartment building with people sitting outside in front and behind the building and children playing around. I see dear faces of women, my neighbors, who used to get together outside in the evening hours and tell stories, jokes, discuss the problems, and share the love and passion for their loved ones and community.

Most of the women in my building were housewives. They would cook food for their families and take care of children. I remember coming home from school and when I got into the building, the smell of food the mothers used to cook. . . . I loved that homey feeling brought by the smell of baked bread, cooked meat, vegetables, and cakes.

I feel such a joy and peace when I think about the life we used to live in Bosnia. People were so happy, it was almost contagious.

But the war, of course, quickly ended that peace and joy. Erupting in the wake of the dissolution of Yugoslavia, the war was primarily a territorial conflict fought along ethnic lines—Muslims (Bosniaks), Serbs, and Croats.

Even though the war officially ended in 1995, after years of bitter fighting, old hostilities and prejudices lingered. The country left in the rubble was just a ghostly shadow of the one Zeljana and her husband Florijan (FLOOR-ee-un) had grown up in. They did not want to raise their two small boys in an environment where people of different faiths and national heritages (like themselves) couldn't live in harmony.

During the interview process with US Citizenship and Immigration Services, Zeljana said she had a friend in Louisville, and that is where the family was resettled in September 1999. Although Catholic Charities and Zeljana's friend were a great help, it wasn't easy adjusting to life in America. "You have to leave your family and friends and everything you are accustomed to," says Zeljana. She and her husband, a mechanical engineer, did not have high expectations of finding employment. Their English was limited, and they knew they would have to take whatever jobs they could get. They felt fortunate when they found work rather quickly—Florijan in a factory, and Zeljana at Catholic Charities' ESL school, tutoring and providing child care to school-age children while their parents attended evening English classes.

Meanwhile, at home, her sons struggled to assimilate. It was particularly hard for her older son, Zeljana recalls, because he was old enough to remember their former life in Bosnia and everything they had left behind. Then her younger son developed a stutter. Zeljana had been encouraging him to speak their native tongue at home, but she realized that this might be contributing to his speech problem, so she told him to speak in whichever language he was most comfortable. Sure enough, his speech slowly improved.

After working in the Catholic Charities child-care room for a few years, Zeljana's hard work was rewarded with a promotion to ESL teacher. She taught beginners and found herself in an optimal position to add to her own language skills and confidence. By teaching a subject, one becomes more proficient at it, and Zeljana felt that, as a nonnative speaker herself, she knew firsthand what her students needed. In 2006 a fellow teacher recommended Zeljana for the job of ELT manager, a position she has held ever since. "I love what I'm doing. It gives me a sense of purpose. I learn so much from our students. I hope that sharing kindness and providing support and education will make a meaningful difference in someone's life. I think we've all been given certain gifts to make this world a better place and to help make one another's burdens a little lighter."

When I visit one Saturday afternoon in late summer to cook *punjene paprike* (stuffed peppers) with Zeljana, she and Florijan, who now works as a mechanical engineer in a manufacturing company, give me a tour of their two-story home near Iroquois Park. Florijan proudly shows off the back deck and screened-in porch he built himself. I can't help but be proud of this couple too. They have taken risks, dreamed big, and worked hard. They are now US citizens and have a say in the direction taken by their country and their community.

Though life is good here, Zeljana still misses her old friends and hav-

Veggies or Vegeta?

Vegeta is an all-purpose seasoning mix made of dehydrated vegetables such as carrots, parsley, celery, and onions; herbs and spices; and flavor enhancers. Invented by a Bosnian Croat scientist and first introduced in Yugoslavia in 1959, Vegeta is ubiquitous in eastern European cuisine and is sold in about forty countries.

According to Zeljana, people in her native country traditionally don't cook with many herbs or seasonings. Primarily, they use salt, pepper, paprika, and Vegeta. Zeljana once asked her grandmother why she didn't use herbs like rosemary or oregano in her cooking. Her grandmother said she was afraid the herbs would dominate the flavor of the food rather than enhance it.

Vegeta can be found in many European markets, in some American groceries with well-stocked ethnic sections, or online.

ing an extended family to rely on. "But I can't complain," she says. "I'm very blessed."

After we've stuffed the peppers with a mixture of meat, rice, and seasonings (including the popular eastern European ingredient Vegeta), we wait in the formal dining room as the dish simmers on the stove and the homemade bread rises in the oven. The sunlight filters through lace curtains, brought from Bosnia. The house feels American, but these soft, Old World touches offer a glimpse into this family's rich heritage.

Florijan checks on our progress, as the peppers we're making are one of his favorite dishes. He and Zeljana speak Bosnian to each other—a language I love to hear because it sounds curiously masculine and feminine at the same time, with its strong, sharp consonants and gentle, round vowels. Although their children are older now and "fully Americanized," the family still speaks Bosnian at home. Zeljana wants her sons to be able to communicate with family and friends on their occasional trips back to Bosnia. "I want them to remember the language of their ancestors," she says.

As the smell of baked bread and stewed tomatoes fills the house,

Zeljana introduces me to her drink of choice, B&B, a mix of brandy and the herbal liquor Benedictine. She pours us each two fingers' worth in Old-Fashioned glasses. We sip our cocktails as we eat fresh bread slathered with strawberry preserves. The Bosnian bread, called *ustipak*, is delicious—light, with just the right amount of "chew," and still warm. We talk about life, Zeljana's sons, the family's upcoming trip to Bosnia, and the drama of male and female relationships.

It has been a good day, and in some ways, I imagine we are not so different from the women Zeljana knew in old Yugoslavia before the war, sharing food and stories and a happiness that is almost contagious, if fleeting.

Zeljana's Punjene Paprike (Stuffed Peppers)

Punjene paprike (poon-YAY-nay PAP-ree-kay) is one of Zeljana and Florijan's favorite dishes. Zeljana remembers this being served primarily in the summer, when peppers were in season in old Yugoslavia (now Bosnia and Herzegovina). If you love peppers and tomatoes, especially paired together, you'll love this dish.

Look for soft, thin-skinned peppers for this recipe; they cook faster and are the kind commonly used in Bosnia. If you can find an ivory-colored variety, that's even better and more authentic. The optional garnishes really bring out the flavors in this dish.

If you can't find Vegeta, substitute some other robust vegetable seasoning mix.

Serves 4 to 5
Ready in about 2 hours

> 10 medium thin-skinned bell peppers (any color or combination of colors), tops and seeds removed (reserve the tops)
> 1½ pounds ground beef, turkey, or pork (lean is fine)
> 2 to 4 cloves garlic, peeled and finely chopped or minced
> 1 small red, yellow, or white onion, finely chopped
> 2 eggs

1 cup rice (uncooked and washed)
2 teaspoons dried parsley or 2 tablespoons fresh parsley leaves
2 tablespoons plain bread crumbs
2 to 3 teaspoons salt
1 teaspoon ground black pepper
2 teaspoons Vegeta (or other vegetable seasoning mix)
¼ teaspoon cayenne pepper (optional)
8 tablespoons canola, vegetable, or olive oil (divided)
¼ cup flour
3 cups water (divided)
3 (15-ounce) cans tomato sauce
Shredded Parmesan cheese (optional)
Sour cream (optional)
Fresh basil leaves (optional)

Wash the peppers.

Mix the next 11 ingredients and 2 tablespoons of the oil in a large mixing bowl. Make sure all the ingredients are evenly distributed, using clean hands to stir.

Stuff the peppers with the stuffing mixture. Pack down just enough stuffing to fill the bottom of the pepper and in between the ribs (slightly more than ¾ full). Do not overstuff. Place one of the reserved pepper tops on top of each stuffed pepper. (This step isn't necessary, but Zeljana doesn't like to waste anything.) Place the peppers in a large bowl or on a platter and set aside. If you have extra stuffing, set it aside to use later.

In a large (8-quart) stockpot, add the remaining 6 tablespoons of oil, or enough to lightly coat the bottom of the pan. Heat over medium-high heat. Add the flour and stir constantly with a wooden spoon until the flour is a light brown (caramel) color (about 2 to 4 minutes), taking care not to overbrown or burn. Remove the pan from the heat briefly. Add 1 cup of water. Return the pan to medium-high heat. Stir until the flour becomes a smooth mixture. Stir in the tomato sauce and the remaining 2 cups of water. If the sauce begins to bubble, lower the heat.

Place the peppers (top-side up) in the tomato sauce, crowding them together so they stand upright. Roll any leftover stuffing into 1- to 2-inch balls and place them in the sauce with the peppers. Bring the sauce to a boil, then turn the temperature down to low. Simmer, covered, for about 1¼ hours. (It's okay if the pepper tops fall off during cooking or some of the tomato sauce gets mixed in with the stuffing.)

About ¾ through the cooking time, test a meatball or pepper for doneness. Taste the sauce, and add more salt and pepper if desired. The dish is done when the sauce's consistency is like tomato soup, the pepper skins are soft, and the rice and meat in the stuffing are cooked through.

This is traditionally served in an oversized bowl with mashed potatoes. Bread can also be served on the side. Garnish with grated Parmesan, a dollop of sour cream, and fresh basil.

Zeljana's Bosanski Lonac (Bosnian Pot)

Lonac (LO-nacs) is a stew-like dish that, according to Zeljana, has no specific recipe, except that it should contain cabbage and either beef or lamb. Traditionally, the ingredients are cut into large pieces and arranged in layers in a clay pot. The pot is then placed over a fire and allowed to gently simmer until all the ingredients are cooked. This dish is a favorite of Zeljana and her mother because they both like cabbage. It's a traditional Bosnian summer dish and very versatile.

Zeljana has simplified this recipe by mixing the meat, vegetables, and seasonings together (rather than having three separate layers). She says it tastes every bit as good as the layered version.

Chicken can be substituted for the beef. In this case, cut the vegetables into smaller pieces, since chicken takes less time to cook.

Feel free to add or substitute vegetables (except for the cabbage) and herbs according to taste. Zeljana often adds fresh green beans, bell peppers, celery, or dried parsley.

If Vegeta isn't available, substitute another flavorful vegetable seasoning or a beef stock cube.

Zeljana usually makes this dish in a pressure cooker, which cuts the cooking time to about half an hour.

Zeljana Javorek, 1999

Serves 4 to 6
Ready in about 2 to 3 hours (depending on the type of meat)

1 green cabbage head (about 1½ pounds), cut into ⅛ sections (about 3-inch wedges)

1 pound veal, beef sirloin, beef stew meat, lamb, or other quick-cooking meat, cut into 1-inch pieces

4 to 5 medium carrots, peeled and sliced into 1½-inch pieces (or about 20 baby carrots)

2 to 3 large Idaho potatoes, cut into large chunks

2 to 3 small white or yellow onions, quartered

2 to 3 garlic cloves, halved or quartered

3 to 4 fresh medium tomatoes, peeled and diced

2 teaspoons salt

2 teaspoons ground black pepper

1 teaspoon whole black peppercorns (optional)

2 teaspoons Hungarian paprika

1 tablespoon Vegeta (or other vegetable seasoning mix) or 1 beef stock cube, crumbled

2 to 4 tablespoons oil (optional, and only if the meat is lean)

2 to 2½ cups water or liquid beef stock (or chicken stock if using chicken)

Place half the cabbage on the bottom of a large (8-quart) stockpot, covering the entire bottom of the pot (or as much of the bottom as possible).

In a large mixing bowl, mix the meat, vegetables, and seasonings, and layer on top of the cabbage.

Add oil (if using lean meat) and 2 to 2½ cups of water or liquid stock. Use enough liquid to almost cover the ingredients, or use less liquid for a more stew-like consistency. (The cabbage and vegetables will also produce some moisture during cooking.)

Lay the remaining cabbage on top of the meat, vegetables, and seasonings. Bring to a boil, cover, and cook on low. Cooking times vary, depending on the meat used. It could take anywhere from 1 hour (for chicken) to 2½ hours. Stir only once, about ¾ through the cooking time, to check the doneness of the meat and the tenderness of the vegetables. Otherwise, leave the layers undisturbed. The dish is done when the meat is tender and cooked through and all the vegetables are soft (but make sure the potatoes don't get mushy).

This is a meal in itself and is generally served without side dishes, but bread and salad would make fine accompaniments.

Prijatno!
(Bosnian for "Have a nice meal!")

7

Rwanda

Nicolas Kiza, March 15, 2000

The first time Nicolas Kiza and I spoke on the phone, I asked him if he was a refugee, a prerequisite for inclusion in my book. He said yes and then corrected himself: "I mean I *was* a refugee." Indeed, it's hard to imagine that the co-owner of Kalisimbi Bar and Grill, located in a vibrant, multiethnic community in Louisville's South End, ever had to run for his life through the jungles of the Democratic Republic of the Congo (DRC) or was ever held in a ten- by ten-foot military prison cell without food for two weeks.

It's early on a Friday evening in late summer. My friend and I are sipping two Belgian beers that Nicolas recommended and poured himself behind the bar at Kalisimbi. We meet Africans from Kenya, Rwanda, and the DRC, and we talk about African cuisine and the best cities to visit in Africa (Cape Town is apparently a must). One of our new friends serenades us with the Kenyan pop song "Jambo Bwana," Swahili for "Hello Mister."

For Nicolas's customers, the majority of whom are Africans, Kalisimbi is a home away from home away from home—a place where they can feel comfortable and accepted, eat their native cuisine, and speak their own language. These are the same things Nicolas always wanted but could never find in the Louisville area.

"You see all this?" Nicolas says, making a sweeping gesture around the renovated space that used to be a pizza parlor. "We did it ourselves." He is referring to his business partner, a childhood friend and fellow Rwandan refugee. He points out the bar shelves they constructed and an

Entrepreneur Nicolas Kiza serving customers at Kalisimbi Bar and Grill.

alcove near the door that converts into a DJ booth on the weekends. "This was our idea," Nicolas says. "We didn't have an expert come in and tell us what to do."

Nicolas also helped create the simple menu, which consists mainly of African dishes such as goat and lamb brochettes, *ugali*, and *sambusas*. However, like any good business owner, Nicolas knew when to get out of his own way: he turned the kitchen over to experienced African cooks.

Kalisimbi, in its first year of operation, is named for the volcano on the border between Rwanda and the DRC, the two countries that have played a pivotal role in shaping the resourceful, strong-willed, courageous man Nicolas is today. But how did Nicolas get from there to here?

* * *

Rwandans are famous for rewriting history, according to Nicolas, but he is here to set the record straight—or at least to share the truth of his own story. It's a quiet Sunday afternoon at the restaurant, and Nicolas (wearing a University of Louisville baseball cap) has just finished delivering food for a catered event. He borrows my pen and a piece of paper and draws a map of Rwanda, one of the smallest nations in Africa. It is nicknamed the "land of a thousand hills." Then he draws Burundi to the south, Uganda to the north, the DRC to the west, and Tanzania to the east. By the end of our nearly three-hour discussion, almost every square inch of paper is covered with statistics of people killed, names of political parties, warring ethnic groups, and key historical dates.

Nicolas came from humble beginnings in Kamembe, a city in western Rwanda along the Congolese border. His grandfather, Nicolas's namesake, was the first to drive a car in his province, and he was the chauffeur to a Belgian administrator (Rwanda is a former French-speaking Belgian colony). For most of Nicolas's childhood, Rwanda was a peaceful place to live, and the two historically opposed ethnic groups, the majority Hutu and the minority Tutsi, lived together in relative harmony. Prior to the early 1990s, Nicolas didn't even know which ethnic group he belonged to. Only when his high school application required him to indicate his ethnicity did he learn, through his father (the side on which ethnicity is determined in Rwanda), that he was a Hutu.

The name Rwanda is derived from the verb *Kwanda*, meaning to enlarge or expand. But the infamous 100-day bloodbath during the spring of 1994 left the country's population utterly reduced. It left an estimated 500,000 to 1 million Rwandans dead, most of whom were Tutsi, as well as some Hutu moderates. The event that triggered the Rwandan genocide occurred on April 6, 1994, when two surface-to-air missiles reportedly struck a plane carrying both the Rwandan and the Burundian presidents (both Hutu), killing everyone on board.

For the sake of brevity, here is an admittedly inadequate synopsis of the conflict: The Hutu had risen to power in the late 1950s and early 1960s after hundreds of years of Tutsi rule. However, they feared the Tutsi might try to regain power, particularly with the rise of the Rwandan Patriotic Front (RPF), a Tutsi-dominated rebel group comprised largely of Tutsi refugees in Uganda. Some believed the RPF was behind the attack on the plane. The combined tensions, suspicions, and fears created a perfect storm, prompting the systematic killing of Tutsi. When the RPF won a military victory in July 1994, as many as 2 million Hutu, fearing Tutsi retaliation, fled Rwanda and sought safety in neighboring countries such as the DRC (then known as Zaire) and Tanzania.

At the time of the plane crash, Nicolas, an only child, was attending boarding school, but fortunately, the students were on Easter break. "That saved me," he says. If classes had been in session, the school could have been an easy target, or fighting could have erupted among the students themselves.

During the first few months of fighting, Nicolas and his parents laid low and tried to hide the Tutsi in their extended family. Eventually, as the fighting spread, Nicolas and his family had no choice but to leave their home and escape across the border into the DRC, where they stayed with relatives. In the beginning of 1996 the family moved again, this time to a refugee camp. They stayed there for a few months, long enough for Nicolas to finish his high school education. When the Rwandan army crossed into the DRC during the First Congo War (1996–1997) and destroyed the camp, the family found themselves on the run again. They fled into the jungle, and not long after their escape, the group of Rwandan refugees who had been traveling together held a meeting to debate their two options: stay where they were, or continue into the depths of the jungle. Nicolas's parents chose to stay, but Nicolas chose to go, reasoning, "I'd rather be killed by a lion than my fellow Rwandans." That decision quite possibly saved his life. Nicolas and his small band of refugees, about twenty in total, traveled about thirty miles a day on foot, trying to outrun the violence that had spilled over from Rwanda into the DRC. By this time, according to Nicolas, no distinct sides existed, and it was unclear who "the enemy" was. It was just pure chaos—humans killing humans.

It took Nicolas and his companions six months to make it to the west side of the DRC and the capital city of Kinshasa. For a time, Nicolas survived with the help of good Samaritans, villagers who allowed him to work on their farms outside the city in exchange for food and shelter. Because Nicolas had grown up on the Congolese border, he knew enough of the local language to pass himself off as Congolese.

In August 1998 another civil war erupted in the DRC. This Second Congo War (also known as the Great War of Africa) was the deadliest conflict since World War II, according to the International Rescue Committee. During this time, Nicolas's luck finally ran out. He was captured and placed in a military camp, where he and about three dozen others were kept in deplorable conditions in a cell no bigger than a small shed. They went for two weeks without food, and they sometimes had to drink their own urine just to survive. What got him through this unimaginably dark time? "Belief in myself," Nicolas tells me. "Perseverance. And my faith."

If not for the intervention of the American Red Cross, Nicolas might not be alive today. The Red Cross took Nicolas and the other political prisoners (as they were classified) to a safer complex just outside the capital. A few months later, the Red Cross transported them to an even safer location—the democratic nation of Benin, in West Africa. Nicolas learned through the Red Cross that his mother was still alive but that his father had died in the DRC. Nicolas wrote to his mother and told her that he was in the process of immigrating to America. He promised to call her when he got there, but it was a full year later, in March 2000, when Nicolas and four others, including his current business partner, finally arrived in Louisville. Nicolas went straight to the local Red Cross office and placed a call to his mother, just as he had promised. He hadn't seen her in three years. During that emotional conversation, he learned about all the other family members who had perished during the years of senseless fighting.

Nicolas got a warehouse job at United Parcel Service (UPS) through the assistance of Catholic Charities. This experience sparked Nicolas's interest in the logistics of moving materials from one place to another and helped pave his future career path. He attended the University of Toledo and graduated with a double major in supply chain solutions and operations management. Soon after, he was working for Honeywell in Ohio as a supply chain planner.

In 2005, a monumental year for Nicolas, he not only became a US citizen but also married Christine, a woman he had met years before at a Rwandan Youth Summit. The wedding also served as a means of getting his mother out of Rwanda. Nicolas wrote a long letter to the US ambassador to Rwanda, recounting all that had happened to him. He concluded his letter as follows: "If my mom is not here for the wedding, you are going to be held responsible." The letter worked. Now, almost a decade later, Nicolas's mother is safe in America, helping to care for Nicolas and Christine's two young children.

Nicolas ended up back in Kentucky when Honeywell outsourced jobs to India and offered him a job at its Louisville office. He stayed with the company for several more years and then decided to cash out his 401k and buy a warehouse with his business partner. Out of this warehouse, the two entrepreneurs run a shipping service, transporting secondhand goods—clothes, shoes, and even cars—to Africa and South America. With the money they made from the warehouse, Nicolas and his partner opened Kalisimbi. "We are very ambitious," says Nicolas. In fact, they hope to open a second restaurant in the future.

Although Rwanda has one of the highest refugee populations in the world, very few Rwandan refugees have resettled in the United States. Kentucky's low numbers reflect the nation's: between 1994 and 2013, only about fifty Rwandan refugees were recorded in the Kentucky Office for Refugees' database. What they lack in numbers, Rwandans make up for in strength of character and desire to succeed. According to Nicolas, almost all his Rwandan friends have advanced degrees and good jobs.

Today, former refugee Nicolas Kiza has made a new home—not only for himself but for others as well: a home away from home away from home. (Sadly, Kalisimbi Bar and Grill met the fate of many new restaurants, ending its operations in March 2014.)

Nicolas's Peas and Potatoes

This is one of Nicolas's favorite dishes, and it is common throughout Rwanda and other parts of Africa. It is so common, in fact, that Nicolas couldn't give it a specific name. Rwandans love to eat mixed foods

Kalisimbi Bar and Grill provided a cultural haven for its largely African clientele.

in general, and this is just one example. Although it may be common in Nicolas's neck of the woods, from an American perspective, this dish has an unusual addition: a seasoned tomato and onion sauce (reminiscent of a Cuban *sofrito*).

Rwandan food is fairly simple, heavy on the vegetables and prepared with locally grown ingredients. Meat and eggs are seldom eaten outside of urban areas due to their cost. Common staples include sweet potatoes, beans, corn, peas, and fruit. Nicolas still eats this dish about once a week in America.

True credit for this recipe must be given to Clarissa Umuhoza, the Rwandan cook at Nicolas's restaurant. She whipped it up for me with no advance warning, using ingredients she had on hand. She tells me there are many variations of this dish in Rwanda. It can be served as a side dish with a meat entree or by itself as a vegetarian main dish, as I ate it. However, I think it would pair beautifully with a flavorful rib-eye steak or smoked sausage.

Clarissa insisted that I season my peas and potatoes with a couple dashes of hot sauce, a condiment customarily served with the dish. And let me say, the hot sauce took it to the next level.

If you don't like tomato peels floating in your sauce, peel the tomatoes. Fresh or frozen green beans can be substituted for the peas, and green cooking bananas (similar to plantains) are sometimes substituted for the potatoes. (See "You Say Banana, I Say Plantain" in chapter 13.)

Serves 4
Ready in about 40 minutes

> 5 medium Idaho potatoes, peeled, quartered, and washed
> 1½ teaspoons salt
> Olive oil for sautéing (about 5 tablespoons)
> ½ medium yellow, white, or red onion, thinly sliced
> 3 medium ripe tomatoes, chopped
> 1 tablespoon tomato paste
> 1 teaspoon sweet paprika
> ½ teaspoon garlic powder
> ½ teaspoon Accent flavor enhancer (MSG)
> 2 cups frozen or fresh peas (or a mix of peas and carrots)
> Hot sauce (optional)

Place the quartered potatoes in a medium saucepan and cover them about halfway with water. Add salt. Bring to a boil over medium-high heat. Cover and simmer for about 15 minutes, or until the potatoes have softened but are not mushy.

Meanwhile, as the potatoes cook, thoroughly coat the bottom of a small saucepan with olive oil. Heat the oil over medium-high heat. Just before the oil gets hot enough to pop, add onions and cook until light brown and soft, stirring occasionally. Lower the heat to medium-low and add tomatoes and tomato paste. Stir often so the mixture doesn't stick to the bottom of the pan. Add paprika, garlic powder, and Accent seasoning.

Stir until well combined. Cook until the sauce thickens slightly. Take off the heat and set aside.

Once the potatoes have softened, add the peas and stir gently, taking care not to break apart the potatoes. Cook on medium-low heat until the peas have softened (about 5 minutes). If there is excess liquid in the pot, drain it off.

Add the tomato mixture to the peas and potatoes. Cook on medium-low heat for about 5 minutes, stirring occasionally.

Serve warm as a main or side dish. Top with a few dashes of hot sauce, if desired.

Nicolas and Clarissa's Chipsi Mayai (French-fried Potatoes and Eggs)

Chipsi mayai (Swahili for chips and eggs) is commonly served in Tanzania, a close neighbor of Nicolas's native Rwanda. It combines what the British call chips and the Americans call steak fries with eggs.

Some Africans consider this dish a luxury due to the cost of eggs. Just about any ingredient you would put in an omelet can be added to this dish: mushrooms, cheese, meat, beans, herbs, and so on. If you're adding meat, place it on top of the fries, before the vegetable layers. Chef Clarissa Umuhoza says this dish can be served for breakfast, lunch, or dinner, but in Rwanda it is often served as a hearty lunch with meat and rice.

I like to make this dish for the sheer fun of flipping the eggs from pan to plate and plate to pan. I also like the unique texture, a cross between an omelet and a frittata.

The size of the skillet is important in this recipe. Use only a 10-inch skillet for the measurements given.

Those who prefer their onions cooked rather than raw may want to brown the onions in a small amount of oil before frying the potatoes; then set them aside and add them at the proper time. If you're in a hurry, thawed frozen steak fries will work just fine. Just be sure to give them adequate time to cook and brown.

Serves 1 (or 2 small portions)
Ready in less than 30 minutes

    4 eggs
    ¼ teaspoon salt
    ¼ teaspoon Accent flavor enhancer (MSG)
    Olive or vegetable oil for frying, plus 1 tablespoon
    1 medium russet potato, cut into 3-inch-long by ¼-inch-wide strips
        to resemble steak fries, or 15 to 20 frozen steak fries
    ¼ small onion, cut into thin slices or chopped
    1 to 2 small Roma tomatoes, sliced into ¼-inch-thick rounds
        (about 6 to 8 slices)
    ¼ small red pepper, cut into thin slices or chopped
    ¼ small green pepper, cut into thin slices or chopped

In a small mixing bowl, whisk eggs. Add salt, Accent, and any other desired seasonings. Set aside.

In a 10-inch skillet, add enough oil to reach about halfway up the sides. Heat the oil over high heat until it's almost popping. Carefully add the potatoes and assemble in a single layer, making sure there's enough oil to just cover them. Fry until the potatoes are soft inside and lightly browned and crisp on the outside (about 2 to 4 minutes per side). Drain the oil. Keep the fries in the skillet and lower the heat to medium-low.

Top the potatoes with the onions. Cover the onions with the tomato slices. Alternate the red and green pepper slices between the tomatoes. Pour 1 tablespoon oil over all the vegetables. Whisk the eggs again and pour evenly over all the ingredients. Cook for 2 to 3 minutes, undisturbed (the eggs should begin to set at this point).

Take a plate large enough to cover the skillet and hold it over the skillet with one hand. With the other hand (working over the sink or a large bowl or plate to collect any runny egg), take the handle of the skillet and flip the skillet upside down. The slightly uncooked top side of the eggs will now be facedown on the plate. Slide and transfer the chipsi mayai off the plate and back to the skillet, using a spatula to replace any ingredients that were disturbed during the transfer.

Cook for another minute or two, pressing down lightly on the already cooked side with a spatula. Flip again, using the plate, transfer back to the skillet, and press down again with the spatula. After another minute or two, check to make sure that the bottom is cooked. Check the center of the omelet with a knife to make sure the eggs have cooked through. Be careful not to overcook. Each side should be only slightly browned.

Flip the eggs once more, this time transferring them to a clean plate for serving.

Serve alone or with ketchup or hot chili sauce.

Muryoherwe
(Kinyarwanda for *bon appétit*)

8

Somalia—Bantu

Amina Osman, November 5, 2004

Perhaps you've eaten a salad at a restaurant in Louisville's East Market District made with African pumpkin fresh from Amina (Ah-MEAN-ah) Osman's garden. Or maybe you've seen her in a colorful head scarf stationed behind a table overflowing with her homegrown cucumbers, tomatillos, bell peppers, and eggplants at a farmers' market around town. She might not know much English, but the fruits of Amina's labor speak volumes.

Amina is a Somali Bantu, an ethnic minority that lives primarily in the southern part of Somalia. Bantus differ culturally, ethnically, and physically from the Somalis, who constitute the ethnic majority. It is believed that Somali Bantus originated in Central Africa and migrated to other parts of the continent, including Somalia, or they may have been brought to the region through the Arab slave trade of the 1800s. During the Somali civil war, which began in 1991, Somali Bantus, a historically marginalized group, were particularly vulnerable to persecution by warring clans due to their lack of any clan affiliation. Amina and her family fled to Kenya, where they stayed from 1992 to 2004 in the Dadaab refugee camp, the largest such camp in the world.

Unlike ethnic Somalis, who are traditionally herdsmen, Bantus are an agricultural people, and farming is their main livelihood. When Amina and her husband, Bakar, and seven children came to the United States in 2004, they never dreamed they'd have the opportunity to work in the

A version of this story appeared in *Edible Louisville*, September–October 2013.

Amina Osman selling fresh produce from her own garden at a farmers' market.

fields again. "Now I'm in the midst of farming," says Amina, who happily spends almost every day during the growing season maintaining her two gardens—one plot designated for commercial sales and the other for family consumption.

Amina has been growing and selling her own produce since 2009 through the Refugee Agricultural Partnership Program (RAPP). The program, which hosts five garden sites in Louisville, began in 2007 as a federally funded, grant-based initiative administered by the Kentucky Office for Refugees, a division of Catholic Charities. One of its goals is to empower refugee families and communities through urban agriculture. With her participation in RAPP, Amina has been able to reduce household food costs and earn supplemental income.

Amina grows a wide selection of produce, including onions, corn, kale, tomatoes, okra, watermelons, and hot peppers—all of which she grew on her farm in Somalia. One crop she can't grow here and wishes she could is sesame, an ancient, drought-resistant oilseed grown primarily in tropical and subtropical regions. She sells to many local restaurants and at several farmers' markets. One of the latter, Growing Forward Farmers' Market at St. Francis of Assisi Church in Louisville, is managed by middle school students and was specifically established to help refugees sell their produce. Amina, who loves to cook, even gave a cooking demonstration to a group of St. Francis students, teaching them how to prepare her unique version of *sambusas*, a meat- and vegetable-filled pastry that she also sells at the church's farmers' market.

Of the active sellers in RAPP, Amina has consistently been its highest earner. Lauren Goldberg, former RAPP project coordinator, believes this is attributable to two factors: more marketing opportunities and Amina's business savvy. "She has been real innovative on her own," says Goldberg, who explains that Amina pays attention to what others are selling and what her customers are buying and then adjusts her plantings the following year. For example, Amina grows a lot of kale—the current "queen of greens"—which is chock-full of nutrients and has a long growing season.

"It's definitely an adjustment, since they are coming from a different soil and climate," says RAPP's volunteer technical adviser Robbie Adelberg. We talk one hot afternoon as he walks barefoot through the program's largest community garden in Louisville's South End, where many resettled refugees live and sixty families maintain individual plots. RAPP tries to make its clients' adjustment to cultivating on "foreign" soil as easy as possible by providing more than a dozen training and educational classes each year. But according to Goldberg and Adelberg, they often find that they are the ones learning new things. "People grow what we consider weeds, but they know they are edible and/or have medicinal uses," says Goldberg.

Adelberg shows me one such plant, amaranth, which is popular among Southeast Asians and Africans. Perceived by some farmers as just a pesky, invasive weed, amaranth can be both a green and a grain (depend-

Farming on "Foreign" Soil

Did you know that hundreds of refugees use their extensive agricultural experience to provide fresh, locally grown produce for their own families and for the Louisville community?

The Refugee Agricultural Partnership Program (RAPP), one of the first of its kind in the country, is dedicated to empowering refugee families and communities through urban agriculture in Louisville. RAPP helps its clients access land, and today, refugees from the Democratic Republic of the Congo, Burundi, Somalia, Bhutan, and Burma (Myanmar) grow crops on five urban agriculture sites in the Louisville area. Ninety percent of RAPP participants also have community garden plots and grow food as a hobby, saving money on produce and reconnecting with their agricultural traditions. In addition, RAPP offers more than a dozen formal training classes so that these growers can augment their agricultural knowledge to achieve optimal yields in this region. Topics include planting, disease control, and soil fertility. Finally, RAPP trains refugees to sell their produce to direct marketing outlets such as farmers' markets, restaurants, and small groceries. As a result of these and other community partnerships, refugees acquire the skills they need to start their own small farm businesses.

If you, your family, your business, or your faith community has access to land or a desire to partner with RAPP, contact Catholic Charities Migration and Refugee Services in Louisville, Kentucky.

ing on the species), and it is an important source of nutrition. It is also used to treat a variety of ailments and conditions—from skin abrasions to hypertension. Amina grows amaranth in her family garden and uses the greens, comparable to spinach, in soups and other dishes. So far, she hasn't sold it commercially, but as more people awaken to the health benefits of amaranth and as refugees continue to arrive in Kentucky through resettlement agencies such as Catholic Charities and Kentucky Refugee Ministries, the demand for this and other traditional plants may increase.

Amina seems at home in her gardens, often joking with her husband as they work side by side. They value the land and appreciate having a place to call their own. Somalia doesn't seem so far away when they

A refugee displays some of the vegetables he grew on his RAPP garden plot.

are engaged in the familiar activity of gardening and can transform their homegrown produce into culturally familiar dishes. Working in her gardens also helps Amina stay active and eat nutritiously, which is critical due to her diabetes. And on the days she sells her produce to the public, she can practice her English. Although communicating basic information (such as price) hasn't posed a challenge yet, Amina says, "I would love to learn more English." Finding the time, however, is the true challenge. "I would also like to learn about American ways of cooking," Amina adds. Being a true visionary and entrepreneur, she imagines combining Somali and American cuisines in a restaurant of her own, where she could serve produce and herbs plucked fresh from her garden.

Although Amina has experienced many benefits from growing and selling her produce, the benefits to the community are just as manifold. Amina's customers are getting a high-quality, chemical-free product grown in Jefferson County, with a harvest time usually within twelve hours of sale. Refugees like Amina help provide healthier, more diversified eating options to the community. They have become a vital link in the farm-to-table chain. "I love working," Amina says with a smile that seems to traverse continents. "What else would I do?"

Amina's Sambusas

Sambusas (also known as *samosas* in some parts of the world, and a close cousin to *empanadas*) are deep-fried, triangular pastries filled with meat, vegetables, or both and a variety of spices and herbs. They are often served as a snack or an appetizer, with or without a dipping sauce, at large gatherings and on special occasions.

Amina's mother taught her how to make sambusas. She uses vegetables from her own garden to make the filling, so every batch differs, depending on Amina's whims and what's in season. However, she almost always adds potatoes—an uncommon ingredient in traditional Somali sambusa recipes. This version also uses a mix of hot peppers and refreshing cilantro.

The amounts in this recipe can easily be halved for smaller gatherings. I fried a half batch of sambusas one day, ate some, and stored the rest in the freezer. A month later, needing a last-minute appetizer, I warmed them in the toaster oven and paired them with a fresh batch of Kamala Pati's spicy Tomato and Toasted Sesame Seed Dipping Sauce (see chapter 11). They tasted as good as the first day I made them. So if you have the time, make a large batch and store them for future snacking.

Vegeta is a popular eastern European ingredient and an all-purpose seasoning mix made of dehydrated vegetables, herbs, and spices (see "Veggies or Vegeta?" in chapter 6). If you can't find Vegeta, use another all-purpose vegetable seasoning mix or a combination of your own preferred seasonings.

Sambusa wrappers can be handmade, but Amina purchases hers frozen at the International Mall in Louisville, which stocks homemade wrappers and dipping sauces made by local Somali women. Spring roll pastry wrappers (not rice paper) and 8- by 8-inch eggroll wrappers can be substituted and are available frozen at many groceries; however, Amina prefers to use real sambusa wrappers. If you're using spring roll wrappers, you want the thicker, doughier pastry wrappers rather than the extra-thin wrappers, which have a crispier texture once they are fried or baked.

Methods for folding sambusas are as varied as the fillings and depend on the size and shape of the wrappers. The main objective is to ensure that all the ingredients are securely tucked inside the folds of the wrapper so that no oil can leak in during frying. You can find demonstrations online, or you can try the method included in this recipe. Once you fold a few, you'll find a method that works best for you.

Amina uses water to wet and seal the edges of her wrappers. I've never had luck doing that, so I used a flour paste, which my African friends tell me is a common method.

Serves about 20, or 2 per person (makes between 40 and 50 sambusas)
Ready in about 1½ hours (with 2 people assembling the sambusas)

5 small, round potatoes, peeled, quartered, and washed
1 teaspoon salt (divided)
2 pounds ground beef
4 to 6 scallions (green or spring onions), sliced into about ⅛-inch
    circles
1 green bell pepper, finely diced
1 to 2 jalapeños (about 2 inches long), finely diced
8 to 10 small cloves garlic, finely chopped or minced
5 stalks fresh cilantro, leaves and stems, chopped
3½ teaspoons cumin
2½ teaspoons Vegeta all-purpose seasoning mix
2 (25-sheet) packages 8- by 8-inch sambusa wrappers, spring roll
    pastry (not extra thin), or eggroll wrappers, room temperature
Flour and water for paste (optional)
Vegetable or canola oil for frying

In a large (8-quart) stockpot, add enough water to cover potatoes. Add ½ teaspoon salt and bring to boil over high heat. Place peeled, cut, and washed potatoes in the pot. Boil on medium-high heat, uncovered, for 15 to 20 minutes, or until potatoes are tender but not mushy (check for doneness with a fork). Drain water and set potatoes aside to cool.

In a large frying pan, add ground beef and cook on medium-high, stirring occasionally. Add the remaining ½ teaspoon salt. Continue cooking, breaking meat into small pieces with a spoon.

In a large mixing bowl, add chopped scallions, bell pepper, jalapeños, garlic, cilantro, and cooked meat.

After the potatoes have cooled, chop them into smaller pieces to match the size of the other chopped ingredients. Add potatoes to the mixing bowl, along with cumin and Vegeta. Stir all ingredients together until well combined. Set aside.

Wrapping the Sambusas

Note: Wrappers have a tendency to dry out quickly, so cover the stack of wrappers with a damp cloth to keep them moist while assembling the sambusas.

In a shallow bowl, place about ¼ cup flour and add a little water at a time until you have a smooth paste that is neither too thick nor too thin. Set aside for sealing the sambusa wrapper edges.

Take a single wrapper and set it on a clean, flat working surface. Fold the bottom of the square up to meet the top edge, forming a rectangle. Keeping the top right corner in place, fold the bottom right corner up to the center of the top edge to form a triangle. Press down on all sides to smooth the pastry. Take the top right corner and fold over the middle seam to connect with the top left corner of the wrapper. Now the wrapper should consist of the two folded triangles that, together, make a small square.

With your forefinger, brush flour paste over the entire square, concentrating on the sides. Take the bottom left corner of the wrapper and fold it up to the top right corner, covering the other triangle. Press down on the sides and smooth the edges. Pinch the bottom point of the triangle between your thumb and forefinger to seal. With the other hand, lift the wrapper off the working surface. Turn the triangle slightly clockwise to reveal the side seam. Brush more flour paste over the seam and press down to get a good seal.

Hold the wrapper loosely in the palm of one hand and let the folds of the wrapper open to form a cone, using your free hand to find the innermost cone. (The backside of the cone will have an extension pointing upward.) Fill the cone with about 2 tablespoons of filling (or ¾ full), pushing down lightly to pack the bottom. Brush more paste over the inner top extension of the cone, and fold the tip of the extension down tightly to cover the cone opening. All the loose edges will come together to form one triangle, which becomes the sambusa shell. Press down and smooth all edges of the wrapper. Pinch all three corners of the triangle to ensure a secure seal. Set the individual assembled sambusas aside for frying later.

Repeat until all the filling and wrappers have been used. See storing instructions below.

Frying the Sambusas

Note: You can also use a deep fryer. Cook for 8 to 10 minutes per batch, turning if necessary for even browning.

In a deep, heavy pan, add enough oil to just cover the sambusas. Heat oil over high heat until it begins to sizzle. (It's important that the oil be the right temperature—hot enough for the sambusas to brown properly, but not so hot that they burn.) After the oil is hot, turn the heat down to medium-high. Test one sambusa in the oil to make sure the temperature is correct. Then cook the sambusas in a single layer, leaving some space between each, for 30 seconds to 3 minutes, depending on the heat of the oil. Before flipping, check the underside of the sambusas to make sure they are golden brown. Flip them over, being careful not to splash the hot oil, and brown the other side for 30 seconds to 3 minutes. (During the cooking process, adjust the heat, cooking time, and amount of oil as necessary.)

Remove the sambusas with a slotted spoon and drain them on paper towels on a large platter.

Serve warm, either plain or with a dipping sauce (try Kamala Pati's Tomato and Toasted Sesame Seed Dipping Sauce in chapter 11). Reheat fried sambusas in a conventional oven or a toaster oven for best results.

Sambusas can be stored, unfried or fried, in a refrigerator for several days. They can also be frozen for a month or so.

Raashiinking Ki Baashaalaa
(Maay Maay, an Afro-Asiatic language, for "Enjoy your meal")

9

Cuba

*Milagros Guzman-Gonzalez and
Lázaro Hondares, May 19, 2006*

Milagros (Me-LAH-gross) Guzman-Gonzalez cracks an egg against the
counter, dumps the golden yolk and white into the meat mixture of her
albóndigas de carne, and tells me something she has never mentioned in
the three years we've been acquainted. In her native Havana, she worked
full time as an accountant for a tourist company, and she misses it—her
professional life. I knew that Milagros's husband, Lázaro (LAH-zah-ro)
Hondares, had been a graphic artist in Cuba, as well as a gifted painter on
the side, but the more reticent Milagros had never shared anything about
her former life with me.

Here in her bright, cream-colored kitchen in Louisville, I see hints
of the discipline, focus, and professionalism that must have served her well
in the fast-paced travel industry. The ingredients for her beef meatballs
have been measured in advance and arranged in sequence on the counter. And, in typical Milagros fashion, she is dressed smartly this hot June
morning in a colorful paisley-print top and a black skirt for our big cooking day. Her beautiful white hair is cut in a short, chic style.

When I first met Lázaro and Milagros (whose name means mira-
cle) at the ESL school where I was teaching at the time, I knew within
minutes that this sociable, enterprising, hardworking, bright, and inquisi-
tive couple, married for almost fifty years now, would assimilate well in
America. Proof of how well they've taken to our local customs is written
on the T-shirt Lázaro wears today: TRUE BLUE FANS BELIEVE. (Yes, Ken-

103

Milagros Guzman-Gonzalez and her husband Lázaro Hondares studied hard to become US citizens. (Photo by Julie Johnston)

tucky, we have another Wildcats fan.) Even greater proof of their assimilation, however, is their recent status as US citizens—a goal toward which they diligently worked for five years. I had the privilege of attending their naturalization ceremony, where everything good and true that America stands for seems to be encapsulated in that one momentous event. "It's like the whole world is here," an awestruck refugee sitting next to me murmured.

As we now gather in the kitchen, Lázaro fixes me with a sheepish look. Something is on his mind. Through our Spanish interpreter and mutual friend, Robin, he asks if my book will be a professional one. I humbly reply that I will certainly try to make it as professional as possible. Lázaro chuckles softly and says he has no doubt the book will be of high quality. What he really wants to know is whether my book will include mainly professional cooks because Milagros is afraid she isn't a good enough cook to contribute a recipe. I reassure them that gourmet cooks and fancy kitchens are *not* what this book is about. I want to share authentic recipes from refugees' native countries; learn more about their cultures, their celebrations, and their food in particular; and cook and share meals together in real, everyday kitchens where families and friends gather, memories are made, and differences are transcended. My response may not have been this well articulated in person, but it was enough to put Milagros at ease and send her back to chopping the ingredients for her *sofrito*.

Maybe it is the distraction of food and the comfort of her own kitchen that make Milagros open up to me now. In addition to missing her career, she misses her native Cuba and living in Old Havana by the bay, with its magnificent colonial architecture, forts, castles, parks, and museums. But especially she misses her two daughters—one a doctor and the other a craftswoman—who still live in Cuba, along with several grandchildren.

She and Lázaro are thankful to have at least two children in the States—a daughter (and grandchildren) in Louisville and a son in Miami. Lázaro Jr. was the first in the family to leave Cuba in 1994 on a balsa, a makeshift raft. Within a day he was picked up by the US Coast Guard and taken to Guantanamo Bay, where he volunteered for the US military and served for a year. Their daughter Milagros Jr., named after her mother and a graphic artist like her father, told me how pleased she was that her mother was contributing the meatball recipe to my book. "My mother makes the best meatballs," she boasted.

Sass It Up with Sofrito

Sofrito is a Spanish word meaning to lightly fry, often by sautéing or stir-frying. The first reference—*sofregit*—dates back to medieval times and one of the oldest European cookbooks from the Catalan region in Spain. Spanish colonists brought this method of cooking with them when they settled in Latin America and the Caribbean.

A fragrant mixture of ingredients chopped into small pieces and slowly sautéed in oil, sofrito provides the foundation for a recipe and determines its flavor. Ranging in color from green to red, and ranging in flavor from mild to spicy, sofrito is often used as a base to season beans, rice, stews, and even meat. In Cuban cuisine, sofrito consists mainly of garlic, onion, tomato, and bell pepper, but it may also include pork, dry white wine, cumin, oregano, bay leaf, and cilantro.

The method is not exclusive to Latin American cuisine. Different methods and recipes can be found throughout the world, including the Philippines, France, Italy, and other Mediterranean countries. Sofrito recipes are as distinctive as the cultures and kitchens that produce them, and they help distinguish one country's cuisine from another's.

Milagros and Lázaro's journey to the United States was not as adventurous as their son's, but it was no less fortuitous. Sometime around 1998, Milagros learned by word of mouth of a lottery whereby Cubans wishing to immigrate to the United States could sign up. (This lottery program is specific to Cuba and is not associated with the worldwide congressionally mandated Diversity Immigrant Visa Lottery Program.) Milagros sent a letter to the US Interests Section in Havana and entered her and Lázaro's names into the pot of randomly selected individuals. *Muchos, muchos años* (many, many years) later, after mounds of paperwork and several rounds of interviews, there was an answer to their prayers: They had been selected. *Adios* Cuba. *Hola* America.

In May 2006 Lázaro and Milagros arrived in Miami and received assistance through Catholic Charities Migration and Refugee Services. When they learned that Catholic Charities had an office in Louisville, where some of their friends lived, they decided to move to Kentucky and arrived in the Bluegrass State on June 15.

Cubans presently constitute the largest resettled refugee population in Kentucky. Since the mid-1990s there has been a steady influx of Cubans each year, ranging from a low of 270 in 1996 to more than 1,000 in 2013. According to the 2010 census, about 9,300 Cubans lived in Kentucky. In 2013 the Kentucky Office for Refugees reported that more than 9,600 Cubans had been resettled in Kentucky, with the vast majority residing in Louisville, followed by Bowling Green and Lexington. However, these statistics do not reflect all the secondary migrants (those who initially resettled in one place before moving to another) or the Cubans who did not apply for and receive assistance from the major resettlement agencies.

For Milagros and Lázaro, life in Kentucky is better than it was in Cuba, and despite their occasional frustrations and homesickness, they realize that these are small prices to pay for the freedoms they now enjoy. They also feel lucky to have had such good teachers and mentors, as well as the support of many fellow Cubans in the area and a strong church community—all of which helped in their successful assimilation.

Milagros now adds fresh-squeezed lime juice to her meat mixture. I scurry over to record the measurement and make sure she isn't adding any other secret ingredients. Milagros explains that the lime is actually a substitute for the bitter (sour) orange she used in Cuba and can't find here. The bitter orange, commonly used in Latin cuisine as a breakdown agent in marinades, helps tenderize the meat while adding a delicious richness and citrus flavor.

When I ask my hosts what foods they miss most from Cuba, their eyes light up as they say simultaneously, "The pork!" Apparently, whenever there is a pig roast in Cuba, the savory scent can be smelled half a mile away. They tell me that Cuban pork prepared in American restaurants just doesn't compare to the pork in Cuba.

The sofrito has begun to simmer on the stove, and the cozy one-bedroom apartment, filled with Lázaro's original paintings, teems with the comforting scents of garlic, onion, and tomato sauce. Milagros rolls the meat into 2-inch balls, lightly coats them in flour, and drops them directly into the sofrito. I note that she doesn't brown the meatballs first. This isn't necessarily a Cuban method, but it is the way Milagros learned from her godmother, who taught her how to cook.

When we sit to eat, Lázaro and Milagros fold their hands to pray, but after a few seconds of awkward silence, Robin says she knows a song, "De Colores," a traditional Spanish folk song. As it turns out, it is the perfect prayer—a celebration of all creation, with its many bright colors. Here is the first verse and the chorus:

De colores, de colores
Se visten los campos en la primavera.
De colores, de colores
Son los pajaritos que vienen de afuera.
De colores, de colores
Es el arco iris que vemos lucir.
Y por eso los grandes amores
De muchos colores me gustan a mí.
Y por eso los grandes amores
De muchos colores me gustan a mí.

In colors, in colors
The fields are dressed in the spring.
In colors, in colors
Are the little birds that come from outside.
In colors, in colors
Is the rainbow that we see shining.
And that is why I love
The great loves of many colors.
And that is why I love
The great loves of many colors.

The traditional Cuban meal is not served in courses; rather, all the dishes are served at the same time. This is exactly how Milagros presents

Milagros's café Cubano. (Photo by Julie Johnston)

our lunch—the salad (*ensalada mixta*), black beans (*frijoles negros*), white rice (*arroz blanco*), and *albóndigas*, all delectably piled onto one plate.

The meatballs are incredibly tender, and I wonder if this is because of the lime juice, the fact that they weren't browned first, or both. I grew up on the quarter-sized Swedish meatballs my mother made for special occasions, handed down from our German ancestors and served in a sweet and tangy sauce, or, when time was limited, those Crock-Pot party meatballs swimming in a sea of melted grape jelly and chili sauce. Needless to say, Milagros's zesty sofrito is a welcome change for my jaded palate.

Over lunch we discuss some of the common fruits in America and Cuba and our personal favorites. Someone mentions papayas, and Lázaro chuckles. "What's so funny?" we ask. He explains that we Americans should take care when mentioning papaya to a Cuban: it's pejorative slang for part of a woman's sexual anatomy. (In case you're wondering, Cuba does have the *fruit* papaya, known as *frutabomba*.)

Milagros offers us some *café Cubano* after our meal. Hers is a milder version of the notoriously bold traditional Cuban coffee (similar to espresso), yet it still packs a powerful punch. She uses a special Cuban coffeemaker and a Cuban coffee brand but tones down the strength by using less coffee or adding more water. She also doctors it up with real sugar and whole cream. The espresso cup holds only a half dozen sips, but I savor each one, imagining that I'm watching a sunrise in a seaside café in Havana.

On the living room wall, one of Lázaro's horse paintings steals my attention. A few weeks before my visit, some of Lázaro's works were exhibited at the Revelry Boutique Gallery in Louisville, and he sold several of them. Lázaro hopes to pursue this artistic passion in America and earn some extra income. He had never painted horses before moving to the United States, but in Kentucky he began to paint this majestic animal as a gesture of appreciation and respect for his new home. His *Kentucky Cuba* is one of my favorite paintings. It is both a tribute to his new country and a bittersweet homage to his homeland. In the foreground is the head of a horse wrapped in an American flag. According to Lázaro, the horse symbolizes the great nobility he and Milagros have found in the United States, specifically in Kentucky. In the background are the ruins of a Cuban home—a reminder of what they have lost but also what they will never forget.

Milagros's Albóndigas de Carne (Beef Meatballs)

The word *albóndigas* comes from the Arabic *al bundaq* (translated "hazelnut" or "a small round object"). It is believed that the Moors, or Muslims, introduced this dish to Spain during their reign (from the eighth to the fifteenth century). Cubans likely adopted this comfort food from the Spanish colonists.

Many people believe, mistakenly, that Cuban food is spicy hot, but that's generally not true. In fact, hot peppers are seldom used in recipes. But what Cuban cuisine lacks in heat it more than makes up for in fullness of flavor.

The meatballs in this dish are so tender that they nearly dissolve in your mouth. Paired with the zesty sofrito (sauce), Milagros's meatballs will send your taste buds salsa dancing! If you prefer your meatballs with a little more punch, add some cayenne pepper or minced garlic to the meat mixture.

Serves about 4 (makes 10 to 12 medium meatballs)
Ready in about 50 minutes

Meatball Mixture
1 pound ground beef
2 tablespoons white or yellow onion, finely chopped
2 tablespoons green bell pepper, chopped
2 eggs, beaten
½ teaspoon fresh-squeezed lime juice
2 teaspoons cumin (optional)
1 teaspoon dry yellow ground mustard (optional)
1 teaspoon salt
1 cup Italian-style bread crumbs or cracker crumbs
Flour for rolling meatballs

Sofrito
¼ cup oil
1 large onion, chopped
1 green or red pepper, chopped
2 cloves garlic, minced
1 (24-ounce) jar pasta sauce (Ragu Chunky Garden Combination)
1 teaspoon salt
⅛ teaspoon pepper
½ cup dry white wine or beef broth

Garnish (optional)
Fresh cilantro leaves, chopped
Freshly shredded Parmesan cheese

Combine all the meatball ingredients (except the flour for rolling) in a large mixing bowl and let sit for 10 minutes.

Meanwhile, start the sofrito. Heat the oil in a 3-quart sauté pan over medium heat. Sauté onions, peppers, and garlic until soft (making sure they don't overbrown). Add pasta sauce, salt and pepper, and wine or broth. Stir.

While the sauce simmers, roll the meat mixture into 2-inch balls (or smaller, if you prefer). Roll the meatballs in flour, covering lightly, and place them directly in the sofrito. If necessary, add enough water so the sauce almost covers the meatballs, but take care not to water down the sofrito.

Simmer for about 40 minutes, covered, over medium to low heat until the sauce thickens and the meatballs are cooked through, gently stirring occasionally. (For smaller meatballs, adjust the cooking time.)

Serve alone or with rice or spaghetti. Sprinkle with fresh cilantro and freshly shredded Parmesan cheese. Accompany with a lettuce salad (see Omar's Ensalada Mixta in chapter 23).

¡Que le aproveche!
(Spanish for "Enjoy your meal")

10

Myanmar (Burma)—Rohingya

Win Khine, March 23, 2008

Win Khine, his friend Sabura (SAB-ur-ah) Lin, and I enter their friend's large eat-in kitchen in Owensboro and instantly start coughing. We soon discover the culprit: a spicy Thai beef dish loaded with hot chili peppers simmering on the stovetop. Win quickly raises both kitchen windows, allowing in the mild mid-October air. American kitchens aren't equipped for Burmese cooking, he explains. The stoves often have insufficient ventilation systems, and the kitchens themselves have either no windows or not enough of them. In his native Burma (Myanmar), kitchens are commonly open air.

Fa Ta Ma (FAH-tah-ma) Bi, who has graciously invited us into her home for our cooking adventure, will serve the Thai dish to her family later. This afternoon, however, the three Muslim friends want to teach me how to make an authentic Burmese dish, a multivegetable bean curry called *the sone pè hine* (THEE-sone-PAY-hane). The bean in this recipe is unfamiliar to many Americans. It is a type of garbanzo bean (or chickpea) known as *chana dal*, which is a split *desi* chickpea (smaller and darker than the canned variety found in American groceries). The yellow-colored split peas we are using today have already been soaking in water for hours to reduce the cooking time, and they are now drained, rinsed, and set on the stove to boil. (See "Chickpeas 101" later in this chapter.)

Sabura and Fa Ta Ma, who met more than a dozen years ago in a Thailand refugee camp, are wearing a whitish cream on their cheeks. Win informs me that this is called *thanaka*, and it is made from ground tree bark. A sunscreen, moisturizer, antiaging cream, and antiacne cream

Win Khine (center) and his Owensboro friends Fa Ta Ma Bi (right) and Sabura Lin (left).

all rolled into one, thanaka is worn by Burmese females of all ages and is applied in circles, stripes, or other designs. It will be interesting to see whether this custom will phase out for future generations of Burmese women in America as they learn about other cosmetic options, or whether it will continue due to tradition, efficacy, or both.

The two women, who speak little English, get straight to work. Fa Ta Ma is at the kitchen table slicing, peeling, and dicing the many vegetables for the soup: okra, eggplant, long beans, hot chili peppers, and opo squash—all of which were grown in her impressive backyard garden. Meanwhile, Sabura sits on her haunches on the kitchen floor and grinds onions, garlic, ginger, and other spices with a mortar and pestle. This base sauce for the curry can also be mixed with a blender or food processor, but according to Win and his friends, the traditional method of grinding by hand yields the best results.

When Win first mentioned that we would be cooking with his two friends, whom he met at Owensboro's only mosque about a year ago, I couldn't help wondering if it was because he didn't or couldn't cook. *Au contraire*. Win is very knowledgeable about the foods and preparation methods of his native Burma. He is like a walking Wikipedia, describing each ingredient, spelling words, and even pulling up pictures on his smartphone for my edification.

Win tells me that Burmese cuisine has Indian, Thai, and Chinese influences, but the food of the Muslim ethnic groups to which he and his friends belong (Win is Rohingya, and Fa Ta Ma and Sabura are Pathis) is more heavily influenced by Indian cuisine because their forefathers migrated from India. Win's first foray into cooking began on the open seas during his days with the merchant marines. "Have you seen the movie *Captain Phillips*?" he asks. The cargo vessels on which Win served as a mechanical engineer and that transported such products as bananas and chickens are similar to the ship in the movie. Unlike in the movie, he didn't encounter any Somali pirates, but he is well aware of the dangers along the Somali coastline, which, he says, most captains try to avoid.

During his ten years with the merchant marines, Win visited Thailand, the Philippines, South America, and Australia. He even picked up some languages along the way, including Japanese, Filipino, and Chinese. Sometimes Win and his shipmates would crave their native food, so at select ports, Win would scout the markets for special ingredients and then help the chief chef prepare Burmese dishes. He had no experience cooking. What little he knew came from observing his mother and sister in the kitchen, but the memories came back to him, and through trial and error, he was able to duplicate some of his family's dishes.

Only when he moved to the United States in 2008 did Win's hobby turn into a necessity. As a single man with no family in his new country, he says, "I had no choice but to learn to cook for myself." In his Chicago apartment, he found an Asian cookbook on his roommate's bookshelf and began studying and experimenting with recipes from his native region. He found that he not only liked cooking but also was good at it.

With all the main ingredients now added to the pot on the stove, there's nothing left to do but let the curry simmer. Win and I take the opportunity to talk more about his native country, his political activism, and his life so far in the States.

Win was born and raised in Taungoo in south-central Burma. His father was a government employee, and his assignments took him to many different locations throughout Burma. Win's Muslim ethnic group, the Rohingya, is one of the most persecuted minorities in the world, according to the United Nations. Burmese Muslims, constituting only 4 percent of the population in Burma, can be found throughout the country but are especially prevalent in the Rakhine and Arakan regions in western Burma. Burma has roughly 135 ethnic groups, many of which aren't formally recognized by the government, including the Rohingya, Burmese Chinese, and Panthay. Such ethnic groups have suffered greatly at the hands of Burma's military dictatorship, which gained power in 1962 after a coup d'état.

Win was a student at the Rangoon Institute of Technology for Mechanical Engineering at the time of the student-led revolution of August 8, 1988 (also known as the 8888 Uprising). In March of that year, events involving the death of a student on his campus and the local police galvanized the opposition movement, which spread by word of mouth to other schools throughout the country and attracted hundreds of thousands of followers from all segments of society. Win became an outspoken activist against the military junta and joined the Democratic Party for a New Society, one of many student-led opposition organizations and the second largest party after the National League for Democracy. He visited outlying areas and conducted secret meetings to educate people about democracy, freedom, equality, and human rights. Unfortunately, the military quelled the uprising in September, but the beating heart behind it never stopped ticking.

I've read about the 8888 Uprising, but Win was *there*, on the front lines. He and others like him played vital roles in the grassroots movement to promote political reform. In 2010 general elections were held in Burma as part of a multistep plan by the State Peace and Development Council to achieve a more modern, democratic nation. Win and many members of the opposition parties saw problems with the new constitution proposed for the nation's new government. In 2007, while on vacation from the merchant marines, he attended a press conference near his hometown where the new government was discussed. Having studied other countries' constitutions, including the United States', Win asked difficult questions at the press conference—questions that the pro-government representatives on the panel couldn't adequately answer. He didn't care that his questions might get him into trouble. "It was my responsibility to my country, my people, and the next generation," he said.

Win was indeed blacklisted for voicing his opinions, and the military's intelligence unit began to investigate Win and his family. He knew that if he didn't flee Burma, he'd be arrested or worse. The merchant marines gave him permission to return to work earlier than scheduled, and when he made landfall in North Carolina after five months at sea, Win jumped ship. But his passport, which he left onboard, was not the only identity he lost that day.

Win is different from the other refugees I interviewed for the book because he sought political asylum in the United States. Although every case is different, the main distinction is that those seeking refugee status apply from outside the country in which they hope to resettle; those seeking political asylum, in contrast, apply for that status after they have already entered the country in which they are seeking asylum. A friend and immigration lawyer in New Jersey helped Win prepare his case. Political asylum is not easy to obtain in the United States. For example, of the approximately 86,000 applicants in 2012, only about 25,000 received it, according to US Citizenship and Immigration Services. Win had a strong case, though, and after a year-long process, the United States granted him political asylum in 2009.

Win arrived in Owensboro in July 2013 by way of Illinois, New Jersey, New York, Maryland, New Jersey again, Texas, and Delaware. By the time he got to Kentucky, he had visited more states than many Ameri-

International Center of Kentucky, Owensboro Office

The International Center of Kentucky, headquartered in Bowling Green, has a satellite office in Owensboro. The center is affiliated with the US Committee for Refugees and Immigrants, which reports to the Department of State's Bureau of Population, Refugees, and Migration and has offices in many cities throughout the United States. The center receives both federal and state funding.

The Owensboro office has resettled several hundred refugees since opening its doors in 2009, according to Martha Little, the present site director for the Owensboro office. The overwhelming majority are from Burma and include the ethnic groups Chin, Karen, Karenni, Tedim, and several Muslim groups.

Owensboro, located in northwestern Kentucky, has a population of roughly 60,000 and is adapting to the needs of its newest community members. The local Tyson Foods factory has employed many refugees. The First Christian Church sponsors a community garden for refugees, and an Asian market stocks native foods. The First Presbyterian Church hosts an annual multicultural festival in August, allowing resettled refugees and immigrants from across the globe to share their foods and native customs.

Martha, a former pastoral associate at a local church for more than twenty years, knows her community well and has many profound things to say about refugees, based on her years of experience. Here are some of her thoughts, quoted with her permission:

- "I hope some of their ways will rub off on us here in America. Refugees have a work ethic like my parents had in the 1950s."
- "Refugees' level of respect for every human life and living thing is beyond our understanding."
- "When people ask me why I should help refugees when there are so many people here at home who need help, I tell them, 'I believe everyone in God's eyes deserves a chance. People here have resources. Refugees don't.'"
- "'Assimilate in America,' I tell new refugees, 'but be who you are.'"

cans ever do. During his first few years in the States, Win had to accept jobs below his skill and education levels: sushi cook, gas station attendant, jewelry salesman, and factory worker at Perdue Farms in Bowling Green. During his short time in Bowling Green, Win provided interpretation services for the International Center of Kentucky. Eventually, he took a case manager position in the center's Owensboro satellite office, where he still works. His duties include helping refugees settle into apartments, find employment, receive medical screenings, obtain Social Security cards, and enroll in assistance programs.

Win estimates there are about 200 Muslims in the Owensboro area, about half of whom are members of his mosque. His faith has helped him meet and unite with Muslims from all over the world, including refugees from Africa and the Middle East. Although Win sometimes contemplates moving to Los Angeles, where there is a large Burmese community and more employment opportunities in his field of mechanical engineering, he is content in Owensboro for now, where he uses his broad world experience to assist his fellow countrymen.

A white bowl of vegetable curry, topped with cilantro and paired with white rice, is placed in front of me. It's the moment of truth. I pick up my spoon, and three sets of eyes anxiously watch my face as I take my first bite.

I've tasted a lot of spicy-hot dishes during the course of researching and writing this book, but this is hands down the hottest, no doubt because of the one-two knockout punch of hot chili peppers and crushed red pepper. My friends are relieved when they see that not only can I take the heat, but I like it too. I particularly like the nice balance between the heat and the sour tomatoes, curry, and cilantro, added in the final stages of cooking.

After our meal, we venture outside to take a look at Fa Ta Ma's garden. In the large, fenced-in backyard, I feel like I've been dropped into the tropics. The run-of-the-mill tomatoes, bell peppers, beans, carrots, and cucumbers typically grown in American gardens are nowhere to be found. Fa Ta Ma's garden feels more like a jungle. Opo vines tower over our

Chana dal (split desi chickpeas) for Win's the sone pè hine.

heads, some of their leaves as big as baby elephant ears. There are pumpkin and gourd varieties I've never seen before, and hot chili peppers are lined up on a bench in the middle of the yard, drying in the sun.

Sabura has a garden plot at the First Christian Church, and Win

Chickpeas 101

Split peas, beans, and lentils (also known as pulses) are the edible seeds of legume plants. Win's recipe for multivegetable bean curry calls for chickpeas, which are also in the legume family. The difference between chickpeas and beans can be confusing. There are two types of chickpeas: *kabuli* and *desi*. Kabuli are the larger, cream-colored chickpeas with a smooth coat commonly found canned in most American groceries; they are also known as garbanzo beans. Desi are smaller and darker colored (ranging from tan to black), with a rough coat. The desi chickpea is more common worldwide than the kabuli, although many Americans are unfamiliar with it. *Chana dal*, used in Win's bean curry recipe, is a desi chickpea split in half with the skin removed. (Yellow split peas can be substituted, but they are technically from a different legume species.) Split peas come in green and yellow varieties and can be interchanged, since there is little to no taste difference, although some say the yellow is slightly earthier.

Split peas don't have to be soaked prior to cooking, but every refugee I've cooked with soaks them. Soaking for several hours or overnight reduces the cooking time and helps remove the phytic acid found in legumes, which can cause intestinal distress and reduce mineral absorption. Split peas absorb a lot of water while cooking, so check the water amounts regularly and replenish as necessary.

hopes to acquire a plot there within the year. In Burma, my hosts explain, almost everyone has a family garden if they don't live on a farm. The gardens cultivated by refugees in America serve a much greater purpose than providing a cheap, healthy, and self-sustaining food source, however. Through these gardens, refugees like Win and his friends are able to transplant a piece of their homeland—a piece of themselves—right here on American soil.

Win's The Sone Pè Hine
(Multivegetable Bean Curry)

This is the kind of soup you want to make when you have a head cold because it's sure to open up the sinuses! It contains quintessential features of Burmese cuisine, including a balance of spicy-hot and sour flavors and common Burmese ingredients such as garlic, onion, and turmeric.

Curry is a broad term used to describe a stew-type dish with a complex mixture of spices and herbs, often including turmeric and cumin. Curries can contain vegetables or meats. They are a true comfort food and are commonly eaten throughout India, Pakistan, and elsewhere in Asia.

Although this may be the hottest dish in the book, the sone pè hine's heat quotient can be toned down and adapted to one's taste. The dish takes on a new character with every ingredient added. You might find yourself mumbling (as I did), "I'm not sure about this one," until you add the sour tomatoes (or other souring agent), curry, and cilantro. Then, magically, all the ingredients seem to be in balance.

Do *not* use the canned, ivory-colored chickpeas typically found in American markets. Make sure to use chana dal or some other type of split pea, which is about half the size and has a rougher coat. These are available in Indian, Asian, and many American groceries.

The vegetables used in the recipe can be adjusted to suit individual tastes, but I think the inclusion of squash, daikon radish, hot peppers, and okra adds to the dish's uniqueness. Opo squash (or bottle gourd) is an Asian member of the gourd family that is similar to zucchini and has a mild taste. Opo grows long and narrow and can range in length from 6 to 36 inches. The fruit has a light green to yellow color and firm white flesh. Opo is most associated with Chinese and Southeast Asian cuisine. The small-seeded squash can be used in salads, stir-fries, soups, and stews. Opo can be found in Asian, Indian, and some specialty markets. Zucchini is a fine substitute.

Chinese long beans (also known as yard-long beans, asparagus beans, or garter beans) are a long, thin Asian bean grown in subtropical and tropical regions such as Southeast Asia, Thailand, and southern China. They have a mild taste, like string beans, but with a softer texture; they are not as crisp or as moist. They can be found in Asian and some specialty markets.

I'm not familiar with the variety of small, greenish, sour tomatoes used in this recipe. Sour-tasting tomato varieties are common in Asian and Indian cooking. According to Win, tamarind powder (made from the pulp of the tart tamarind fruit) can also be used as a souring agent. And vinegar is sometimes used as a substitute for tamarind. Because I think the acidity and texture of the tomatoes definitely enhance this curry, I tried the following: I took about four Roma tomatoes, cut them into small chunks, put them in a bowl, drizzled them with lime juice, and let them sit for about 10 minutes. Then I added the tomatoes to the recipe, along with 1 to 2 tablespoons of vinegar. I have no idea if this is a culinary no-no, but it worked like a charm as a souring agent.

I like to garnish my curry with a cooling dollop of sour cream or plain yogurt in addition to the cilantro.

Serves 6
Ready in about 1¼ hours (plus a minimum of 4 hours to soak the chickpeas)

1 pound desi chickpeas (chana dal or yellow split peas)
1½-inch ginger root, peeled and chopped into small chunks
5 to 6 garlic cloves, halved
1 medium yellow onion, chopped into chunks
1 teaspoon turmeric powder
¾ to 1½ tablespoons Spanish paprika
1 to 2 tablespoons ground red pepper
10 tablespoons vegetable oil
4 medium potatoes, peeled and cut into 1-inch chunks, washed
1 daikon radish, peeled and cut into ¼-inch slices
1 tablespoon salt
10 Chinese long beans (or string beans), ends removed and cut into
     1-inch pieces
2 eggplants cut into 1-inch chunks (optional)
15 to 20 okra, ends removed (smaller okra can be left whole, and
     larger can be cut in half)
1 opo squash (or zucchini), peeled and cut into ¼-inch slices
3 to 5 green chili peppers (medium heat), ends removed and cut
     into 1-inch pieces

1 cup sour green baby tomatoes (or 2 tablespoons tamarind powder
  or 2 tablespoons vinegar)
2 teaspoons curry powder
20 stems fresh cilantro, with leaves

At least 4 hours prior to preparing the curry, soak chickpeas in water in a large bowl. Drain and rinse.

In a large (8-quart) stockpot, add chickpeas and enough water to just cover the peas and bring to a boil over medium-high heat. Cook for about 30 minutes, or until peas are tender but not mushy. (Add more water if necessary.)

While the peas cook, combine ginger, garlic, and onion in a blender or food processor or with a mortar and pestle. Grind until almost soupy, but leave some chunky pieces. Add turmeric, paprika to taste, and ground red pepper. Combine and set aside.

After the chickpeas have cooked, rinse in a colander, drain, transfer to a bowl, and set aside. Using the same large pot the peas were cooked in, heat oil over medium-high heat. Add 1 cup water. Stir in the ginger, garlic, and onion mixture. Cook on a low boil for about 10 minutes. Add potatoes and daikon radish and cook for about 10 more minutes. Season with salt. Cover and simmer for 15 to 20 minutes, stirring a couple of times to keep the sauce from sticking to the bottom of the pan.

Add long beans, eggplant, okra, squash, and chili peppers. Add more water if necessary so that the liquid just covers all the ingredients. Simmer, covered, for 10 minutes, stirring occasionally. Add sour tomatoes and cooked peas. Add more water if necessary. Cook another 10 minutes, stirring once or twice. Add curry powder and cilantro (reserving some cilantro for garnish). Stir to combine. Keep soup on low heat until ready to eat. Serve with rice.

Sar kaung bar zay
(formal Burmese expression for "May you have a good appetite")

11

Bhutan

Kamala Pati Subedi, July 29, 2008

It is a midsummer evening when I visit Kamala Pati (KAH-ma-la PAH-tee) Subedi's home. He is sitting in a lawn chair on a small covered porch—as if he's been there, waiting patiently for me, all day. (And considering that he was one of my most conscientious students—the only one who would complain when I did *not* assign homework—he might have been.) He pops up as soon as he sees me and begins waving wildly. On the porch steps, we control our excitement long enough to bow and exchange *Namastes*, the traditional Nepalese greeting.

You can't look into Kamala Pati's bespectacled brown eyes without seeing the kindest of souls shining through. His whole family confirms this kindness as they tell me more about this big-hearted Bhutanese in the ensuing hours. And I mean his *whole* family—three generations strong. At one point, there are nine people in the spacious kitchen—men and women, old and young, even a baby. Accompanying me this evening is my photographer friend Julie, and the family tells us that this gathering isn't just for our special cooking day; it's a common occurrence. At least once a month the extended family gathers in someone's home and makes a large meal that often includes *momos* (dumplings) and *dhakane* (rice pudding). Both are on the menu tonight. Socializing in the kitchen is an important part of their culture and daily routine. As one of Kamala Pati's daughters also notes, "It's just more fun to cook together."

Like most refugees I know, Kamala Pati's family doesn't follow recipes in a cookbook or measure quantities of ingredients. Instead, they determine amounts based on experience and the number of people who will

"It will be my greatest happiness to raise the American flag in my hand and say proudly, 'I am a citizen of this great nation.'" —Kamala Pati Subedi (Photo by Julie Johnston)

be eating. They shop for groceries about twice a week but don't plan menus in advance.

Kamala Pati is already at the stove browning rice in butter for his dhakane. Several other family members form an assembly line at the kitchen island. One mixes the momo filling, which contains cabbage, ginger, onion, cilantro, curry, and cumin. Another scoops the filling into the center of prepackaged round wrappers. Still another folds the wrappers into half moons and pinches the edges into perfect pleats. All this is accomplished with a beautiful rhythm and synchronicity.

Thirteen family members, including Kamala Pati, currently live in this five-bedroom house located in a fairly new subdivision in southeast Louisville. About thirty other Bhutanese home owners live in the same

Momos prior to steaming. (Photo by Julie Johnston)

neighborhood. This home, owned by Kamala Pati's niece, Tika, and her husband, Oma Kafley, is large by most refugees' standards. A new house is being built down the street, and Kamala Pati, his wife Bishnu, and several other family members will move into it later in the year.

It is typical for more than one Bhutanese family and more than one generation to live together, sharing resources and saving money. The sense of "mine" and "yours" doesn't exist, according to Oma, who is interpreting for us today. In Bhutanese culture, all family members come together and pitch in wherever and whenever necessary for the good of the family and the household. Moreover, here in America, men and women have had to adopt nontraditional roles. Women, for example, have joined the workforce and are going back to school, and men are taking over household and child-care duties as needed.

Kamala Pati's family has assimilated particularly well because of this communal approach to living, their work ethic, smart saving and spending habits, and their strong English skills, especially among the younger generations. Many Bhutanese refugees learned English beginning in kindergarten in the Nepali refugee camps, where a large percentage of their ethnic group, the Lhotsampas (La-SAM-pas), fled in the early 1990s.

Oma's family was one of the first to settle in Kentucky, in June 2008. He tells me, "The story will be too long to describe, but in short it was a religious and political problem that forced us to leave our motherland."

Bhutan is a small Himalayan country sandwiched between India and China. Comparable in size to Indiana, but with a population closer to Alaska's, it is the last independent Himalayan Buddhist kingdom in the world. Since breaking away from its northern neighbor Tibet in the eighth century, Bhutan has enjoyed centuries of isolation from the outside world and has been slow to modernize. The first road wasn't built until the early 1960s, and official television broadcasts didn't air until 1999.

Today, Bhutan is a constitutional monarchy and one of the world's youngest democracies. It held its first general elections in 2007 and 2008. Although it has been touted as one of the happiest countries in the world, Bhutan can hardly claim a blemish-free history. In the 1980s the Buddhist-majority kingdom began to view the Lhotsampas (who are primarily Hindu and of Nepali origin) as a political and cultural threat. The situation escalated in 1989, according to Oma and Kamala Pati, when authorities burned all Nepalese books. Soon after, the harassment campaign against the Lhotsampas began in earnest.

Kamala Pati grew up in Gellephu, a mountainous region in south-central Bhutan on the Indian border. He came from a wealthy family and was a member of a high caste. A prosperous farmer, he had twenty-five acres of land on which he raised cattle and goats. He also had two one-acre fish ponds and a rice mill. Oma says that before he ever met his wife's uncle in America, he knew Kamala Pati by reputation as a well-respected member of the Bhutanese community. I had already noticed this deference at the ESL school where I taught: when Kamala Pati talked, the other Bhutanese students sat up and listened.

Kamala Pati began to volunteer in his Bhutanese community at age fifteen and later became his village's leader-elect. For seventeen years he performed a number of roles: advocate, mediator, problem solver, lender.

He even led a community program to help clean up local ponds and rivers and to raise awareness about forest preservation. (About 75 percent of Bhutan's land is forested, and it is one of the most biodiverse nations in the world.)

Once the government's harassment campaign started, Kamala Pati was among the first Lhotsampas targeted. In October 1990, thanks to a neighbor's warning that the army was on its way for him, Kamala Pati was able to escape Bhutan. Wearing only his pajamas, he headed south on foot to India, just a few miles away, where he hid for the next year and a half. Other Lhotsampas weren't as lucky. Some were thrown in jail and tortured until they renounced their homeland and turned over their possessions. Sometimes the army would throw a family's possessions out the door and burn everything, including the house.

Kamala Pati and his family were reunited in July 1992 in India. From there, they journeyed together to Nepal and spent the next sixteen years in a refugee camp. The camps had no electricity, and large families were squeezed into one small house. They cooked using coal and read by lamplight.

Kamala Pati suffered another devastating loss when his mother died a short time after they arrived in the camp. "I felt a separation in my heart from losing my home, my mother, and my community where everyone knew and respected me," Kamala Pati says.

In America, that separation in his heart has grown wider. Because of the language barrier, he feels that he can't help others. He misses being able to serve his community as he once did. If anything speaks to Kamala Pati's character, it is this.

In their formal dining room, the family waits on Julie and me like we're royalty. They fill our plates with vegetarian momos, accompanied by a spicy tomato and toasted sesame seed dipping sauce, and with dhakane, which is often served with the main meal rather than as a dessert. While we eat the healthy, steamed dumplings and the sweet, cardamom-spiced rice pudding, I ask Kamala Pati to tell me more about his writing.

During class one day, he had shown me a small paperback book

The Big Crisis in Little-Known Bhutan

Many Americans have never heard of Bhutan, a small Himalayan kingdom in Southeast Asia. Even fewer know that, as of 2012, the United States had resettled about 55,000 Bhutanese refugees, according to the United Nations High Commissioner for Refugees (UNHCR). Most of these refugees are Lhotsampas, an ethnic group of Nepali origin whose members are primarily of the Hindu faith. They began immigrating to southern Bhutan in the late nineteenth century.

From about the mid-1980s to the early 1990s, refugees say that Bhutan's Buddhist-majority government, which viewed the Lhotsampas as a political and a cultural threat, carried out a harassment campaign. As a result, the Lhotsampas were pressured to renounce their homes and their homeland, forced to flee, or expelled. Torture, rape, and child labor are just some of the egregious injustices reported by refugees.

The UNHCR reported in 2008 that more than 107,000 Bhutanese refugees were living in seven camps in southeastern Nepal. Yet the Bhutanese refugee situation received little worldwide attention at the time, as it was overshadowed by larger refugee crises elsewhere (Afghanistan and Rwanda, to name two such places). In 2008 several countries, including Canada, Australia, New Zealand, Denmark, and the United States, began to receive Bhutanese refugees from the inundated camps, with the United States accepting the majority. The United Nations called this one of the world's largest resettlement efforts.

Between 2008 and 2013, roughly 1,900 Bhutanese refugees were resettled in Kentucky, according to the Kentucky Office for Refugees. However, a 2013 census conducted by the Bhutanese Society of Kentucky, a nonprofit organization established in 2009 to help preserve the Bhutanese culture, reported that approximately 2,000 Bhutanese were living in Kentucky. The majority resided in Louisville, followed by Lexington and Bowling Green.

written in Nepalese, and from what I could discern, he had authored it. Kamala Pati had initially planned to write a personal memoir about his memories of Bhutan, but when he asked elder refugees in the camp about their nation's history, no one seemed to have any answers, so he decided to find the answers himself. In 2005, after two years of research and writing, he published *Bhutan Aajako Parepakshama* (Bhutan in This Time). As a fellow writer and book lover, I was heartsick to learn that, shortly before he moved to the United States, a fire in the refugee camp destroyed the 200 books he had printed. As far as anyone knows, the paperback he showed me is the only existing copy.

Since arriving in Kentucky by way of New Mexico (what is known in refugee resettlement circles as a "secondary migration"), Kamala Pati has published several articles in overseas Nepali newspapers and magazines. His writing is mainly academic, and his goal, in part, is to educate younger generations about Bhutanese customs and culture, such as the religious importance of the Hindu festival Diwali, the autumn "festival of lights."

After dinner, Kamala Pati, Oma, Julie, and I talk outside on the lawn. As dusk descends, Kamala Pati shares his yearning to become a US citizen, and tears fill his eyes. "My citizenship was stripped from me in Bhutan," he says. Now he is without a country to call his own. For Kamala Pati and many other immigrants and refugees, attaining US citizenship provides a sense of belonging and having a place to call home. "It will be my greatest happiness to raise the American flag in my hand and say proudly, 'I am a citizen of this great nation,'" says Kamala Pati.

Before we leave, Julie takes a photo of me with the family. Suddenly her shoulders start to shake from giggling so hard. "What?" I ask. "You," she said. "You don't exactly blend right in." Whenever I look at that picture now and see my blonde-haired, fair-skinned self alongside my dark-haired, dark-skinned friends, I can't help smiling too—not because of how different I look, but because of how little it matters.

Kamala Pati's Vegetarian Steamed Momos (Dumplings)

Momo is a traditional delicacy in South Asian cuisine, particularly in Bhutan, Nepal, Tibet, and northern India. It may be as ubiquitous a fast food in Nepal and the Himalayan states of India as hamburgers are in America.

The dumplings, which are usually steamed, can be made with a vegetarian or nonvegetarian filling, such as any ground meat. They are commonly served with a tomato-based chutney or dipping sauce. Kamala Pati's family makes momos once or twice a month and often serves them at large family gatherings or for special occasions such as weddings, festivals, and birthdays. Ideally, this recipe requires a steamer or a rice cooker with a steamer basket.

I've sampled many momos over the years, but I think these might be the best I've ever had. The spicy heat coupled with curry and ginger and the crunch of the cabbage . . . you'll see why 10—or more—per person is considered an average serving size!

Dumpling shells can be made from scratch, but the prepackaged kind work just fine, are less time-consuming, and prevent waste (some dough is lost when shaping homemade dumplings). Prepackaged dumplings can be found in Vietnamese or Asian markets and even in some American groceries.

Several methods for shaping the dumplings can be found online. Kamala Pati's family prefers the half-moon method. There are even fancy kitchen gadgets that will mold the dumplings for you. When making large amounts, it is best to recruit some kitchen assistants to help stuff the dumplings, or you can halve the recipe for smaller gatherings. You can also make the full filling recipe and save half for future fresh-steamed momos. Leftover cooked dumplings can be stored in the refrigerator and used within a few days. However, momos are best served fresh and warm.

Serves about 10 (makes about 100 dumplings)
Ready in about 1½ hours (with several helpers assembling the dumplings)

> 3 medium heads green cabbage, grated
> 2½ tablespoons salt
> 2½ cups chopped cilantro
> 1½ large red onions, chopped
> 1 tablespoon cumin powder

Kitchen is home for Huong "CoCo" Tran at her Roots and Heart & Soy restaurants. (Photo by Julie Johnston)

CoCo Tran's soft spring rolls and peanut sauce.

Azar Akrami puts the finishing touches on her tachin.

Like many refugees, Mirzet Mustafić has his own garden in the United States.

Mirzet Mustafić's ćevapi on lepina. (Photo by Mirzet Mustafić)

In Bhutanese families, multiple generations often cook large meals together. (Photo by Julie Johnston)

Hot chili peppers are a staple in Bhutanese cuisine. (Photo by Julie Johnston)

Goma Acharya and her sister Auodya
in traditional Nepalese dress.

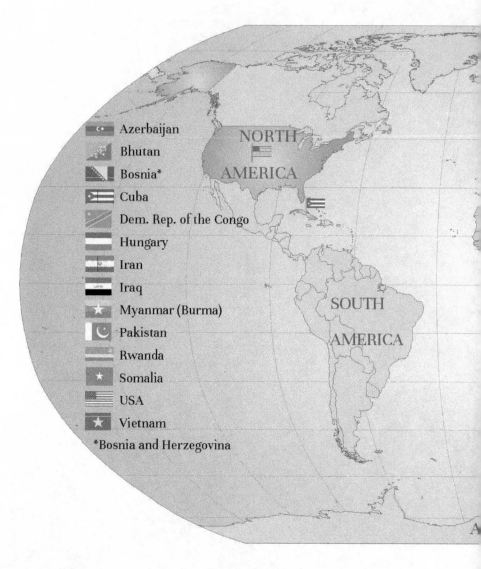

Azerbaijan
Bhutan
Bosnia*
Cuba
Dem. Rep. of the Congo
Hungary
Iran
Iraq
Myanmar (Burma)
Pakistan
Rwanda
Somalia
USA
Vietnam

*Bosnia and Herzegovina

NORTH
AMERICA

SOUTH
AMERICA

National flags are powerful symbols. For some refugees and immigrants, their native country's flag still inspires a sense of identity and national pride. For others, it might represent a government, political regime, or way of life they can no longer support or

do not identify with. The flags featured here are meant to reflect the diversity of the countries represented in this book and to honor each contributor's unique cultural heritage.

Amina Osman
grows her own
vegetables through
Louisville's
RAPP-sponsored
communal gardens
for refugees.

Amina Osman's sambusas.

Sofrito for Milagros Guzman-Gonzalez's albóndigas de carne. (Photo by Julie Johnston)

Pastor Thomas Kap and Esther Sung's Burmese pork curry.

Dr. Gulalai Wali Khan's gazaro halwa.

Elmira Tonian's chopped pork with mushroom cream sauce and whipped potato rosettes.

William Thang's khyan-gyin thee thoke.

Cooking is often a family event for Zainab Kadhim Alradhee, her husband Barrak Aljabbari, and their two children.

Zainab Kadhim Alradhee's chicken biryani.

1 teaspoon chili powder

1 tablespoon turmeric

2 tablespoons curry powder

1 tablespoon Ajinomoto (umami seasoning) or Accent flavor
enhancer (MSG)

4 tablespoons unsalted butter, melted, or vegetable oil, plus more to
grease the steamer basket

1½ cups peeled ginger, grated

4 (14-ounce) packages dumpling wrappers (25 wrappers per
package)

In a large bowl, mix cabbage and salt to taste. Place in a colander
and squeeze out excess water by pressing down on the cabbage. Drain
well. Add cilantro, onion, cumin powder, chili powder, turmeric, curry
powder, and Ajinomoto (or Accent) to taste. Stir. Add melted butter or oil
and combine well. Add ginger. Stir and set aside for 20 minutes to let all
the flavors combine.

To Fill the Dumplings

Wet one side of the dumpling wrapper with water and put 1 tablespoon filling mixture in the center of the wrapper. Fold the wrapper in
half and pinch the top together with one hand. With the other hand,
bring all the edges together to the center by making small pleats. Pinch
and twist the pleats slightly to ensure that the stuffing stays inside the
dumpling.

To Steam the Dumplings

Heat water in a steamer and bring to a full boil. (The amount of
water depends on the capacity of the steamer. Follow the manufactur-
er's instructions, but don't let the water touch the momos.) Generously
oil the bottom and sides of the steamer rack (this is an important step to
prevent the dumplings from sticking). Arrange the uncooked dumplings
in the steamer in one layer, leaving some space between them to prevent
sticking. Cover and steam until the dumplings are cooked through, about

15 minutes. (The dumplings become soft, transparent, and moist when done; however, the cooking time can be adjusted based on the texture you prefer.)

Remove the dumplings from the steamer and serve immediately with Kamala Pati's Tomato and Toasted Sesame Seed Dipping Sauce.

Kamala Pati's Tomato and Toasted Sesame Seed Dipping Sauce

This dipping sauce is a perfect accompaniment to momos, and the great thing about it is that you can easily modify it to suit individual tastes. If less heat is desired, use all mild chili peppers or reduce the amount of peppers. For additional heat, use hot peppers or increase the amount. If a sweet sauce is desired, add 1 tablespoon brown sugar or honey instead of the chilies, or try a combination of sweet and spicy flavors. Mustard oil, made from mustard seeds, can be found in Indian markets, but a smaller amount of ground mustard can be substituted. This dipping sauce also goes well with Amina's Sambusas (see chapter 8).

Makes about 1½ cups
Ready in about 15 minutes

> 7 medium tomatoes, quartered
> ½ to 1 tablespoon salt
> ½ cup toasted sesame seeds
> 1 to 3 small hot chili peppers, finely chopped
> 1 to 2 small mild red chili peppers, finely chopped
> 2 teaspoons fresh ginger, peeled and finely chopped
> 1½ tablespoons mustard oil
> ½ cup cilantro
> Juice from half a lime (optional)

Place tomatoes in a medium bowl and sprinkle with salt. Microwave until softened, 5 to 15 minutes, depending on size and ripeness.

Meanwhile, toast the sesame seeds in a small skillet over medium-low heat, stirring constantly and taking care not to burn them. Toast the seeds until they are lightly browned and produce a nutty aroma (about 5 minutes).

In a blender, grind sesame seeds into a powder. Add tomatoes and mix until soupy. Add chili peppers, ginger, mustard oil, and cilantro. Mix and taste; adjust seasonings if necessary. Add lime juice, if desired, and blend until the sauce is well combined.

Serve in a dish with Kamala Pati's Vegetarian Steamed Momos (dumplings).

Kamala Pati's Dhakane (Rice Pudding)

Dhakane (dah-KAH-nee) is slightly different from its sister dish *khir*, another sweet rice pudding, in that it is made by frying the rice in butter. Rice pudding is probably the most famous food in Nepalese culture, and countless versions of it can be found throughout Nepal, Bhutan, and parts of India. Kamala Pati learned how to make this dish from his mother and father, who learned how to make it from their parents, and so on.

This rice pudding is an integral part of any party, festival, or ceremony, including the two largest Bhutanese holidays, Dashara (also known as Dashain) and Diwali. Dhakane is also eaten during the Hindu holy month of Shrawan (celebrated July through August). Though it can be a dessert, dhakane is also served with the main meal as a side dish, as a snack, or even as a breakfast treat.

Use whole milk for best results. Use slightly less milk if you prefer a thicker, more pudding-like consistency.

Freshly crushed cardamom seeds are much more flavorful and aromatic than packaged ones, which can quickly lose their freshness. I highly recommend that you obtain cardamom pods and extract the seeds by crushing the pods with a mortar and pestle. Pick out the pieces of pod shell and then grind the small black seeds with a mortar and pestle or spice grinder. Both seeds and pods are available in Asian, Indian, and some American groceries with well-stocked ethnic sections. (See "Carda-mom: The Spice Queen" in chapter 19.)

Serves 4
Ready in about 1 hour

> 6 cups whole vitamin D milk
> ½ stick unsalted butter
> 1 cup basmati rice
> ⅓ cup fresh coconut, grated (or packaged Angel Flake sweetened
>   coconut)
> ½ cup sugar
> ½ teaspoon freshly ground green cardamom seeds (or 1 to 1½
>   teaspoons bottled cardamom powder)
> ¼ cup almonds, slivered
> ¼ cup cashew nuts, slivered
> ½ cup golden raisins

In a medium pot over high heat, bring milk to a full boil, stirring a few times. Lower the heat or remove the pan from the heat altogether so the milk doesn't overflow or overcook.

Meanwhile, in a large (8-quart) stockpot, melt butter. Add rice to the melted butter. Cook, stirring frequently, for 8 to 10 minutes, or until the rice browns and gives off a pleasant aroma. (Be careful not to over-brown or burn the rice.)

Add grated coconut to the stockpot and stir to combine with rice and butter. Transfer the milk to the stockpot and bring the mixture to a boil. Simmer on a gentle boil for 30 to 35 minutes, or until the rice is softened, the milk is reduced, and the overall mixture has thickened. Stir frequently so the milk doesn't burn or overflow. (Remove any milk film that forms on the surface.)

Add sugar and stir until completely dissolved. Taste and add more sugar if desired. Add cardamom and stir to combine. Add almonds, ca-shews, and raisins and simmer for 3 to 4 minutes.

Remove from heat and serve warm or chilled. Optional garnishes include coconut flakes, raisins, nuts (toasted for additional flavor), or a dash of cardamom or cinnamon.

Dhakane can be made 2 to 3 days in advance and warmed in the microwave.

Krishnarpan
(Nepalese for "Have a nice meal")

12

Myanmar (Burma)—Chin

Pastor Thomas Kap, September 6, 2008

I visit Pastor Thomas Kap on Labor Day, a day meant for rest and re-laxation. But for the pastor, it's just another workday. In fact, since this morning he has been trying to fix the brakes on his car with the help of a fellow Burmese refugee. It's a perfect example of neighbor helping neigh-bor—or, in this case, Chin helping Chin. If there's anything I take away from my visit with the pastor and his wife, Esther Sung, it's this: Chin do not abandon their own.

In the kitchen of their second-floor apartment in Crescent Springs, I'm introduced to the ingredients for the pork curry that Esther is going to teach me to make. These are common staples in the Burmese culinary arsenal: garlic, ginger, turmeric, paprika, chili pepper, cilantro. The pork curry quickly wins over my heart when I see Esther throw all the ingredi-ents into one large sauté pan and place it on the stovetop to simmer. That's my kind of cooking: quick and easy.

Esther, whose smile would instantly calm a screaming child, loves to cook, and she starts to make another dish, a pumpkin leaf soup. Cooking with pumpkin leaves is unfamiliar to many Westerners, but it is common in some South Asian and African regions. However, Esther and I decide against including this recipe in the book because of its obscure and hard-to-locate ingredients, including a small, mysterious gourd whose name even Esther doesn't know. Esther makes both the pumpkin soup and the pork curry frequently, just as her mother, who taught her how to cook, still does back in Burma (now Myanmar). Their native foods now bridge the great physical divide between them.

Pastor Thomas Kap, his wife Esther, and hundreds of other Chin refugees have made Crescent Springs their new home

As the house fills with a potpourri of scents, my hosts and I gather in the living room. On the wall opposite me is a framed picture of Jesus. Beneath my bare feet (I kicked my shoes off at the door, following my hosts' lead) is a large woven grass mat from Thailand. According to Esther, almost every home in Burma has one just like it. On another wall is a large map of the United States. I am surrounded by the symbols of the things that have shaped this family's identity: their faith, their native country and culture, and their new life in America.

In September 2008 Pastor Thomas, Esther, and their daughter Glory arrived in Florence, Kentucky, where some of the pastor's relatives lived. They knew nothing about Kentucky other than that it was a US state. Pastor Thomas found work in the Levi Strauss factory in nearby Hebron. After two years in Florence, the family relocated a few miles northeast to Crescent Springs, just across the Ohio River from Cincinnati. It is here that the pastor would return to his true calling in the ministry.

Turmeric: The Healthy Spice with a Bright Yellow Splash

Turmeric, related to the ginger family, comes from the root of the *Curcuma longa* plant. The rhizome has dark, rough skin and bright orange flesh. Turmeric is usually sold in powdered form in the West.

Native to Indonesia and tropical India, turmeric has been harvested for 5,000 years and has long been used to dye textiles, heal the body, and flavor and color foods. It is commonly used in Indian, Asian, and Middle Eastern cuisines, especially in curries, and it gives basic yellow mustard its vibrant color. Turmeric is slightly bitter, pungent, and peppery.

Though it has long been used in Chinese and Indian medicine, including the Ayurvedic system, turmeric is slowly gaining popularity in the West as more research points to its many therapeutic benefits. The yellow or orange pigment in turmeric, known as curcumin, is believed to have anti-inflammatory and antioxidant properties. Curcumin is also found in curry powders.

Take care when using turmeric because it can easily stain. To prevent temporary stains on fingernails and hands when cooking with turmeric, wear kitchen gloves.

Pastor Thomas, who is wearing a T-shirt with Isaiah 54:2 printed on it, tells me that it was never his intention to start a faith community when he first came to the United States. If anything, that faith community—or at least the need for one—found *him*.

"When I came here there were only about fifteen Burmese people," Pastor Thomas explains. They met once a week for worship services in someone's basement. Within a year, however, the Chin worshippers had grown to between 50 and 100—too many to continue to meet in a member's home. The informal congregation rented space from a Presbyterian church, but in two years' time they numbered 200 and had outgrown their worship space again. This time they found a larger facility, Erlanger Baptist Church, just a short jaunt down the highway. And they gave their faith community an official name: Calvary Chin Baptist Church. "By the grace of God we grow in members, and now we are 315 people," the pastor says.

Many of the current church members knew Pastor Thomas prior to coming to the United States. Some settled in Crescent Springs because they learned by word of mouth of the vibrant church community in the area. The pastor quickly rejects my suggestion that he is the reason so many Chin have flocked to northern Kentucky. "We take care of each other," he says modestly.

Pastor Thomas and Esther grew up in Hakha, the capital of Chin State. In 1899 the first American Baptist missionaries arrived in the remote, mountainous region in western Burma—the country's poorest state today and home to the majority of the world's Chin people. Within fifty years, Christianity had gained a strong foothold in Chin State, and today an overwhelming majority of people living there are Christian.

Pastor Thomas and Esther don't remember much fighting in the region until 1988, when a student-led uprising against the military regime ignited in Rangoon and spread like wildfire throughout the country. In the midst of this external chaos, Pastor Thomas took an inward journey, turning his life over to Christ and being baptized in 1991. He went to a Bible college, and in 1999 he and Esther married.

At the time of this writing, despite some encouraging political reforms, Burma is still considered one of the worst violators when it comes to religious freedom. For Pastor Thomas, this bleak statistic was part of his daily reality. For seven years he served as pastor of a church in Burma, but preaching the Christian gospel in a Buddhist-dominated country proved to be an uphill battle. His and other Christian clergy's sermons were edited by government censors. When he couldn't get a permit to build a larger church for his growing congregation, he was forced to apply for one under the pretense of constructing a building for personal, nonreligious purposes. And he could only stand by helplessly as the government offered cash incentives to Buddhist men to marry Christian women and convert them to the Buddhist faith, or as the children of poor Christian families were offered a free education in exchange for their indoctrination into Buddhism.

In 2005 Pastor Thomas and Esther decided to move to Malaysia, where they ministered to the many Chin people who had fled there. Today, Pastor Thomas's ministry goes far beyond addressing his people's spiritual needs. They need interpreters, and he is one of the few Chin in the area who can speak English well. They need help applying for green cards, health insurance, and jobs. They need help getting to and from doctors' appointments, finding affordable housing, locating suitable schools for their children. The list goes on.

As of 2014, northern Kentucky lacked an official, federally designated refugee office. The Kentucky Refugee Ministries (KRM) office in Lexington, which opened in 1998 and became an official satellite to KRM's Louisville headquarters in 1999, can resettle only those refugees who have a US connection—someone willing and able to help support them. Moreover, most of the Chin in northern Kentucky are secondary migrants who have moved to the area from somewhere else, such as Ohio, and KRM isn't always informed of their arrival. The Lexington office does its best with limited resources to serve those refugees who qualify for its services. It also strives to identify new partners, such as the Junior League of Cincinnati, and additional sources of aid. From 2007 through 2013, according to statistics compiled by the Kentucky Office for Refugees, slightly more than 700 Burmese Chin had been resettled in Kentucky through official resettlement agencies. The Chin are the second largest Burmese refugee group resettled in Kentucky, after the Karen.

Pastor Thomas is appreciative of KRM's help, especially the regular office hours it keeps once a week at a Presbyterian church in Crescent Springs. But the Chin community, particularly the newcomers, still requires more support. Recently the church hired one of its own, a student studying social work at Northern Kentucky University, to assist Pastor Thomas as he tries to meet the growing needs of their faith community.

Despite the challenges facing the Chin in their new community, they have assimilated remarkably well in a short time. Most of them become self-sufficient within 120 days of arrival. Pastor Thomas says that four Chin families have bought homes ranging in price from $130,000 to $230,000. He and Esther hope to purchase a home of their own within the year.

But why have the Chin been so successful? For one thing, they are excellent savers and rarely spend beyond their means. But they are also hard workers. "They like to work very much," says Pastor Thomas. It helps, too, that they have been able to find work. Northern Kentucky is home to many large factories where employees require little English to perform rote tasks such as sorting and packaging. Club Chef in Covington, a fresh produce distributor, and Levi Strauss have employed many Chin as well. Esther, who is presently employed at Levi Strauss, works four days a week, ten hours a day, and sometimes earns overtime.

"We love America," Pastor Thomas tells me. "America is the land of opportunity. It is for everybody. Those who work hard and those who study, they have their opportunity. That is what I like. . . . Everybody is free."

Pastor Thomas checks his watch and informs me that he must go; he has a church commitment. He leaves me in Esther's capable hands, and she proudly models some of her native Chin attire, including a multicolored striped skirt and shirt woven by her mother. Pastor Thomas and Esther believe strongly in preserving their culture and passing it down to the next generation. Every summer the Calvary Chin Baptist Church teaches its youth about Chin dress, dance, language, and other customs to help keep their native traditions alive.

With the pumpkin leaf soup and the pork curry now cooked to her satisfaction, Esther serves me a hearty helping of each. I imagine the brothy soup, with its nutrition-packed pumpkin leaves, nurturing my body with every spoonful. The pork is exceptionally tender and flavorful, and the fresh cilantro and hint of ginger balance the heat of the chili pepper. Esther knows little English, but few words are needed. She can tell by my *oohs* and *ahhhs* and my eagerness for another helping of each dish how much I appreciate all the time, effort, and *heart* that went into the meal.

When Pastor Thomas returns from his church obligation, he checks to make sure that I got everything I needed. I can tell that he is tired, and he excuses himself to go rest, at long last.

After I return home, I look up the Bible passage (Isaiah 54:2) printed on Pastor Thomas's shirt. It couldn't be more well suited to the life the pastor, his family, and his faith community have built for themselves in the United States:

> Enlarge the place of your tent,
> stretch your tent curtains wide,
> do not hold back;
> lengthen your cords,
> strengthen your stakes.

Pastor Thomas and Esther's Burmese Pork Curry

Burma shares a border with many neighbors—India, Bangladesh, China, Laos, and Thailand—and its cuisine has been heavily influenced by these countries' ingredients and cooking styles. Yet it's the combination of these ingredients and styles that makes Burmese cuisine as unique as a thumbprint.

Esther serves this traditional Burmese dish (usually accompanied by rice) at least once a week in her home. It is both delicious and easy to prepare. Burmese curries don't always use curry powder, but they do typically use onion, garlic, turmeric, ginger, and some form of chili pepper.

I suggest that you select a cut of meat with plenty of fat. The first time I made this dish, I used a piece of pork with most of the fat trimmed off, and it wasn't as flavorful as Esther's and didn't produce enough juices to make gravy. If you like, you can trim any excess fat after cooking. For spicy heat lovers, add more chili pepper flakes. The cilantro garnish, though optional, really brings all the flavors together.

Serves 4
Ready in about 1½ hours

> 1½ to 2 pounds boneless pork loin roast, fat untrimmed
> ½ large tomato, cut into chunks
> 1 tablespoon Spanish paprika
> 1 teaspoon salt
> 1 teaspoon chili pepper flakes

¼ teaspoon Ajinomoto (umami seasoning) or Accent flavor
    enhancer (MSG)
½ teaspoon turmeric
1 inch ginger, peeled and grated
½ medium white onion, finely sliced
10 cloves garlic, halved
3 tablespoons vegetable oil
Fresh cilantro leaves (optional)

Wash the pork, blot dry with paper towels, and cut into bite-size cubes. Put the pork in a large sauté pan, add the next 9 ingredients to the pan, and top with vegetable oil. Mix well and place on the stove over medium-high heat.

Cover and cook for 15 to 20 minutes, stirring occasionally. Check periodically to see if there is enough liquid (it should reach about half-way up on the ingredients; if it doesn't, add a little water). Lower heat to medium-low and simmer for another 30 minutes, or until the meat is tender, stirring occasionally to prevent the juices from sticking to the bottom of the pan. The dish is ready when the meat is tender and the liquid has reduced to a stew-like consistency. Garnish with fresh cilantro and serve with white rice.

Mein mein saa
(informal Burmese expression for *"Enjoy a delicious meal"*)

13

Democratic Republic
of the Congo

Aline Bucumi and Genevieve Faines,
December 12, 2008

Genevieve Faines, wearing a red sundress, plops down on the kitchen floor with a large stockpot and a dozen green bananas and begins peeling them one by one. I sit across from her and start peeling too.

These aren't what most Americans consider green bananas—the sweet variety a few days shy of ripe—which can be peeled with the hands and eaten raw. These are "cooking bananas," which are similar to plantains and eaten like a vegetable. They are a special variety grown only in the eastern regions of the Democratic Republic of the Congo and East Africa. Their tough skins must be removed with a sharp knife, and once cooked, they taste a lot like boiled potatoes.

"Am I taking too much off?" I ask, afraid I'm removing more flesh than peel.

Genevieve inspects the banana in my hand, chuckles softly, and confirms my hunch with a shy smile.

Aline (Ah-LEAN) Bucumi, Genevieve's mother, is resting on the living room couch. She likes to cook but is not feeling her best today, so Genevieve has taken her place as my African culinary tour guide.

My new friend, a recent graduate from Louisville's Central High School, explains that young people from her region of Africa are largely self-taught cooks. They are given the basics and then slowly take on more cooking responsibilities, often figuring it out as they go along.

"Everyone farms in Africa. If you aren't farming, you aren't eating." —Aline Bucumi (with her daughter Genevieve Faines)

"Do you eat goat?" she asks. Her family eats a lot of goat, and she plans to add it to the *matoke* (ma-TOE-ka) she's preparing today, an East African dish made with bell and chili peppers, onions, garlic, tomatoes, and—you guessed it—cooking bananas. I tell her that I do eat goat (although, to be honest, I'd never eaten goat meat prior to writing this book). I like the taste of it, and I also like the fact that it has lower calories, fat, and cholesterol than traditional meats like chicken and beef. (See "Here a Goat, There a Goat" in chapter 14.)

"What about stomach?" Genevieve asks, smiling and nodding toward the pot on the stove's back burner, where the organ is simmering for a dish she will later serve the family.

"I'm adventurous, but not *that* adventurous," I say.

I hear Genevieve's younger brother Adonisi (ADD-oh-NEE-see) in the next room, goofing off with my friend Robbie Adelberg. I met the family through Robbie, who met them through his role as technical adviser for the Refugee Agricultural Partnership Program (RAPP), administered locally by Catholic Charities Migration and Refugee Services. RAPP provides refugees the opportunity to learn about American agriculture and helps them grow and sell their own produce (see "Farming on 'Foreign' Soil" in chapter 8). Robbie first met Adonisi at one of RAPP's five garden sites, located on the south side of Louisville. They became fast friends, and Robbie is now like a member of the family, helping transport the kids to activities and Aline to doctor's appointments. He is just one of many behind-the-scenes volunteers across the country who help ease refugees' transition into American life and support the efforts of resettlement agencies.

Genevieve and her mother are both from the Democratic Republic of the Congo (DRC)—one of the poorest countries in the world. When Genevieve was a small child, she and her mother fled to a refugee camp in Tanzania. They feared for their safety in the war-ravaged DRC, which has the disreputable distinction of being the "rape capital of the world." According to a Refugees International 2013 report, about 2.5 million people from the DRC have been internally displaced due to the ongoing conflict, primarily in the country's eastern provinces, and more than 260,000 have fled to nearby countries such as Tanzania.

Genevieve's father died in the DRC when she was just a baby, and she tells me the circumstances are too involved to get into. She turns quiet, and a look of pain suddenly washes over her face. I don't press, knowing that I'm treading on sacred ground.

Aline thought she would spend the rest of her life in a refugee camp, and she actually has fond memories of the camp where she and her daughter lived for more than a decade in Tanzania. It is where she gave birth to her son. "If not for refugee camp, I would not have come to America," she says.

And if she hadn't come to America and received good health care, Aline, who suffers from back pain associated with a herniated disk and other health problems, believes she might not be alive today. Aline was so sick during one of her refugee resettlement interviews that she asked her caseworkers, "Would you like to take my children? Because I'm not sure I can make the trip to America."

She describes the day when she and her two children finally, after a five-year process, made landfall in Louisville: "We were so happy," she says. "We thought we were in another heaven."

While we wait for the matoke to finish cooking, we gather in the living room, where an action movie is playing on the flat-screen TV. I'm hoping to discuss the family's life so far in America, and Genevieve and Adonisi interpret for their mother. The family speaks Swahili, one of four national languages in the DRC, although more than 200 languages are reportedly spoken in the country. I'm impressed by the amount of English Genevieve and Adonisi have learned in just a few short years in the United States. When the family came to America, they knew little to no English. Aline still speaks very little, but as is often the case with refugees and immigrants, she understands more than she can speak.

Adonisi is still in high school, and Genevieve wants to go to community college to continue to learn English. She dreams of a career in the medical field, perhaps as a physical therapist.

I ask if becoming an American citizen is also a dream, since the family will soon be eligible. "We must first pay off our plane tickets," Genevieve explains. (Refugees are responsible for repaying the cost of their plane tickets to America, usually within a few years of their arrival.) The family's involvement with RAPP has propelled them a little closer to that goal. Having a garden plot where they can raise their own produce—corn, beans, tomatoes, winter squash, onions, and a unique variety of African pumpkin—has allowed the family to save money on groceries. "It helps us a lot," says Aline, noting that they probably save between $200 and $300 a year. RAPP has also helped the family sell their produce to restaurants in the area and to a local food wholesaler. One chef in particular likes to use Aline's winter squash in creative seasonal salads.

Additionally, this past spring, Robbie took Adonisi and Genevieve out to collect ramps and sell them for profit. Ramps, also known as wild leeks, are native to the Appalachian Mountains and taste similar to spring onions. They have a strong odor, reminiscent of garlic. Restaurants re-

You Say Banana, I Say Plantain

One of the little mysteries I came across while writing this book is the difference between plantains and bananas. I'm not referring to the sweet bananas commonly consumed raw in the United States—the Cavendish variety. The banana in question is the variety of green cooking banana used to make matoke, a popular East African stew. To me, it looks and even tastes like a plantain. Not so, several of my East African friends insist.

Part of the confusion is that, throughout the world, people generally make little or no distinction between cooking bananas (and sometimes bananas in general) and plantains, and they use the words interchangeably. For example, when I asked Africans from outside East Africa, they told me that cooking bananas and plantains are the same, as far as they knew. But as one explained, "Africa is a huge continent with different cultures based on tribal affiliation. Foods and cooking practices can vary widely within the same region."

After hours and hours of research, here's what I learned: Hundreds of different types of bananas exist, and more than 55 million tons of bananas are consumed worldwide each year. Bananas grow best in humid, tropical regions such as Africa, Central and South America, and Southeast Asia. East Africa is the leading banana-producing and -consuming region in the world, and bananas are a critical food crop in Uganda, Tanzania, Burundi, Rwanda, and eastern portions of the DRC.

The diversity of plantain (or cooking banana) cultivars in Africa alone is astounding. Apparently, the plantains in West Africa differ markedly from East African cooking bananas. The variety Aline and Genevieve use is the East African Highland banana, which has many subvarieties. These bananas are referred to locally as matoke, the same name as the dish made from them. The East African Highland banana (or at least a close equivalent) can be found in some African and Asian markets and even some American groceries with well-stocked ethnic produce sections.

People in East Africa eat bananas at almost every meal, an average of three bananas per day, according to Aline and Genevieve. Bananas are also an important source of income, and in addition to being eaten, they are used to make beer, juice, and many other products. For Africans and many other people worldwide, bananas are much more than an occasional healthy snack; they are a critical, life-sustaining part of the daily diet.

ally like ramps, according to Robbie, but they are in limited supply. "They pretty much like to grow only where they want to grow," he says. Ramps are typically found in wooded areas, as they prefer shade and moist soil. Robbie and his two young friends made a deal with a local landowner: they would dig up and collect the ramps from the owner's property and share a portion of their profits. During this project, Genevieve and Adonisi used a shovel for the first time. It was difficult work, but Genevieve made $280 and her brother made $200. With the money she earned, Genevieve bought a beautiful strapless white gown and had professional graduation pictures taken.

Aline loves to work in her garden. In addition to the physical and mental health benefits it offers, communal gardening provides a social outlet for many refugees. Aline has made friends from different countries, and she can continue to do the work she was accustomed to in Africa. "Everyone farms in Africa," Aline says. "If you aren't farming, you aren't eating."

When she's feeling well, Aline spends three to four days a week in her garden. I ask whether tending her garden is a relaxing activity or feels like work. "It feels like work," Aline replies, "but I like to work."

Presently, Aline must rely on government assistance, but she wants to become healthier so she can earn her own money and provide a better life for her children. She is thankful to America and to her doctors for giving her the chance to make that dream come true. "My hope is to be healthy and stay with my kids until they are old enough to be on their own. If I was able, I'd provide anything for them for the future. I need them to go to school and to go far. I want them to become self-sufficient."

Later that afternoon, as I enjoy a warm bowl of wholesome matoke made with fresh tomatoes and bell peppers from the family's garden, I look at Genevieve's graduation pictures adorning the living room wall. In that beautiful, hopeful smile and the white gown she bought with her hard-earned money, I can see Aline's hopes and dreams for her children already taking root.

Aline and Genevieve's Matoke (Banana Stew)

Matoke refers not only to the starchy green cooking banana grown in East Africa but also to the stew-like dish made from it. It is the national dish of Uganda, but many versions of matoke are served throughout the DRC, Rwanda, Burundi, Tanzania, and Kenya. The bananas in the stew, which taste similar to boiled potatoes, are cooked until softened.

According to Aline and Genevieve, this is a very common dish in their part of Africa, and it is eaten many times a week. Even in America, if they have gone several days without eating matoke, they miss it. It is a true comfort food for them, and it is almost always served with a sticky, dough-like starch called *fufu*. (See Sarah Mbombo's fufu recipe in chapter 22.)

The greenish semiripe bananas found in the average supermarket won't work in this recipe. This special type of cooking banana (the East African Highland variety) is usually a little larger than sweet bananas but not quite as large as plantains. For most American palates, plantains can be substituted in this recipe, but African cooking purists say that only green cooking bananas should be used. I've tried both in the stew, and I prefer the cooking banana, but for me, the difference is almost imperceptible. The banana is slightly sweeter and a tad less starchy than the plantain. These cooking bananas can be found in some African and Asian markets and even some American groceries with well-stocked ethnic produce sections; they're usually found with the Cavendish bananas and plantains. They are generally not labeled, so you have to go by sight and texture. Press down firmly on the skin of the green banana; both the skin and the flesh underneath should be hard and not give way.

The amount of bananas specified here is based on 2 whole bananas per serving. I prefer to either slice the bananas into ½-inch-thick rounds or cut them in half crosswise. If you do this, reduce the amount of bananas to roughly 8, or according to your own preference.

Aline's family serves this dish with cooked goat meat, fish, or a small dried fish called *ndagala*. Chopped steak, stew meat, lamb, or some other rich meat is an acceptable alternative. Any of these can be prepared on the grill or browned in a skillet while the stew is cooking. I highly recommend adding a meat or other protein to this dish to enhance the flavor and texture (but ground beef didn't add enough flavor or texture for my personal taste).

Peel the tomatoes if you don't like peels floating in your stew. Feel free to experiment with other vegetables and seasonings to create your own personalized matoke!

Serves 6
Ready in about 1 hour

> 12 green, hard cooking bananas or plantains (fewer if slicing)
> Vegetable oil for sautéing (about 7 tablespoons)
> 1 small white onion, sliced lengthwise
> 1 green bell pepper, sliced lengthwise
> 1 to 2 chili peppers, sliced lengthwise
> 4 Roma tomatoes, cut into large chunks
> 2 to 4 cloves garlic, minced (optional)
> 1 (5- to 6-ounce) can tomato sauce
> 1 tablespoon salt
> 1 pound goat meat, stew meat, fish, or other protein, cut into bite-size pieces, cooked (optional)

Peel the bananas carefully with a sharp knife, cutting off the ends and running the blade down the length of each banana by sections, making sure to remove the thick rind underneath the skin. If desired, slice the bananas, or keep them whole. Place the bananas in a large (8-quart) stockpot. Fill the pot with cool water and wash the bananas. Drain the water and refill the pot with just enough cool water to cover the bananas (too much water will produce a thin soup). Place the pot on the stove over medium-high heat. Cover and cook on a low boil for about 10 to 15 minutes (reduce the cooking time if you're using sliced bananas).

Meanwhile, in a small saucepan, add vegetable oil (enough to coat the bottom of the pan) and warm over medium-high heat. Add onions and cook, stirring often, until they are tender and slightly browned, about 10 to 15 minutes.

Test the bananas for doneness by inserting a fork. All the bananas should be cooked through and tender. Add bell peppers and chili peppers. Stir, cover, and cook for 10 to 15 minutes on a low boil.

Add chopped tomatoes and garlic to the onions in the small saucepan. Stir, cover, and cook for 5 minutes over medium-high heat. Stir again and add about 7 tablespoons tomato sauce (for a thinner stew, add water to the tomato mixture, which can be taken from the boiling water in the stockpot; for a thicker stew, add more tomato sauce). Add salt. Stir and cook the tomato mixture, covered, on medium-high heat for 5 to 10 minutes.

If you prefer a thicker stew, remove some of the boiled water from the large stockpot at this time. Add the tomato sauce mixture in the saucepan to the bananas and peppers in the stockpot. Stir gently. Check the stew consistency again, and adjust by adding more water or more tomato sauce as desired. Add cooked meat or fish (optional). Cover and simmer for another 5 to 10 minutes to allow the meat or fish to warm and flavor the stew. Lower the heat and keep warm until ready to serve.

Serve matoke on individual plates or in shallow bowls with fufu, rice, or bread.

Bon appétit

(This French expression for "Enjoy your meal" is also used in the DRC.)

14

Bhutan

Goma Acharya, June 23, 2009

Goma (GO-ma) Acharya looked at me with her penetrating, dark brown eyes and pushed her notebook across the table. "Here," she said, "write phone number." That's Goma for you—intense, assertive, determined.

The year was 2009, and it was my first day as a volunteer teaching assistant at Louisville's Catholic Charities Migration and Refugee Services' ESL school. Although I hesitated to give my phone number to a student, Goma's persistence finally wore me down. She called me twice that same day, announcing each time, "I, Goma, and you, be friends." It was not a request or even a suggestion. Looking back now, it was pure prophecy.

In the years I have known Goma, she has experienced several major life changes: giving birth to a second baby, moving twice, learning how to drive, and purchasing her first home—a ranch in a quiet neighborhood just minutes from Walmart, where she and her husband Tek work.

When Tek and Goma were house-hunting, Goma asked about the new house I had just bought. When I told her I lived in a condo, she fell silent. Then she said in her just-above-a-whisper voice, "Aimee, did you say *condo*? I should tell you . . . in my country, condo is a very bad word." This is just one of the things I love about my friendship with Goma—we are each other's teacher and student.

When I tell people that I work with many Bhutanese students, one of their first questions is, "Where the heck is Bhutan?" Bhutan is a small Himalayan kingdom in South Asia, located between India to the south, east, and west and Tibet (China) to the north. To the west of Bhutan, di-

157

"Everything has advantages and disadvantages. Life is better here but a struggle."
—Goma Acharya

vided by a slice of India, is Nepal. The population of Bhutan is made up of many ethnicities, including the Lhotsampas, who are of Nepali origin and are primarily Hindu. The state religion in Bhutan, however, is Buddhism.

That's where things got a little thorny. The Lhotsampas began to settle in southern Bhutan in the late nineteenth century. They prospered in their new land but were eventually seen as a threat to the Bhutanese government, which wanted to protect its Buddhist culture and identity. From about the mid-1980s to the early 1990s, refugees say that Bhutan's government carried out a harassment campaign in which the Lhotsampas were forced to renounce their homes and homeland or flee; those who didn't were expelled. Torture, rape, and child labor are just some of the egregious injustices refugees have reported.

According to statistics compiled in 2008 by the United Nations High Commissioner for Refugees (UNHCR), more than 107,000 Bhutanese refugees were documented in seven camps in southeastern Nepal. As of 2013, a large percentage of these refugees had been resettled in several host nations, with the United States accepting the majority. (See "The Big Crisis in Little-Known Bhutan" in chapter 11.)

Goma was just a young girl during this unfortunate time in Bhutan's history. She grew up in the valley region of Daga in southern Bhutan. Her family's home was made of stone and mud and covered by a thatched roof. On their ten-acre farm they raised sheep, cows, goats, and chickens, and they grew corn, rice, wheat, peppers, pineapples, bananas, oranges, and lemons. But that's as much detail as I can gather from my friend. "We don't like to recall our past," she once told me. "It is painful."

In 1993, after the conflict in her native country escalated, Goma's family decided to leave their home before they were forced to do so—or worse. They had heard stories of houses being burned and people being captured by the army and taken to jail. Carrying only the bare necessities on their backs, Goma and her family set out for India, traveling five hours on foot and another three by truck. They lived in India for one month before they continued on to Nepal, where they eventually settled in a refugee camp. That's where my friend spent the next sixteen years of her life.

Most Americans can't imagine living even a day in a refugee camp, much less getting married and having a baby in one. Food rations were meager, and Goma and her family cooked using firewood and charcoal. Sometimes thirteen people slept in a single hut. There were no phones or TVs. Once, when I asked Goma what she liked most about the United States, she replied without hesitation: "Electricity."

Even though Goma and Tek received some English (British) instruction in the refugee camp, language was still a barrier when they arrived in the States in 2009. They took some English classes in America but picked up most of their English in the workplace. Whether they were cleaning out bathrooms in a bar or washing windows in a hotel, Goma and Tek have always been grateful for every job they've had. "Everything has advantages and disadvantages," Goma says. "Life is better here, but a struggle."

But those struggles have definitely paid off. When they bought their first home in 2012, Goma and Tek, then in their early thirties, accomplished what many Americans only dream of—and in only three years' time. They invited me over for a blessing of their new home. In the unfinished basement, guests sat in a circle on the floor during a multihour prayer ceremony while Hindu priests chanted mantras in the soft glow of candlelight.

To visit a Bhutanese home is to never be lonely—or hungry. Extended family is always dropping in, often without knocking. And there is always food. The first time I visited Goma, she served me delicious sweet milk tea seasoned with black pepper, followed by a large platter of rice pudding. She entertained me with Nepalese folk music videos of beautiful dark-haired women in bright pink and red saris, dancing to the lilt of flute notes and deep, repetitive drumbeats.

On another occasion, I had the honor of receiving a blessing from Tek's parents, Tanka and Tila, during the celebration of Dashain, a Hindu festival held in the fall. Culturally speaking, Dashain is similar to Christmas—a joyous time when relatives from near and far gather together to feast and exchange gifts. What I especially love about this festival is the blessing younger generations receive from their elders. The prayer Tanka and Tila said over me as they applied *tikka* (a red mark made of red powder, yogurt, and rice) on my forehead is interpreted as follows: "May you live a long life. May your life be god-like. May you have no enemies, trouble, or sickness upon you." Afterward, they served me a delicious split pea curry soup with rice. Bhutanese cuisine is some of the spiciest in the world, and hot chilies are consumed as part of the daily diet. But Goma graciously lowered the heat quotient for me. The curry was accompanied by a side dish of goat, a delicacy in Nepalese cuisine. It was my first introduction to this lean and tasty meat, and although I was a little hesitant to try it, I found goat more flavorful than beef and less rich than lamb.

Here a Goat, There a Goat

Goat meat accounts for 63 percent of all red meat consumed worldwide, according to the Alabama Cooperative Extension System. It is becoming more accessible in the United States, perhaps to meet the growing demands of immigrants and refugees who have arrived in recent decades from the Middle East, Africa, Southeast Asia, and Latin America, where goat meat is often an important source of animal protein.

Considered the new lean meat, goat is lower in calories, fat, and cholesterol compared with beef, chicken, pork, and lamb, according to the US Department of Agriculture. Most of the refugees I cooked with don't buy their goat meat from stores. Rather, they buy a whole goat from a local farm (sometimes sharing the meat and the cost with another family) because it is more economical, healthier, and more environmentally sound.

In addition to serving only native Bhutanese cuisine in her household, Goma insists that her children speak Nepalese at home as a way to keep them steeped in their cultural heritage. Tek's mother and father, who live with the family and help with child care, also work to keep the old traditions alive. But one afternoon while I'm visiting Goma, she walks into the kitchen and rolls her eyes. She has just come from checking on her toddler in the other room. I can hear the thump-thump of a booming bass beyond the doorway. "They don't like Nepalese music," she says with a sigh. "They will only listen to American." Despite Goma's best efforts, she worries that her children will lose their cultural heritage. Even Goma herself, who has just served me a beverage in a Kentucky Derby commemorative glass and has been periodically checking her iPhone, has adopted many of the cultural habits and customs of her new land. It is one of the greatest challenges refugees face: how to embrace the new while still honoring the old.

I ask Goma if she ever wants to go back to Bhutan. She laughs and immediately says, "No." But then she admits she has never considered it. "Maybe in the future," she says. "If I can."

Goma's Ema Datshi (Chili and Cheese Soup)

I cannot tell a lie. Fast and easy to prepare, *ema datshi* (EM-ma-DOT-chi) is one of my all-time favorite Bhutanese dishes. I've never been to Bhutan, but when I cook and eat this curry, I feel like I'm halfway there.

Ema datshi literally means chili and cheese. Considered the national dish of Bhutan, this traditional vegetarian curry of hot peppers and cheese is extremely unusual and spicy, although the heat can be modified according to taste. But don't be misled. This is not a thick, creamy sauce like a Tex-Mex *chile con queso*. There are limitless variations of this dish. Goma uses additional vegetables and a homemade yogurt in her recipe.

Daikon radish is a large, mild white radish that can be bought at most Asian or Indian markets, organic markets, and some American groceries. If daikon radish isn't available, substitute thinly sliced potatoes.

Because the cheese traditionally used in ema datshi can't be found outside Bhutan (it's a local farmer's cheese made from the milk of cows or yaks), substitute a thick, creamy, plain yogurt; a good melting cheese; or a combination of the two. Romano and smoked Gouda cheeses work well. For a more authentic dish, add a crumbled farmer's cheese or a Dutch feta at the final stage of cooking over low heat and gently stir until just combined, or use this same cheese as a garnish. I have also added shredded Mexican cheese to thicken the soup and used it as a dip with tortilla chips.

If you can't take the heat in this dish (no, don't get out of the kitchen!), use milder peppers such as poblanos or none at all—but then it won't be true ema datshi. I highly recommend the garnish to get the full ema datshi experience.

Serves 4
Ready in about 30 to 40 minutes

> ⅓ cup vegetable, canola, or olive oil
> 1 teaspoon cumin seed
> ⅛ teaspoon turmeric powder
> 1 medium red, yellow, or white onion, sliced
> 1 red bell pepper, sliced

1 green bell pepper, sliced

2 or more hot green chili peppers, cut lengthwise into 2 or more slices, seeds and ribs removed, if desired, for less heat

1 daikon radish (or potato), thinly sliced

2 medium tomatoes, peeled (optional) and sliced

1 tablespoon salt

3 cloves garlic, minced (optional)

2 cups plain Greek yogurt (the creamier the better)

Cheese to taste, crumbled or shredded (Dutch feta, Romano, smoked Gouda, or other)

1 tablespoon Spanish paprika

⅛ teaspoon cumin powder

⅛ teaspoon cayenne pepper

Few dashes ground brown or black mustard seed (optional)

Garnish (optional)

2 tablespoons cilantro, leaves and stems

¼ red onion, chopped

1 small hot green chili pepper, chopped

In a large (8-quart) stockpot, heat oil over medium-high heat until it begins to smoke slightly. Add cumin seed, turmeric, and onion. Stir. Add bell peppers, hot peppers, radish, and tomatoes. Stir and add salt. Cook for 10 to 15 minutes, or until vegetables are soft, stirring occasionally. Add garlic. Lower heat to medium or medium-low. Add yogurt and cheese and stir. If a thinner soup consistency is desired, add a little water. Add paprika, cumin powder, and cayenne pepper to taste. Stir and cook, covered, over medium-low heat for 10 to 15 minutes, stirring occasionally. Add ground mustard seed. Stir to combine.

Garnish if desired and serve with basmati, jasmine, or Bhutanese (Himalayan) red rice; *sel roti* (a ring-shaped sweet rice bread or doughnut); or a bread of your choice.

Krishnarpan
(Nepalese for "Have a nice meal")

15

Somalia

Abdiaziz Haji, September 3, 2009

Abdiaziz (Ahb-DEE-ah-ZEEZ) Haji rolls out a large, clear plastic tarp over the area rug in the living room and says, half apologizing, "We usually just eat on the floor." In the small kitchen of their Florence, Kentucky, apartment, Abdiaziz's wife Hafsa (HAHF-sa) prepares our lunch. Their dimple-cheeked four-and-a-half-year-old son Naji (NAH-gee) tries to steal my attention, head and hips wiggling in opposite directions as he strums his toy electric guitar. Naji is running at full throttle this Sunday afternoon, the first day of fall. In addition to the excitement of having a female American stranger in his home, he will be starting preschool tomorrow. His father plans to take him shopping for a new backpack later.

Education is a priority for Abdiaziz. Although he can speak several languages, including two Somali dialects, Swahili, and English, and can read and write in Arabic, he never finished high school. Abdiaziz spent almost two decades of his life in refugee camps. "This life is better," he says. "You are missing a lot of stuff in refugee camp. No job. No education."

Hafsa, wearing a vibrant orange *garbasaar* (a shawl that covers her head and upper body), refuses my offers to help as she makes several trips from the kitchen to the living room to deliver our picnic fare: lettuce topped with sliced onions and lime wedges, goat meat with bell peppers and onions, a colorful vegetable relish, and bananas. The attractive, twenty-something couple tells me that this is a typical lunch in their native Somalia in East Africa. The midday meal is the largest, and meat-based dishes and pasta are commonly served. Dinners are generally small, often

165

"All the things people want in life . . . you can get in the United States." —Abdiaziz
Haji (with his wife Hafsa and their two children)

comprising rice (a staple food for Somalis), legumes, soup, and *anjero* (or *canjeero*)—a light, chewy homemade bread resembling a spongy pancake, similar to Ethiopian *injera*.

Somali cuisine varies from region to region and has been influenced not only by English, French, Italian, and Indian cuisines but also by the predominant religion in Somalia: Islam. Pork and alcoholic beverages, for example, are prohibited, and only *halal* meals are eaten. *Halal*, Arabic for "lawful" or "permissible," refers to the food and the preparation method that follows Islamic dietary law. Somalis drink tea (*shaah*) two to three times a day, and they like it sweet, with milk, and flavored with spices such as cinnamon, cloves, nutmeg, and cardamom—often ground by mortar and pestle in the home. Hafsa and other refugees have taught me the value of grinding my own spices, and I've incorporated this practice in my own kitchen.

I join my hosts in eating with my hands. Who knew such a simple salad of crisp iceberg lettuce paired with onions and drizzled with lime juice and a touch of salt could be so tasty? Likewise, I find the flavorful, lean goat meat the perfect accompaniment to our rice and vegetable side dishes. Apparently, this American girl has gained a fondness for goat meat while sampling recipes for this book, or maybe Hafsa's preparation of it is particularly top-notch. I'm also intrigued by the combination of flavors and textures in the vegetable dish—sweet golden raisins mixed with pungent red onion and small chunks of potatoes—and I insist that we include it in the book. Hafsa, a gracious host and a good sport, agrees to make it again after we eat, along with *doolsho subug*, a cardamom-spiced butter cake.

Like the majority of refugees I've interviewed, Abdiaziz's family rarely eats anything but their native cuisine at home, but this wasn't always the case. Abdiaziz immigrated to America a few years prior to his wife and son, and he didn't know how to cook. He quickly fell into the fast-food trap. He started out with chicken at McDonald's—the first go-to fast food for many new refugees, he tells me. Then, little by little, he experimented with hamburgers, french fries, fried fish, and sub sandwiches. When his wife and son joined him in the States in April 2012, one of the first things he asked Hafsa to do was teach him how to cook some Somali dishes. He never wanted to be without his native food again.

Abdiaziz and Hafsa were both born in the south-central Somali city of Baidoa. Somalia, which constitutes the cap of the Horn of Africa, is the most homogeneous country in Africa. The majority of people are ethnic Somalis, like Abdiaziz. They are predominantly Sunni Muslims, speak the Somali language, and share many of the same customs. Unfortunately, this ethnic and cultural cohesiveness hasn't stopped decades of civil war and unrest.

In 1991, when Abdiaziz was about seven years old, fighting broke out between different clan-based factions, resulting in the ousting of the long-term military government. These clashes disrupted agriculture and livestock production, which in turn contributed to the 1992 famine that killed hundreds of thousands of Somali people. Hundreds of thousands more fled to neighboring countries during this crisis. Abdiaziz and his family headed to a refugee camp in Mombasa on Kenya's east coast. After six years, the Kenyan government and the United Nations High Commissioner for Refugees (UNHCR) resettled them in a camp in Kakuma (Swahili for "nowhere"), an arid, isolated town in northwestern Kenya. That camp has played host to tens of thousands of refugees since 1992, the majority of them from Somalia, Ethiopia, and Sudan. In fact, many of the "Lost Boys of Sudan," a group of roughly 20,000 young boys orphaned or displaced during the Second Sudanese Civil War, ended up at Kakuma.

Abdiaziz tells me that malnutrition, malaria, and other communicable diseases were common in the camp. The houses were constructed of sticks, and the roofs were made of *makuti* (palm tree leaves); they provided protection from the sun but not from the harsh dust, the rain, and the thieves from the host district of Turkana. Nevertheless, Abdiaziz chose to stay in the Kakuma camp when the rest of his family, for various reasons, opted to move on. If not for this decision, he might never have reconnected with his childhood acquaintance, Hafsa. They met again when Abdiaziz visited Nairobi, Kenya's capital, where Hafsa had fled during the civil war to stay with her sister.

What's in a Name?

The naming system in Africa varies from region to region and even from village to village. Names might be based on clan or family names, birth time, birth order, physical characteristics, or religious figures. Muslim names, for example, are especially common in northern Africa, whereas in central and southern Africa, Christian and European names (influenced by colonists and missionaries) are prevalent.

Somalis usually have three names: the person's own given name, the father's given name, and the grandfather's given name. Thus, Abdiaziz's son's name is Naji Abdiaziz Mohammed—his given name Naji, his father's name Abdiaziz, and his grandfather's name Mohammed. Because Somali names are often similar, many men and women are identified by nickname in public.

Abdiaziz tells me that in America, Somali refugees often drop the middle (father's) name and use the grandfather's name as a surname. However, back in Somalia, Somalis use their middle name as their surname and drop the third name. Somali women traditionally keep the names they were born with.

After a brief courtship, Abdiaziz and Hafsa married, but then came some good (and not so good) news. Abdiaziz, who had begun the resettlement process when he was single, had finally been approved to relocate to the United States. He hated to leave his wife and four-month-old Naji behind, but he couldn't pass up the opportunity to move to America, get a job, and pave the way for a brighter future for his family.

Because Abdiaziz didn't have any friends or relatives living in America, the resettlement agency selected a city for him: Minneapolis. But Minneapolis, known as "Little Somalia" because of its high percentage of Somalis, didn't suit Abdiaziz. He had no car, and the Catholic Charities office was twenty miles from where he lived. Plus, it was cold (even Kentucky winters are too cold for him, he admits). So when he learned that there were job opportunities in northern Kentucky, he packed his few possessions and headed to Florence. For someone descended from a nomadic people and accustomed to not having a permanent home, what was one more move? At first, he accepted whatever jobs he could get. He worked as a garbage collector and as a packer at a fresh produce distributing company. Eventually he found employment at Levi Strauss in neighboring Hebron, where he still works. When his wife and son finally moved to Florence, he picked up a second job, prepping rental cars at Enterprise. Currently he works seven days a week. "This is a busy world compared to Africa," he says. "Twenty-four/seven, people are working." Abdiaziz, out of necessity, is now part of that American grind.

He and Hafsa face many of the same quandaries and anxieties experienced by average Americans. One of their early dilemmas was whether Hafsa should work outside the home. She did for a while, but then she and Abdiaziz decided it would be more cost-effective for her to stay at home with Naji and their baby girl Naima, rather than paying for child care. Abdiaziz ticks off the things they're still paying for: a beautiful dark chocolate living room sofa, the couple's bed, and the family's airplane tickets to America, the cost of which refugees are obliged to repay to the US government.

They also worry about how to conscientiously raise their children in a culture where youngsters seem to grow up far too quickly. One rule they've established in their home is limiting Nafi's television viewing to only an hour or two a day, per their doctor's suggestion. On the flip side, Abdiaziz says, "You are not worried about fighting and war. If you call the police, they will come help you. In Africa, sometimes they come and sometimes they don't."

Abdiaziz also likes the fact that a nonnative can get a job, just like an American. "If you are qualified, you can get the job. No discrimination." And unlike in Africa, Americans try to improve things. "If people see a problem, they will work to solve that problem." Hafsa says she likes American law the best. Abdiaziz teases her, "Is it because in America a man can only have one wife?"

Sometimes Abdiaziz considers moving his family to a bigger city, like Louisville. Few Somalis live in Florence, and Abdiaziz is afraid his children will miss out on cultural opportunities and the ability to interact with other Somalis. But for now, he is content simply to be in America. "All the things people want in life—to have a job, to have the opportunity to be educated, and to live in a peaceful country—you can get in the United States."

Abdiaziz and Hafsa's Zabib Qudaar (Raisin Vegetable Mix)

I fell in love with this dish the moment Hafsa served it to me for lunch with a side of rice and goat meat. She makes this easy dish several times a week. It reminds me of a cross between chutney and relish.

Somalis like their meat, and they have few vegetarian dishes. But in the southern parts of the country in particular, where Abdiaziz and Hafsa are from, there is more agriculture, and more vegetables are consumed. This dish has endless variations. I particularly like the combination of textures and the pungency of the onion balanced by the sweetness of the raisins.

Serves 4 to 6
Ready in about 40 minutes

> 2 medium white baking potatoes, peeled, washed, chopped into
>   small pieces (about the size of large, plump raisins)
> 2 tablespoons vegetable or canola oil
> 1 small red onion, peeled and finely chopped
> 1½ cups classic frozen vegetable medley (carrots, corn, green beans,
>   and peas)
> 2 chicken bouillon cubes, crumbled
> 1 cup golden raisins

Bring a small amount of water (about ¾ cup) to a boil in a medium saucepan. Add chopped potatoes. Turn heat down to medium-low and cover. After about 3 to 5 minutes, stir and make sure the heat isn't too high and the potatoes aren't sticking. (There should still be some water in the pan.) The potatoes are ready when they've turned tender but not mushy.

Add oil and half the onions. Stir. Continue cooking on medium to low heat, covered. After 5 to 10 minutes, add mixed vegetables and crumbled chicken bouillon cubes. Gently stir to combine. After another 5 to 10 minutes, add the raisins and the rest of the onions. Stir, cover, and remove from heat. Before serving, let the dish sit for a few minutes so the onions can soften a bit.

Serve warm over rice, eat it alone for a light bite, or serve as a side dish with a main entree.

Abdiaziz and Hafsa's Doolsho Subug (Butter Cake)

Somali cuisine is an interesting fusion of East African, Arab, and Indian cuisines, with a sprinkling of English, French, and Italian influences. Sponge and pound cakes, believed to have originated in the United Kingdom, are popular in Somalia, but butter cakes, long associated with American cuisine, have also staked a claim in some African countries. Though similar to pound cakes, butter cakes are a little less dense and rich.

This incredibly easy cake is mixed by hand and uses melted butter. Instead of vanilla, a common ingredient in American butter cakes, Somalis typically use the slightly cheaper cardamom to flavor their sweets.

Butter cake is often served to visitors with a cup of tea. On holidays or other special occasions, the cake may be given as a gift. Hafsa makes this cake a couple of times a month. Sometimes she gives a slice to Abdiaziz to take to work as a snack.

Hafsa uses freshly ground cardamom seeds removed directly from the pods, which produces an almost poppy seed–like texture. Cardamom seeds (already extracted from the pods) are also available in stores, but they aren't as fresh. I like to use a mix of freshly ground cardamom seeds (for texture and a more pronounced cardamom flavor) and a good-quality cardamom powder (see "Cardamom: The Spice Queen" in chapter 19).

Somalis usually serve this cake plain, but it can be dusted with powdered sugar or drizzled with a glaze. I used a simple coconut glaze recipe I found online, and it was delicious. I also like to add lemon zest to the batter. Because this cake is reminiscent of a quick bread, I sometimes bake it in a loaf pan instead of a Bundt pan, but that's not how Somalis generally serve it. Also, if you use a loaf pan, the cake will be moister.

Serves 8 to 10 (fewer if using a loaf pan)
Ready in about 45 minutes to 1 hour

2 teaspoons ground cardamom (preferably freshly ground)
4 large eggs, room temperature
1 cup sugar
1½ sticks butter, melted
1 tablespoon baking powder
½ cup whole or low-fat milk, warmed
1½ cups flour, sifted, plus extra to dust the pan
½ to 1 tablespoon vegetable oil

Preheat oven to 350° F.

Grind fresh cardamom seeds in a blender, food processor, spice grinder, or with mortar and pestle. The goal is a fine powder consistency, but with some slightly larger grounds. Set aside.

In a medium bowl, beat eggs with a whisk. Add sugar and melted butter. Beat until well combined.

In a small bowl, add baking powder to warm milk. Beat lightly to combine. Add this to the egg mixture. Whisk. Add ground cardamom and half the flour. Whisk again. Add the rest of the flour slowly, whisking until well combined.

Generously grease a Bundt, tube, or loaf pan with oil and dust it with flour. Use your hand to spread the oil and flour around the entire surface of the pan, including the sides. Drain any excess oil out of the pan.

Pour batter into the pan. Bake for 35 to 40 minutes, or until a toothpick inserted in the cake comes out clean. (Adjust cooking time, as necessary, if you're using a loaf pan.) Watch carefully during the last few minutes to avoid burning.

Cool the cake before serving. If desired, dust with powdered sugar or ice with a glaze of your choice.

Ku baashaal cuntada
(Somali for "Enjoy your food")

16

Azerbaijan

Elmira Tonian, April 16, 2010

For Elmira Tonian, cooking is not just a pastime; it's a passion. Some might even argue that it's an obsession. "Every time I go to bed at night," Elmira says, "I think about what I'm going to make the next day."

I met Elmira through the Elder Refugee Program where I was teaching. I knew her by reputation, from the delicious dessert creations she often brought to school and shared with the teachers and students during break time. "Elmira brought a cake!" I would hear someone shout down the hall before class, and the mere thought was enough to sweeten the rest of our morning.

So when it came time to identify potential contributors for this book, Elmira's name was at the top of my list. When I called Elmira to set up a time to meet, I quickly discerned that she understands more English than she speaks. So we arranged for an interpreter—her good friend, Arina (Ah-REEN-ah) Saforova, an Armenian immigrant (1991) who co-owns the Golden Key international grocery store in Louisville.

Elmira greets me at the door of her third-floor apartment. In her early sixties, she is short and exhibits a pleasant maternal plumpness, with an outward seriousness that seems to mask an inner shyness. Arina has not yet arrived, but Elmira and I are able to communicate through simple sentences, pantomime, and visual aids.

Elmira teaches me how to properly pronounce Azerbaijan, the country where she was born and raised. She says it slowly so I can repeat: Ah-zer-BYE-zhon. She pulls out a Russian-English dictionary, finds the word, and shows me the spelling. Then she locates a world map, spreads

"Every time I go to bed at night, I think about what I'm going to make the next day."
—Elmira Tonian (Photo by Julie Johnston)

it out on the dining room table, and points to her native country, situated at the crossroads of Europe and Asia. Elmira's show-and-tell presentation continues as she turns on her computer in the living room and surfs the Internet. Soon we are watching a video of Baku, the capital of Azerbaijan and the largest city on the Caspian Sea. The video, set to fast-paced techno music, shows stalwart ancient buildings and fortresses juxtaposed with modern architecture and elaborate cascading fountains. "My home," Emira says softly, never taking her eyes off the screen. Her words are thick with nostalgia and the accent of her mother tongue: "My home."

When Arina arrives, the energy in the room immediately shifts from second to fourth gear. A commanding but entirely engaging presence, Arina wears a black poncho draped over her shoulders, her black hair pulled back in a clip. She introduces herself, apologizes for her delay, and then begins chitchatting with Elmira in Russian, a language that is commonly spoken in Baku and other parts of Azerbaijan.

I have an affinity for the Russian language. I love how the vowel sounds are held heavy in the mouth and then spill forth as if coated in liquid gold. "It's because when we talk, we *feel* it," Arina says.

Elmira and Arina met at the Golden Key shortly after Elmira arrived in the United States in the spring of 2010. Ever since that chance meeting, Arina has played a vital role in helping Elmira assimilate. Take, for example, the warm, dark-wood furniture, the cheerful flower arrangements, and the knickknacks in the apartment. Arina helped find and arrange these. Arina also found Elmira's apartment itself, complete with elevator and secure "buzz in" entrance. When Arina first visited Elmira's former apartment and witnessed a workman painting over a cockroach on the wall, she quickly got her friend on the waiting list of the apartment complex where she now resides, which is occupied by many senior Russian immigrants.

"Since Elmira is a true refugee and was without a home of her own for so long," Arina says, "a big goal of mine was to get her into her own place."

Arina also helps the other Russian residents in the apartment complex. For instance, she offers a mini-market on-site several days a week, stocked with goods from her grocery store. There, the residents can conveniently purchase fresh produce and other ingredients from their homeland.

I ask Elmira what it has meant to have Arina in her life. "It has meant a lot," Elmira says. "A lot," she emphasizes. "Before I didn't have anyone. I was all alone."

"My father used to say, 'The fish stinks from the head.'" This is the proverb Arina uses to explain the Nagorno-Karabakh War in the late 1980s and early 1990s, a continuation of the ongoing Armenian-Azerbaijani conflict over a piece of land in southwestern Azerbaijan in the South Caucasus. The war commenced after the dissolution of the Soviet Union, when the ethnic-majority Armenians living in the Nagorno-Karabakh region wanted to secede and join Armenia, Azerbaijan's western neighbor.

In Arina's interpretation of the fish proverb, it's the corrupt people in power who cause the little people to suffer. "I don't even want to think about that time," Arina says. "It was horrible."

But life in their native country wasn't always difficult. Elmira and Arina, who were both born and raised in Azerbaijan and attended college there, can recall a time when there were no problems, the economy was good, and people of multiple nationalities got along peaceably.

Like so many ethnic Armenians living in Azerbaijan during the war, Elmira and Arina were persecuted and forced to flee. They went to Armenia, the land of their ancestors—Arina in 1988, and Elmira and her husband in 1989. This relocation was only a temporary solution, however, and the timing couldn't have been worse. Armenia was still dealing with the aftermath of an earthquake that had hit the country in December 1988. In addition, no refugee camps had been established to accommodate the influx of refugees, and the Armenian economy was in shambles. In fact, many people left Armenia and went to other countries such as Ukraine and Russia—wherever they had friends or relatives who could help support them.

Elmira waited it out for a few years, but she finally left Armenia in 1995 and joined a nephew in Ukraine. Just a couple of years later, however, her husband passed away, and Elmira was left to support herself. Although she had worked for years as an accountant, jobs were hard to come by, especially for refugees. What could she do?

Elmira had always enjoyed cooking. She had started cooking with her mother as a six-year-old, and by the time she was a third-grader, she was making stuffed cabbage leaves (*dolma*), a notoriously time-consuming dish, on her own. She decided to put her talent and passion for cooking to practical use and opened a small food stand in Ukraine, selling to workers and passersby on the street.

While Elmira prepares tea and a snack for us in the kitchen, Arina scrolls through the pictures on her camera, boasting of Elmira's culinary talents and showing me some of her friend's multitiered cakes and decorative salad molds. Sweets and salads are among Elmira's favorite things to make.

Elmira's cooking can't be tied to any one culinary style, and she adds her own creative flair to everything she makes. But from what I've observed and tasted, her dishes, like Azerbaijani cuisine in general, seem to be heavily influenced by Persian cuisine (with its signature use of greens, vegetables, fruits, and nuts).

Displaying the hospitality Azerbaijanis are known for, Elmira emerges from the kitchen with black tea (Azerbaijan's national drink) and an apricot fruit roll she made that morning. "See?" Arina says. "This woman is a magician." The apricot fruit roll is a perfect blend of sweet preserves, crunchy nuts, and flaky pastry.

When Arina first tasted Elmira's cooking, it was love at first bite. So when Elmira offered to cook for Arina's full-service catering business (an offshoot of her international market) as a way to repay her friend's many kindnesses, Arina could hardly refuse. Elmira's brain is always churning with new recipes and designs. Sometimes she will call Arina and say, "Okay, I have an idea." Their win-win business partnership gives Elmira not only a sense of purpose but also an outlet for her creative spirit.

On another day when I visit Elmira, Arina's teenage daughter, Izabel, is there. Arina wants Izabel to get some practice interpreting. When

I ask Izabel which of Elmira's dishes is her favorite, she throws back her head and sighs. "Oh, goodness, that's hard." Apparently, every time Elmira makes something it comes out a little different, but it's always exceptional. Izabel finally lands on a favorite: the spinach- and cheese-stuffed chicken breasts Elmira is making today.

While I stand over Elmira's shoulder, diligently trying to take notes on the several dishes she is making simultaneously, I ask if she ever tires of cooking. "No," she says. "Never." We have been in the kitchen for hours, and I ask her if her feet are hurting, because mine sure are. Her reply: "When I'm cooking, nothing hurts."

Americans are always watching the clock, according to Arina. The Armenian (and Azerbaijani) cooking process is slower and healthier. All dishes are made from scratch, using garlic and greenery, especially herbs such as mint, cilantro, basil, dill, and parsley. Many of these Elmira grows in pots on her balcony. Today she uses them to garnish two of the dishes she has prepared—dill for the whipped potatoes and basil for the chicken.

When we finally sit down to eat, Elmira barely touches her food. "I got full just off the smell," she says, and we all laugh.

I discover for myself the truth of Arina's words: Elmira is indeed a kitchen magician. The chicken oozes with clear juices and melted cheese. The pork's mushroom sauce is an addictive amalgam of vegetables, curry, garlic, and cream. I take more than one helping of everything, including dessert: walnut meringue puffs that are golden brown on the outside, light as air on the inside, and bursting with sugary-nutty goodness. I can't stop at two or even three. (I'm sorry, readers. I tried to duplicate these later, and I even asked an excellent baker to test them, but we could never get them to mirror Elmira's heavenly little puffs.) I ask how to say "I love it" in Russian. *Ya lyublyu*, they tell me.

After a while, even Elmira succumbs to her own cooking. She takes a bite of the tangy mushroom and bell pepper salad—a dish she invented for the first time today. She closes her eyes, savoring what she has put her heart and soul into all morning. "Mmm," she says. "Mmm mm mm." It's an utterance that requires no interpretation.

Elmira's Spinach and Cheese Rolled Chicken

This is one of Elmira's original creations. She uses American cheese, but feel free to use other cheeses. Personally, I like a mix—Swiss in the chicken and mozzarella on top. The basil garnish provides the perfect finishing touch.

Serves 4 to 6
Ready in about 1 hour

> 8 small to medium boneless, skinless chicken breasts
> 2 teaspoons salt
> 1 teaspoon ground black pepper
> ¾ cup mayonnaise
> 1 cup chopped baby spinach leaves
> 8 pieces Swiss, mozzarella, American, or other cheese, about
>   ¼ inch thick and 2 inches long
> 1 tablespoon olive, corn, or vegetable oil to grease the pan
> ¾ to 1 tablespoon sweet paprika
> 1 teaspoon curry powder
> 4 ounces Swiss, mozzarella, American, or other cheese, grated
> Fresh basil leaves (optional)

Heat oven to 400° F.

Wash chicken and pat dry. Place chicken pieces, one by one, on a piece of plastic wrap on a flat surface. Cover with another piece of plastic wrap. Use a meat pounder (tenderizer) or a small, heavy saucepan to beat each piece flat. Place chicken on a large plate. Combine salt and pepper in a small dish and sprinkle over one side of each piece of chicken. Set aside.

Spread about ½ to ¾ teaspoon mayonnaise over the seasoned side of each piece of chicken, coating lightly. On top of the mayonnaise, place enough chopped spinach to generously cover the entire piece of chicken. On top of the spinach, place 1 piece of sliced cheese at one end. Beginning with the cheese end, roll the chicken tightly until the spinach and cheese filling is covered. (If some of the filling escapes, simply stuff it back into the chicken.)

Lightly coat the bottom of an 8- by 8-inch baking dish with oil. Place the chicken pieces snugly in the dish. Spread the remaining mayonnaise over the rolled chicken to lightly cover. Sprinkle with paprika and curry powder. Top with grated cheese.

Bake for about 20 to 30 minutes, taking care not to overcook the chicken. The chicken is done when the internal temperature reads 165° F and the juices run clear. Garnish with basil leaves. Serve with Elmira's Whipped Potato Rosettes.

Elmira's Chopped Pork
with Mushroom Cream Sauce

This is another Elmira original. Instead of cooking the pork chops whole, Elmira cuts the meat into very small pieces and combines it with the other ingredients, allowing all the flavors to meld together and the mushroom sauce to penetrate the pork. The curry is a wonderful complement to the overall dish.

Save yourself some tears: Elmira places whole peeled onions with the ends removed in cold water for a short time to cut down on the pungent smell before cutting them.

Elmira purees her mushroom sauce in a food processor, but I like a chunkier texture, so I forgo this step and just pour the mushroom sauce from the pan directly over the pork, add a bit of water, and then bake. If you do this, mince the garlic cloves and add them with the mayonnaise and half-and-half.

Serves 4 to 6
Ready in about 1¼ hours

Pork
6 boneless, thinly sliced pork chops or cutlets
½ medium onion, finely chopped
1 teaspoon salt

1 teaspoon ground black pepper

1 egg

1 tablespoon mayonnaise (not fat-free)

2 teaspoons cornstarch

Canola or vegetable oil for sautéing

Mushroom Sauce

Vegetable or canola oil for frying

½ medium white onion, sliced into 1-inch pieces

1 cup carrots, peeled and cut into bite-size pieces

1 (8-ounce) container small to medium white button mushrooms
   (champignon), sliced

½ teaspoon salt

½ teaspoon ground black pepper

2 shakes curry powder

2 tablespoons sour cream (not fat-free)

2 tablespoons mayonnaise (not fat-free)

5 tablespoons half-and-half

2 cloves garlic

Preheat oven to 400° F.

To Prepare the Chopped Pork

Trim any fat off the pork chops and cut the meat into very small pieces (about ⅛ to ¼ inch). Place in a large mixing bowl. Add onions, salt, and pepper. Stir to combine. Mix in egg, mayonnaise, and cornstarch. Stir again and set aside.

In a frying pan, add enough oil to fully coat the bottom of the pan. Heat oil over high heat. When the oil begins sizzling, use a slotted spoon to drop the chopped pork mixture into the pan, arranging it into individual patties (about the size of the original pork cutlet). To avoid overcrowding the pan, keep a small space between each pork patty (fry them in 2 batches, if necessary). When the bottom of each patty is golden to dark brown and slightly crisp, flip it carefully, taking care to keep the patties intact (if they break apart a little, reassemble into a patty shape). Cook the meat only about ¾ through; it will finish cooking in the oven. Transfer the patties to an unlined plate to drain, reserving the juices. Set aside.

To Prepare the Mushroom Sauce

Add enough oil to a large sauté pan to fully coat the bottom. Heat the oil over medium-high heat. Add onions and carrots. Sauté until onions are transparent and lightly browned and carrots have softened. Add mushrooms. Cook over medium-high heat, stirring often, until mushrooms are softened and lightly browned. Add salt, black pepper, curry powder, and sour cream. Stir. Remove pan from heat. Add mayonnaise and half-and-half and stir until well combined.

Transfer mushroom sauce to a standard-size food processor or blender. Add garlic. Fill the frying pan with a small amount of water, swish it around to collect the juices, and add this mixture to the food processor. Blend ingredients to create a thick sauce.

Place the pork patties in a 9- by 12-inch glass baking dish, leaving space between each. Drizzle any extra juices from the plate over the pork. Spoon the mushroom sauce over the pork patties. Use a spatula to lightly spread the sauce around.

Bake for 20 to 30 minutes, or until the sauce bubbles and lightly browns. (Cover the baking dish with foil, if necessary, to keep the pork and sauce from overbrowning.) Serve with Elmira's Whipped Potato Rosettes.

Elmira's Whipped Potato Rosettes

The presentation of these potatoes is impressive, and they can accompany just about any entrée. The egg is an interesting addition, giving the potatoes an almost cream puff flavor.

To create the rosette mounds, Elmira uses a piping bag with a large star tip. Alternatively, you can use a large Ziploc bag with one end snipped off, but make sure to cool the potatoes first. If you aren't too concerned about the design, you can just use a tablespoon to form the mounds.

Serves 4 to 6
Ready in about 1 hour

1 teaspoon salt
3 medium baking potatoes, peeled and quartered
1 egg
3 tablespoons butter, cut into pieces
Fresh chopped dill or rosemary (optional)

Preheat oven to 400° F.

Fill a medium pot about ¾ full of water, add salt, and bring to a boil. Add potatoes and cook over medium-high heat until they have softened (about 15 to 25 minutes, depending on their size). Drain the potatoes in a colander, then transfer them back to the pot. Mash well with a potato masher or a fork until there are no lumps. Add egg and butter. Stir, making sure the butter is completely melted.

Fill a piping bag or Ziploc bag with the potatoes and squeeze them out onto an ungreased baking sheet. Use a circular motion, starting from the outside and working in. Form about 8 swirled rosettes or mounds.

Bake for about 20 minutes, watching closely for the last 5 minutes. The tips of the potatoes should become lightly browned. Transfer to a serving platter. Sprinkle with dill or rosemary.

Prijatnovo appetita
(Russian for bon appétit)

17

Iraq

Hasana Aalarkess, April 29, 2010

Hasana (Huh-SAH-na) Aalarkess and I are watching, of all things, Mel Gibson waxing his legs while wearing a pore strip on his nose in *What Women Want*. This Iraqi mother of seven likes American actors: Mel Gibson, Tom Cruise, Brad Pitt, Angelina Jolie. Her occasional soft laughter reminds me of ripples on calm water as I speak with her youngest daughter, Lamia, on the other side of me. On an adjacent couch are her eldest daughter, Hiba, and her son, Mohammed, who are helping Lamia interpret for their mother this June afternoon.

Through a special modem on the TV, Hasana switches the movie over to English with Arabic subtitles for my benefit—one of the family's many gracious, hospitable gestures. In fact, I had never personally met any of them before my visit, yet they were willing to allow a complete stranger into their home to ask prying questions and consume their food.

When I had first entered their immaculate, well-furnished apartment in a popular, centrally located Louisville suburb, I hastened to take off my sandals (after seeing the family's shoes lined up neatly by the door). Then a slim woman with graying hair tied back in a low ponytail strode out of the kitchen, arms opened wide: Hasana, the woman who was going to show me how to cook Iraqi style. The hug she gave me felt like it carried the full blessing of her home country.

Now, lounging on the couch, Hasana asks if I've ever had Iraqi tea (*chai*). When I tell her no, she and her children begin an animated description of how unique and delicious it is, and they insist I have some.

"That looks like a fancy contraption," I call to Lamia out in the kitch-

187

Hasana Aalarkess still loves to cook her family's favorite Middle Eastern dishes in the United States. (Photo by Hiba Shnawa)

en. I'm referring to a red-handled, stainless steel, double-stacked kettle on the stove. Lamia gives me one of her beautiful ear-to-ear, pearly-white smiles and explains that it's a Turkish teapot and can be found online.

A spicy, nose-tingling aroma eventually wafts from the kitchen. I hear cupboard doors opening and closing and silverware clinking. "Would you like your tea in an *istikan*?" Lamia asks. I have no idea what that is, but I say I'll take it however they normally serve it. When in Rome (or Baghdad), as they say.

When a quaint tea set is placed before me, I discover that an istikan is an elegant, clear, hourglass-shaped tea glass. This particular one has gold detailing, and a dainty spoon rests beside it on a glass saucer, also festooned in gold. According to Lamia and her siblings, more Iraqis, especially the young, are using mugs rather than istikans. I ask if they fear

Iraqi chai with a Turkish teapot. (Photo by Lamia Shnawa)

losing their Iraqi traditions in America, and Lamia laughs, not unkindly. "We're too old," she says. If she and her siblings were young children, this might be the case, but at their ages, these traditions are more than a way of life; they're a part of who they are.

The family advises me to add sugar to my tea—at least one to two teaspoons. This is how Iraqis traditionally drink chai, the sugar balancing the tea's intensity. And let me say, Iraqi tea does not disappoint. The "secret" ingredient added to most Iraqi tea, imparting its characteristic flavor, is cardamom. But Hasana's family has doctored up this batch with mint as well, providing a smooth, refreshing aftertaste.

As I sip my new favorite tea, Hasana (which means beautiful and fair) proudly shares with me the few English words she knows: cup, spoon, saucer. Her keen, sharp gaze tells me that she is a clever, resourceful woman and nobody's fool. The children's father is deceased, and she is clearly the matriarch of this family, but a playful, generous one.

As we talk, Hasana occasionally pats me on the forearm, fluffs the ruffles of my shirt sleeve, or plays with the back of my hair. She speaks directly to me, as if I can understand every word she is saying, often not waiting for her children to interpret. In a strange way, I feel like I have known this family for years and that I am the prodigal daughter returned.

But I am not the one who has journeyed far from home. A framed photo of the Gates of Babylon across the room is a reminder of what this family has left behind—not only friends and family but also the sacred heritage and treasures of their ancestral land. Lamia tells me they would like to go back to Iraq someday, but only if the situation improves and their lives are no longer in danger.

Hiba and Lamia worked at the US embassy in Baghdad and were the first in the family to arrive in America in 2007. They and Mohammed, who worked for NATO and arrived two years after his sisters, were awarded special immigration visas, available to eligible individuals who were employed by or on behalf of the US government in Iraq. The rest of the family, including Hasana, followed shortly thereafter, as refugees. One brother lives in Louisiana, and another sister still lives in Iraq (in a safe place), and they try to connect on a daily basis, using Skype and other digital-era tools. Overall, the family has found that Americans are nice, but every now and then they run across an ignorant person who thinks that all Muslims are terrorists.

Our conversation eventually turns to the business at hand: cooking. I'm curious about what differentiates Iraqi cuisine from that of other Middle Eastern countries. The family recognizes that it's hard to put a finger on the exact differences, since the cuisine has been so heavily influenced by nearby countries such as Turkey and Iran, and it varies from region to

Eggplant: The "Vampire" of Oil

Hasana and her family refer to eggplant as a "vampire" because it is notorious for soaking up cooking oil.

Native to India and cultivated for millennia in Asia, eggplant is technically a botanical fruit, but it is eaten as a cooked vegetable. The name *eggplant* comes from earlier varieties whose fruits were white, round, and the size of eggs. The eggplant is a member of the nightshade family and is related to the potato and tomato. Varieties cultivated after the eighteenth century lost their extreme bitterness and began to emerge in European cuisine, particularly in Italy, Greece, Turkey, and France. Today, the most common variety is the tear-shaped, dark purple Western or "globe" variety. The globe eggplant is valued for its glossy, deep purple skin as well as its distinctive taste and texture. The smaller Japanese eggplants are long and narrow with fewer seeds, a thinner skin, and a milder flavor. Eggplant is an excellent source of nutrition, and it also makes a good meat substitute.

A process called "disgorging" can be used to remove excess moisture from eggplant before cooking. This can also help lower oil absorption during the cooking process and improve the eggplant's texture and overall taste, including reducing the bitterness of some varieties. (Generally speaking, the long Asian varieties are less bitter than the large Mediterranean varieties and don't need to be presalted.) To disgorge, cut the eggplant into the desired size and shape. Salt it, and let it sit for about 30 minutes. Blot the excess salt and moisture with a paper towel before cooking.

region within the country itself. Some culinary scholars have gone so far as to suggest that Iraq lacks a distinct cooking style, but this is a point of debate. For Hasana's family, it's all about the spices. I press them on this point because I've read that many countries use the same spices in their cooking: turmeric, cardamom, and curry, to name a few. It's not the actual spices, they clarify, but rather their concentration and intensity. The spices in Iraqi cuisine are apparently more subtle than those of neighboring countries.

Perhaps it's best to turn to a few signature Iraqi dishes for some culinary insights. *Masgouf* (or *masgûf*), considered Iraq's national dish, is a delicacy that, the family tells me, cannot be replicated in the home. It is a whole fish sliced open butterfly style; marinated in a mix of olive oil, rock salt, tamarind, and turmeric; and skewered and slowly smoked on an outdoor grill. Hasana's eyes sparkle as she describes this dish, the one she misses most from her homeland. I am reminded of Remy, the mouse in the movie *Ratatouille*, as Hasana waves her hands in front of her nose, trying to conjure up the intoxicating smell. The family hopes to get a taste of masgouf soon, on an upcoming trip to Dearborn, Michigan, where there is a large Iraqi population.

When the family first arrived in the United States, they didn't like American food. If they ate out, they gravitated toward restaurants that reminded them of their own cuisine. I'm astonished when they tell me that Mexican food was the closest match—Taco Bell in particular. But they have branched out over the years and are now more accustomed to our food. Some of their favorite dishes? Macaroni and cheese and chicken fettucini. Their favorite restaurant is Olive Garden, but they have to watch what they order, since some of the dishes and sauces are prepared with wine. Being Muslim, they consume no pork or alcoholic beverages.

We discuss which recipes Hasana would like to contribute to the cookbook and teach me how to make. The family tosses around several ideas in Arabic. *Dolma* (stuffed grape leaves)? Or perhaps *bigilla*, a traditional bean dish served over torn pieces of bread and topped with a fried egg for breakfast? Hasana makes several trips to the kitchen to collect and show me the ingredients mentioned, including flatbread and spice blends for *biryani* (a rice dish), dolma, and *kari* (curry), all of which they bought at a local Arabic market.

Finally the family reaches a consensus: *maklouba* (translated "upside down"). It is a popular Middle Eastern dish that typically includes meat, rice, fried eggplant and other vegetables, and sometimes nuts or dried fruits. The layered dish is artfully flipped onto a plate before serving.

Hasana, who loves to cook and learned from her mother at age twelve, knows many recipes—all by heart. I'm told that Iraqis don't use cookbooks or recipes much, if at all. This is ironic, considering that tablets found in ancient ruins in Iraq contain recipes for religious festivals, suggesting that Mesopotamia was the home of the first cookbooks in the world. Most Iraqi cooking, the family tells me, is done by instinct, memory, observation, and experience. That's exactly why I want to record their recipes, I tell them. So these dishes won't be lost, and so others can know what an authentic Iraqi dish tastes like.

I ask whether they might try some of the other recipes featured in the book. Sure, they say, albeit hesitantly, still loyal to their native cuisine. Nevertheless, I can't help smiling at the thought of Iraqis rolling Cuban meatballs, Somalis stirring a pot of hearty Hungarian goulash, and Burmese flipping over a perfectly layered Iraqi maklouba.

Hasana's Iraqi Chai (Tea)

Iraqi-style tea is generally stronger than Iranian and Turkish tea (although the latter is a close equivalent). The brewing method involves a tea concentrate, which is commonly enhanced with cardamom and slowly steamed in a small kettle stacked on top of a larger kettle or a samovar. (A samovar is a metal urn used to boil water; it may have an attached teapot to heat a tea concentrate.) Iraqi tea is traditionally served very sweet, to balance the strength of the tea. Some say that Iraqi chai is the tea equivalent of espresso.

For best results, a Turkish (double-stacked) teapot or samovar is needed for this recipe. A French press or kettle with a tea infuser is sometimes used as a brewing alternative.

Feel free to experiment with the proportions of tea, water, cardamom, and mint until you arrive at the perfect blend for your personal taste.

Serves 4

    5 cups water
    3 teaspoons tea leaves (this amount is for a full-bodied black tea
        such as Ceylon or Earl Grey)
    ½ teaspoon cardamom seeds

2 to 3 large fresh mint leaves, plus additional for garnish (optional)

Boil 5 cups water in a large kettle. Put tea, cardamom, and mint in a small kettle. Pour 4 cups of boiled water from the large kettle into the small kettle. Turn heat to low, and place the small kettle on top of the large kettle (which should still contain 1 cup water). Brew for at least 15 minutes, or longer for stronger tea.

Serve in a small, clear tea glass (Iraqis traditionally use istikans) to show off the tea's deep color. Set the empty glass on top of a saucer, add sugar (1 to 2 teaspoons) to the glass, then pour the tea concentrate (strained) over the sugar. Top off with the remaining hot water from the large kettle, the amount depending on the desired strength of the tea. Stir the tea to dissolve the sugar. The glass will be hot, so hold it at the top between your thumb and forefinger. Add a sprig of mint to each individual tea glass if desired.

Hasana's Maklouba
(Upside-Down Chicken, Rice, and Vegetables)

Maklouba is a traditional Arabic dish with ancient origins and many variations. It typically includes a tasty combination of meat such as lamb or chicken, rice, fried vegetables, and sometimes nuts or dried fruits. The ingredients are placed in a pot and flipped upside down when served, making a striking and mouth-watering presentation.

This is not a difficult recipe, but it involves the use of several pans and the performance of several steps at once. Read the recipe thoroughly before getting started.

The fried vegetables can be drained on paper towels to remove the excess oil before layering them in the sauté pan, if you like. Peeling the vegetables is optional, except for the onions. If some of the larger chicken pieces are taking up too much room in the sauté pan, cut the meat from the bone, discard the bone, and layer the meat with the rest of the chicken pieces.

I like to add a few dashes of cayenne pepper to the rice along with the chili powder, for extra heat.

Serves 4 to 6
Ready in about 2 to 2½ hours

    8 to 10 pieces chicken (a variety of pieces, with skin and bones)
    Vinegar (optional)
    4 teaspoons salt (divided), plus ¾ tablespoon salt
    2 cups basmati rice (preferably an aged, high-quality brand from an
        Indian or Arabic market)
    1 medium eggplant, sliced into ¼-inch rounds
    ½ large green bell pepper, sliced into ¼-inch rounds
    3 medium white potatoes, sliced into ¼-inch rounds
    1 medium yellow onion, peeled and sliced into ¼-inch rounds
    Olive oil for frying (do not substitute canola or vegetable oil)
    4 medium red tomatoes, sliced into ¼-inch rounds
    Chili powder to taste

Place chicken pieces in a large (8-quart) stockpot and cover with water. Add 2 teaspoons vinegar and 1 teaspoon salt. (The vinegar helps take away the smell of the cooking chicken.) Bring to a boil and cook for 20 to 30 minutes, or until all the pieces are cooked through. (Take care not to overcook the smaller pieces; remove them early if necessary.) Drain and set aside. If preferred, the skin can be removed after the chicken cools.

Meanwhile, wash the rice, then soak it in water (enough to cover the rice) in a medium bowl for 20 to 30 minutes. Drain and set aside. Sprinkle sliced eggplant and green pepper with about 2 teaspoons salt, and sprinkle potatoes and onions with about 1 teaspoon salt. Let these vegetables sit while the rice soaks and the chicken cooks.

In a medium fry pan (with a lid), heat olive oil (enough to coat the bottom of the pan) over medium-high heat.

At the same time, in a 3- or 4-quart sauté pan (with a wide, flat base and preferably a fairly short handle for easier flipping later), heat about 2 teaspoons olive oil. Over medium to low heat, cook the tomatoes in a single layer (make sure to put the ends of the tomatoes skin side down). When the tomatoes soften, flip them, being careful to keep them in a single layer. If necessary, remove the first batch and set aside on a plate to make room for additional batches. Then transfer all the tomatoes back into the sauté pan.

Meanwhile, after the oil in the fry pan has heated, fry the potatoes in a single layer (this might take a couple of batches). When the potatoes are slightly brown, flip them. After the potatoes have cooked, transfer them to the sauté pan, in a layer on top of the cooked tomatoes. (It's okay if some of the vegetables, such as the potatoes and eggplants, form more than a single layer. Just make sure that each vegetable has its own distinct layer.)

Next, fry the onions and then the peppers in single layers. Transfer them both to the sauté pan, and layer them on top of the potatoes. During this process, add olive oil to the fry pan as often as necessary so the vegetables don't stick to the bottom.

Taste the eggplant to make sure it is well salted. Blot up extra moisture with a paper towel, then fry the eggplant until it is dark brown but not burned. Transfer the eggplant to the sauté pan, topping the other layered vegetables.

Brown the cooked chicken in the fry pan and transfer it to the sauté pan, topping the vegetable layers.

Cover the maklouba stuffing (everything in the sauté pan) with a lid to keep it warm.

To the still warm fry pan, add enough olive oil to the remaining grease and juices to equal about 2 tablespoons.

Add the soaked, drained rice to the oil in the fry pan, along with 1½ cups water. Add ¾ tablespoon salt to the rice, stir, cover, and cook on medium heat for about 5 minutes, letting it boil slightly. Stir, switch to low heat, and continue cooking, covered, until the rice has softened. Check it often to avoid overcooking.

When the rice is done, sprinkle it with chili powder and stir. Transfer the rice to the maklouba stuffing in the sauté pan, layering it over the vegetables and chicken pieces.

Now for the flip: Make sure you have a large enough serving plate to accommodate the layered contents in the sauté pan. It is best if the plate has a slight lip to catch any overflow. Carefully, using potholders if necessary, flip the maklouba over onto the serving plate. (You might want to recruit a helper if the pan is heavy.) Use a fork to replace any pieces that escape their appropriate layers.

Hasana likes to serve this dish with a tossed Mediterranean-style salad topped with a simple lemon and olive oil dressing and sprinkled with dried mint.

Belafia
(Iraqi-Arabic for bon appétit)

18

Iran

Baharieh Moosari Arabi, June 7, 2011

"I love it very much, this country," says Baharieh (BAH-hah-ree-AY) Moosari Arabi. She smiles with girlish delight over a cup of Starbucks plain black coffee that her son, Arash (AH-rash) Taarifi, has just delivered to our table. Arash, who is in his midthirties, moved to the United States from Iran in 2007. He likes to take his parents on as many outings as possible, even if it's just a quick trip to the local coffee shop in Louisville. He wants to expose them to real-life America, "not life you see in the movies," he says.

Baharieh pulls out a small notebook filled with English vocabulary translated into Farsi, her native language, so she can jot down any unfamiliar words that come up during our discussion. "She loves to learn new words," Arash says.

An old 1970s disco tune with a catchy beat begins to play, and we all pause for a moment, as if on cue, to dance in our seats. That's what I love about Baharieh and her whole family: their love of life. "I don't like to get old," Baharieh says.

I remember the first time I met Baharieh and her husband, Kiummars (Koo-MARS) Taarifi, at the Elder Refugee Program (a joint effort between Kentucky Refugee Ministries and Catholic Charities Migration and Refugee Services). The students had gathered for their midmorning snack in the cafeteria, and I saw two unfamiliar faces across the room. They were the first Iranians I had ever officially met, and they served as excellent ambassadors for their native country—polite, friendly, stylishly dressed, and obviously well educated. When the students do their morn-

Baharieh Moosari Arabi dancing with her husband of over fifty years, Kiummars Taarifi. (Photo by Julie Johnston)

ing exercises, led by one of their classmates (an Iraqi swimmer rumored to be a former Olympian), Baharieh is typically smiling, laughing, and clapping her hands, fully immersed in the moment. But I know that behind the smiles, Baharieh, like all refugees, has experienced a heartache that most Americans can't fully imagine.

Baharieh and her family asked that I not discuss the politics involved in their story; consequently, I can't say how and why they came to the United States. Their request stems partly from their Baha'i faith. The Baha'is I know are some of the most positive, upbeat people I have ever met. Their faith centers on unity—the oneness of God, all religions, and humanity. Arash explains that his family doesn't view their past as good or bad. "It is our journey," he says.

Baharieh's phone rings, and she excuses herself to take a call from her daughter Mojgan, who also lives in Louisville. Mojgan, who is the mother of one child, works at one of the hospitals in town. "I am the second choice," Arash says good-naturedly. "There is a saying in our country, 'I wouldn't trade one hair of a girl for a thousand boys.' That's how much we value females in our society."

Arash is chief engineer and maintenance manager for Residence Inn Marriott, where he is on call twenty-four/seven and sometimes works ten- to twelve-hour shifts. He recently took on a second job, working the grill and cash register at Shiraz Mediterranean Grill in Louisville, so he doesn't have much time for a social life. He works hard and saves his money to buy a home someday, which he will share with his parents. "It's tough," Arash confides, "but it's a blessing too."

Baharieh returns to the table and overhears us talking about one of Arash's proudest moments: when he became a US citizen in 2012. She chimes in excitedly, "I love to become a citizen right now!" Arash explains that she won't be eligible for citizenship for a couple more years.

When Baharieh and Kiummars arrived in the United States in 2011, they were eager to join their son and daughter and start a new life together in a free land. But within ten days of their arrival, Kiummars, fourteen years Baharieh's senior and a former architectural engineer in Tehran, lost a kidney. Suddenly, the couple's dreams of exploring America were thwarted. On the plus side, Kiummars's health problems have made the family more health conscious. They now eat better and exercise more, a trend that started about a decade earlier when Baharieh, who was a nurse in Iran, had open-heart surgery.

Their interest in eating nutritiously is apparent when I visit their East End apartment for the first time. They immediately serve me tea and Iranian dates—some of the best I've ever had. They boast of the dates' high nutritional content and assure me that they will give me energy for the entire day. They tell me about a great Iranian grocery store in town where I can get these dates and other Persian goodies.

The Summer Olympics are on TV. I tell them that I love to watch the American teams file past during the opening ceremony's Parade of Nations because we don't have a particular physical "look." Arash agrees and says that's what he loves about America—its diversity.

Getting to the Bottom of Tahdig

Tahdig (tah-DEEG) comes from the Persian *tah*, meaning "bottom," and *dig*, meaning "pot." It is the crispy, browned—sometimes even borderline burned—bottom layer of flatbread (such as lavash or pita), rice, or sliced potatoes cooked in a pot. Considered the best part of a dish such as adas polo ba gosht, tahdig is generally reserved for guests. (Perhaps the American equivalent would be the brown, crusty edges of a baked fruit cobbler or a cheesy macaroni casserole.) However, because we Americans tend to think of anything crunchy and nearly burned as a "mistake," the concept, and taste, of tahdig might take some getting used to.

This specialty crust of Persian and Mesopotamian cuisine relies on the delicate fusion of several factors, including the correct amount of oil and a dry-heat cooking method that transfers enough heat to the bottom of the pot to brown the tahdig while maintaining a minimal moisture content. To help control and absorb the moisture, Persian cooks often wrap the lid with a kitchen towel or a special fabric covering.

Tahdig is not easy to master, so don't get discouraged if your first (or even second) attempt is less than stellar. Even seasoned Persian cooks can have a hard time achieving the perfect crispy brown crust, and there seems no consensus on the best way to prepare tahdig. It is all about experimentation.

We continue our conversation in the kitchen so Baharieh can begin preparing *adas polo ba gosht*, a common Persian dish featuring rice, lentils, and some type of meat. Today, Baharieh is using lamb, my favorite for this particular dish because it adds richness and depth to the subtle seasonings.

"I love cooking," Baharieh announces.

"Good," I say, "because I love to eat."

Baharieh was the eldest of six children, and she helped raise her siblings and did much of the cooking and cleaning. Her mother, a woman who had "magic hands," taught her how to cook. Everything she made, according to the family, was delicious.

Arash says the greatest thing about adas polo ba gosht is its versatility. "You have to make it your own," he repeats adamantly whenever I ask about exact ingredients and measurements. Like the majority of refugees I've cooked with, Baharieh rarely, if ever, measures quantities or uses a recipe. Everything is done by, and with, heart.

Baharieh explains that the key to properly steaming the rice and achieving a nice *tahdig* (the crispy, browned flatbread at the bottom of the pot) is to use an absorbent buffer to catch and control the moisture in the pot. Baharieh uses a special fabric pot cover she bought in Iran.

While we wait for the lamb, onions, lentils, rice, and raisins to meld, Baharieh shows me some of her other handiwork around the house: a needlepoint tablecloth on the dining room table, a crocheted blanket on the back of the sofa, and several beautiful scarves. After Baharieh lost her job in Iran due to circumstances surrounding her faith, some of her friends who owned stores let her sell her handmade pieces so she could earn extra money for the family.

When the adas polo ba gosht has finished cooking and has been crowned with its signature saffron-infused water, the family and I take our seats at the dining room table. This is my first home-cooked Persian meal, and let me tell you, I don't just eat it—I devour it. I find the mix of sweet raisins and onions and just a hint of heat from the cayenne pepper flavorful and well balanced. And, of course, I love the crunch of the tahdig, of which I am given a generous serving, as the honored guest.

Arash plays some Turkish music on his cell phone. Baharieh and Kiummars start swaying in their seats. Finally, succumbing to the music, they rise from the table and dance together. Surrounded by the sights, smells, tastes, and sounds of their homeland, I can't think of a more perfect ending to a perfect meal: watching this loving couple, together for more than fifty years, as they embrace a new country and a new life with dignity and grace—and in each other's arms.

Baharieh's Adas Polo Ba Gosht
(Lentils and Rice with Meat)

Baharieh likes this dish because it's light and versatile, and the lentils are a good source of protein and iron. This is a traditional Iranian meal and is often served at celebrations, memorial services, or any large gathering.

This dish has multiple steps and uses many pans at once. It isn't difficult, but it takes some organization. The entire dish can be made in advance, warmed just before serving, and refrigerated for up to 3 days.

Lavash is a soft, thin flatbread originating in Armenia and popular in Iran, Turkey, Azerbaijan, and throughout the Caucasus. It can be found in some European, Persian, and Middle Eastern markets. Other thin flatbreads can be substituted.

If you're using a good-quality, aged basmati rice, it's best to soak it in advance. If you prefer subtle flavors, follow the spice measurements as directed. For additional pizzazz, add cinnamon, cardamom, cumin, or a packaged Persian rice seasoning mix to the meat or to the cooked rice. The Persian rice seasoning mix I found was labeled *Advieh Poloi*, or Rice Seasoning; it's available in Persian stores or online. It has become the one spice I can't do without, and I use it in a variety of dishes and different types of cuisines.

Serves 6 to 8
Ready in about 1¼ hours (not including the time to soak the rice)

> 2 cups long-grain basmati rice
> 1 teaspoon saffron threads, ground
> 8 tablespoons vegetable oil (divided; or more as needed)
> 1 large white or yellow onion, diced
> 1½ pounds ground lamb or ground beef
> 1 tablespoon turmeric
> 1 to 2 teaspoons ground cayenne pepper
> 1 teaspoon salt
> 1 cup lentils
> 1 cup golden raisins (or dried cranberries, cherries, or a mix)
> 1 lavash, large round tortilla shell, or any soft, thin flatbread
>   (enough to cover the bottom of an 8-quart stockpot)

Between 30 minutes and 2 hours prior to preparing the dish, soak the basmati rice in a large bowl with enough water to cover the rice plus ½ to 1 inch. (If you're using another type of rice, follow the package instructions.) After soaking, rinse and drain the rice well until the water runs clear. Set aside to boil later.

Grind saffron threads with a mortar and pestle and put in a small jar. Add 3 to 4 ounces hot water to the saffron and stir (this should produce a bright golden yellow color). Set aside.

In a large skillet, heat 1 tablespoon oil over medium-high heat. Sauté onions until translucent (about 15 minutes). Add meat, stirring often to break up the large chunks. When meat is about halfway cooked, add turmeric, cayenne pepper, salt, and any other preferred seasonings. When the meat is cooked through, set aside.

Meanwhile, in a medium saucepan, cook lentils per package directions (about 15 minutes). Lentils should be tender but not mushy. Simultaneously, in a large (8-quart) stockpot, cook rice according to package directions (15 minutes or less), but do not cook it completely (this is important, because the rice is cooked more at a later stage).

While the rice and lentils cook, put raisins and enough water to cover them in a small bowl and soak for 15 minutes. Set aside.

Drain and rinse the cooked lentils. Combine them with the meat and onion mixture in the large skillet, then set aside. Drain and rinse the rice and set aside.

Drain the raisins. Wipe out the medium pan used to cook the lentils (to avoid dirtying another pan) and add the raisins plus 1 tablespoon saffron water. Cook over medium heat, stirring often, until the raisins are plump and juicy. Set aside.

Wipe out the large stockpot used to boil the rice and add 2 tablespoons vegetable oil. (Some cooks suggest adding a little water to the oil to achieve a nice tahdig.) Cover with the flatbread. (It is best to keep the flatbread in one piece, but if it's not large enough to cover the bottom of the pot, break it into large pieces to cover the bottom in a single layer.) Cook over medium heat, flipping once or twice, until both sides are lightly browned.

Add half the meat, onion, and lentil mixture, covering all the flatbread. Add half the rice on top of the meat. Repeat the meat layer and then the rice layer, ending with the rice on top. Pour 4 tablespoons oil over the entire dish and lightly poke a few holes into the mound of rice, lentils, and meat, but do not pierce all the way to the bottom (this helps vent the steam). Wrap the pan lid with an absorbent kitchen towel or special fabric cover and cover the pot (this helps control the moisture content in the pot). Cook an additional 20 to 30 minutes on medium-low heat. (Check the bottom of the flatbread about halfway through the cooking time to see if it is browning sufficiently. If not, increase the heat for a few minutes.) When done, the bottom layer of flatbread (tahdig) should be crisped and browned but not burned.

Use a large serving spoon to transfer the rice mixture from the pot to a serving platter and fluff with a fork. Place the tahdig pieces on top and around the sides of the rice mixture. Top with raisins and drizzle with the remaining saffron water. This dish is often served alone as a main meal.

Nooshe jan
(Farsi for "May your soul be nourished")

19

Pakistan

Dr. Gulalai Wali Khan, June 14, 2011

In a Mediterranean diner a block from her workplace at Kentucky Refugee Ministries (KRM), Dr. Gulalai (Goo-LAH-lay) Wali Khan tells me she shouldn't be alive today. On August 9, 2010, as she was leaving her health clinic in the crowded Karachi Market in Khyber Bazaar, a gunman on a motorcycle fired three bullets at her, one of which hit her in the arm. How the gunman failed to kill her at such close range is a mystery. What isn't a mystery is why Gulalai was targeted. Just a day after she was shot, the Taliban issued a statement claiming responsibility for the attack. The reason? Bloodlines.

Gulalai grew up in a prosperous political family in Peshawar, a valley region near the Pakistan-Afghanistan border. Gulalai's grandfather was Khan Abdul Ghaffar Khan, known as the "Frontier Gandhi" for his non-violent opposition to British rule and his close friendship with Mohandas Gandhi. He spent twenty-eight years in British jails for his political beliefs. Gulalai's father was president of the leftist, secular Awami National Party (ANP) and spent eight years in jail. At the time of the attack on Gulalai, her brother was president of the ANP. After 9/11, the ANP publicly opposed the Taliban, and the Taliban, in turn, claimed that the ANP was in cahoots with America. It began targeting party members and then their blood relations. But this attempt on Gulalai's life was by no means her first brush with death.

On this frigid January afternoon over a plate of pita bread and hummus, Gulalai's striking green eyes widen as she recounts the time when, months prior to her shooting, a suicide bomber entered her father's home.

"Foods have such strong smells. They are part of our identity. Spices and smells identify us as people." —Dr. Gulalai Wali Khan

She, her family, and their guests had gathered there for Eid, a celebration marking the end of Ramadan, the Islamic holy month of fasting. The principal target of that attack was Gulalai's brother, who survived thanks to the heroic efforts of his security guard. The guard, who had grown up in the household, died, as did six guests. "It was awful," Gulalai says, but she tried to rationalize the tragic event: *This is what happens if you stand up for your beliefs . . . you will hurt some people.*

Not long afterward, she experienced another narrow escape when she was buying floor tiles and a bomb exploded not thirty feet from her.

She was saved by the fortuitous fact that she had gone upstairs to shop. Everyone on the store's ground floor perished.

Even after such close calls, Gulalai would still tell herself, *Well, this is my country. It's just bad. I will just go along.* Her thinking radically changed, however, when she realized that even she—a professional with no blatant political ties—could become a target. "If someone tells you, 'Don't do the following,' you may be able to change it. But if someone tells you, 'I target you because of your genetics,' it can't be changed."

Our waitress delivers our lunch: Greek salads and "atomic" falafels. If not for Gulalai's recommendation, I never would have tried such an ominously named dish, but the sliced jalapeño peppers give the pita-wrapped chickpea patty just the right punch.

I inquire into Gulalai's cooking background. She laughs and smoothes back her thick mane of gray hair from her forehead. "I am not very good at cooking actually because I haven't done it for most of my life." Even when she moved away from home to take a postgraduate fellowship at the Royal College of Surgeons of Edinburgh (where the female-to-male ratio was 8 to 200), she didn't cook. There was no time. "I'd open a can of baked beans and get a disposable spoon, so I didn't have to do anything."

Fortunately, Gulalai's mother had insisted that her children learn the fundamentals of cooking. So when Gulalai moved to the United Kingdom, she was armed with at least some basic culinary knowledge. "I knew how to bake a cake," she jokes.

But one morning she woke up craving her own food. When it comes to cooking native foods outside one's native country, "finding the right ingredients is the key—and the problem," says Gulalai. She managed to acquire the ingredients for one of her favorites—*pulao*, a rice dish steamed in meat stock and seasoned with aromatic spices. Suddenly, in her home away from home, the smells and flavors of Pakistan—cumin, cinnamon, cloves, and cardamom—came back to her.

When she moved back home after completing her fellowship, Gulalai had difficulty finding a job as a surgeon because she was a woman. In fact, she was the first female surgeon to graduate from her hometown's Khyber Medical College. She believes the only reason she was allowed to

Cardamom: The Spice Queen

Cardamom, known as the "queen of spices," is a tropical, shade-loving perennial native to India, Sri Lanka, and parts of Southeast Asia.

In the first century, Rome imported huge amounts of cardamom. In addition to being one of the most popular Oriental spices in Roman cuisine, it was used to clean the teeth and freshen the breath. Even today it is found in some chewing gums. Guatemala and India are currently the world's largest producers and exporters of cardamom. It is the third most expensive spice by weight, after saffron and vanilla.

There are two types of cardamom: green and dark brown (black). The green is more popular. Its dark seeds exude a camphor, eucalyptus, orange peel, and lemon fragrance. Cardamom is best bought in whole pod form, as the seeds lose their flavor quickly. Because of cardamom's unique sweet and savory flavor, it is a versatile ingredient used in desserts, drinks, curries, and fruit and rice dishes. A little goes a long way.

Research continues on the diverse health benefits of cardamom. The spice has been used to treat mouth ulcers, digestive problems, depression, cancer, blood pressure problems, and hiccups. In the ancient world it was even used as an aphrodisiac.

receive that training was because the professor of surgery was a relative. "He was obliged to take me because he couldn't say no to his wife," she teases.

She worked as an assistant professor of surgery at the postgraduate institute in Peshawar, and once she was settled in her career, she married one of her classmates from medical school. For many years, life was good as she practiced and taught surgery, doing what she loved.

"Honestly, for me, that was the most important part of my life because women suffer really badly in societies like [Pakistan]. We would see breast cancer in its final stages because no woman would show her breasts to a man because it is a very conservative society. We would see rectal cancer in its final stages because no woman would show her bottom to a man. When people ask me what was my specialty, I tell them, 'These ends'"—

Gulalai points to her chest and bottom—"because these are the ends no [woman] would want to show anybody."

After the attempt on Gulalai's life that fateful August, life turned upside down for her family. Gulalai and her sons—aged nineteen, sixteen, and ten at the time—were assigned security guards and had to stagger their comings and goings. The most devastating aftershock came when police told Gulalai she would have to quit her job; they couldn't guarantee that a gunman wouldn't walk into her clinic and kill innocent people. Then the police chief shared tapes of a recorded conversation between the two men supposedly involved in Gulalai's attack: one man told the other that he'd botched the job and had better get it right the next time.

On the heels of this disturbing information came the news that Gulalai's first cousin, the vice-chancellor of Islamia University, had been kidnapped by the Taliban. This event, more than any other, solidified in Gulalai's mind what she had to do. If the Taliban could target her cousin, who was to say her children wouldn't be next? "I worked three-quarters of my life toward a career that really mattered to me, and yet it took me a split second to walk away when the decision came down to my career or motherhood."

She told her brother about her decision to leave Pakistan with her sons, and he set the wheels in motion. The International Organization of Migration (IOM), working through the United Nations High Commissioner for Refugees (UNHCR), handled the details, but due to the high security risks, Gulalai wasn't told when or where she and her sons would be going or what to expect when they got there. "Two hours before the flight they handed me my paperwork," Gulalai recalls. "There was an address in Louisville, Kentucky. I thought, *Where the hell is Louisville? I haven't heard of Kentucky in my life other than Kentucky Fried Chicken.*"

Gulalai describes the leap of faith they took the day they boarded the plane: "It's like stepping out of a window and you don't know how far the ground is below. You just get on this flight and hope you hit the ground standing up."

The family arrived in Kentucky in June 2011, without Gulalai's husband. Because his life wasn't in danger in Pakistan, he stayed behind to help provide for the family. This is one of the things Gulalai misses most in America—there's no one to help shoulder the daily responsibilities and demands of raising children in an unfamiliar land and culture.

For the first year or so after arriving in Louisville, Gulalai pounded the pavement, speaking to hospitals, licensing boards, and potential employers, but to no avail. To practice medicine, she needs a two-year residency in surgery, and preference is given to American medical school graduates. She feels fortunate to have gotten a job as a medical caseworker at KRM, although working there has been an eye-opener. Once, when she took a client into a doctor's office, she saw the following notice posted at the reception desk: "All copays due at time of service. If you have no insurance or no ability to pay, no service will be provided and there are no exceptions to this rule." She was shocked. "I couldn't imagine that someone would actually put up something like this and call themselves a doctor," Gulalai says. "You take the Hippocratic oath. You will treat [patients] even if they are your worst enemy or whether they have the ability to pay or not. . . . For me, medicine was never about what it is in this country—money, litigation."

As much as Gulalai misses her career as a physician, her job at KRM has made her appreciate all that she still has. "I see people who are worse off than me. People who have language problems, who can't get a job, who have no means to support themselves, and whose kids are having problems."

When I visit Gulalai's two-story apartment in a low-income housing neighborhood where many other refugees reside, I can't help thinking what a stark contrast this must be from her former lifestyle. But here, she has things money can't buy. Gulalai's sons spent their first few days in Louisville just walking the streets, enjoying the freedom to do so without security guards and without fear of the next suicide bombing. "That's what I tell people in this country," Gulalai says. "They don't know how much they have to be grateful for. The peace. The law. The order."

Today, Gulalai is teaching me how to make two family recipes: *boorani* (a layered eggplant and yogurt dish) and *gazaro halwa* (carrot dessert). While we wait for the cardamom pods to toast on the stove, emitting their eucalyptus and citrus notes, Gulalai observes, "Foods have such strong smells. They are part of our identity. Spices and smells identify us as people. When you walk through the door of a home, you can almost identify who the family is and where they are from based on the smells."

I meet Gulalai's dark-headed sons as they meander through the kitchen, one by one, monitoring our progress. When they first moved to the United States, they sought out American fast food—burgers, chicken wings, pizza. But lately, like Gulalai so many years ago in the United Kingdom, they are craving their native food again. And Gulalai has been obliging them, filling her kitchen with the soothing smells and tastes of home.

Gulalai's Boorani
(Layered Eggplant, Yogurt, and Spicy Tomato Sauce)

Gulalai's boorani (also spelled borani) is a vegetarian yogurt dish passed down from her mother's paternal grandmother, who was a member of the royal family in Afghanistan. (Gulalai's hometown of Peshawar shares much of its cultural heritage with Afghanistan.) Boorani probably originated in Persia and is particularly popular along the Pakistan-Afghanistan border. It is traditionally served as a side dish with the main meal, but the freshness of the yogurt coupled with the heat of the sauce makes it an excellent choice for a lively spring or summer appetizer.

This dish can be made in advance and refrigerated, but the layers shouldn't be disrupted. Ideally, prepare boorani 3 to 4 hours ahead of time, which allows all the ingredients to meld and the eggplant to soften slightly. (Making it 24 hours in advance might result in a dish that's too soggy.)

For easier dipping when serving, cut the eggplant slices in half before frying, especially if they're large. Try sprinkling the cut eggplant with salt prior to cooking and letting the slices sit for 20 to 30 minutes. This helps draw out the excess moisture and keeps the eggplant from absorbing too much oil and becoming limp (see "Eggplant: The 'Vampire' of Oil" in chapter 17). As a time saver, use a large griddle to fry all the eggplant at once. For those who don't like eggplant, substitute fried zucchini instead.

Serves 4 to 6
Ready in about 1 hour

Eggplant
Vegetable or olive oil for shallow frying
2 medium eggplants, sliced crosswise into circles (¼-inch thick)

Sauce
Vegetable or olive oil for shallow frying
2 garlic cloves, minced or finely chopped
1 medium onion, chopped (or 1 cup thinly sliced green onions)
1 tablespoon cilantro stems, chopped, and ½ cup cilantro leaves, combined (divided)
¼ teaspoon cayenne pepper, crushed red pepper flakes, or a mix
2 teaspoons ground turmeric (or curry)
¼ teaspoon salt
1 cup fresh Roma tomatoes, chopped (use more for a long casserole dish)

Yogurt
2 cups natural, plain, Greek-style yogurt (the thicker and creamier the better)
½ teaspoon salt
1 teaspoon cumin seed

To Prepare the Eggplant
Fill a large frying pan with enough oil for shallow frying and heat over medium-high heat. When the oil is hot enough to sizzle, fry the eggplant pieces in a single layer until both sides are golden brown. Remove from the pan and drain on a plate lined with paper towels.

To Prepare the Sauce

In a medium saucepan, heat about 2 tablespoons oil over medium heat. Add garlic and cook until fragrant and golden brown, taking care not to burn it. Add onions and half the cilantro and cook, stirring, until the onions are soft and translucent. Add cayenne pepper, turmeric, and salt. Stir and cook for a few more minutes. Add tomatoes. Turn heat to low and cover, allowing tomatoes to cook in the juices for 5 to 10 minutes, stirring occasionally. Remove lid. Continue to cook until the oil separates from the solids and most of the liquid has evaporated. (If there is oil remaining, you can drain it.) Cool slightly.

To Prepare the Yogurt

Empty yogurt into a medium bowl and add salt and cumin seed. Whisk lightly until smooth.

To Combine the Layers

Pour yogurt mixture into a 1½- or 2-quart glass, flat-bottomed, oval or rectangular serving dish or 8-inch pie dish (a clear dish shows off the layers). Top with eggplant slices in a single layer, overlapping slightly if necessary so the yogurt layer doesn't show. Cover the eggplant layer with sauce. Chill. Garnish with the remaining cilantro.

Serve either at room temperature or chilled with a flatbread such as pita, naan, or *paratha*. Baked pita chips or blue sesame chips are other, nontraditional accompaniments.

Gulalai's Gazaro Halwa (Carrot Dessert)

This dessert is light enough to serve during the warmer months, but it's also an excellent alternative to traditional fall and winter desserts. In fact, carrots are a winter vegetable in Gulalai's part of the world, so the dish is usually served warm.

Two (15-ounce) cans of pumpkin can be substituted for the carrots. For a shortcut, in place of the milk and sugar, use 1 (14-ounce) can of Eagle brand sweetened condensed milk (or less if you prefer less sweetness).

Cardamom is the only true flavoring in this dish, so don't be skimpy with it. If you don't want to bite into whole cardamom pods, remove the seeds from the pod after toasting and mix the seeds into the dish.

Gulalai prefers to buy almonds (with skins) and blanch them herself for a fresher taste. Even though they're optional, pistachios are the perfect finishing touch for this dish, providing color contrast and textural interest.

This dish could also be served as a side dish on special occasions or to counterbalance a salty entree.

Serves 6
Ready in about 45 minutes

> 2 pounds baby carrots (organic or the brightest orange available)
> 2 tablespoons vegetable oil
> 5 to 6 green cardamom pods
> ½ cup sugar
> 1 cup whole milk
> ½ cup fresh whole or halved almonds (skins removed)
> Pistachio nuts (optional)

In a medium saucepan, add carrots and just enough water to cover them. Bring to a boil over medium-high heat. Cook until soft. Drain any leftover water. Mash carrots with a fork or potato masher. (If you prefer, leave a few chunky pieces for texture.) Set aside.

Heat oil in a large wok or saucepan until it sizzles. Add cardamom to taste. Open a couple of pods to expose the seeds. Lightly toast the cardamom pods and seeds, stirring to avoid sticking. Add carrot pulp. Cook on medium heat for 15 to 20 minutes, until the quantity of carrots is slightly reduced. Stir often to avoid burning or overdrying. Add sugar and stir until it is completely dissolved. Reduce heat to medium-low and add milk and almonds.

Cook for 5 to 10 more minutes, stirring occasionally, until the milk has been fully absorbed and the oil begins to separate from the solid ingredients. (Make sure not to overcook the halwa during this last stage, or it won't be as tasty.)

Transfer to a serving bowl and top with pistachios. Serve warm or chilled. Store in the refrigerator.

Nasseb dey shaa
(Pashto for "As may it become your fate" or
"May you digest what you eat")

20

Myanmar (Burma)—Chin

William Thang, November 4, 2011

Ask the average American if they've ever had Burmese cuisine, and chances are they haven't. Even US cities with large Burmese populations, such as Los Angeles, San Francisco, and New York, have few restaurants featuring solely Burmese food. William Thang wants to change that. He has a dream of opening a Burmese restaurant in Louisville someday, and even if he wasn't my friend, I would be one of the first through the door. William introduced me to Burmese food, and I couldn't have asked for a better culinary guide. That's because William knows his way around a kitchen.

When I first visited William's apartment in Louisville's Southeast End, the family had been in the United States for only eight months. After kicking our shoes off at the door, William showed me binders filled with menus from his many cooking jobs in Malaysia. He and his wife Rin, both from the Chin ethnic group, fled to Malaysia in 2008 to escape religious persecution in their native Burma (Myanmar). Malaysia has no formal refugee camps, and during the nearly four years they lived there, William found employment as a cook and gained experience with a wide variety of cuisines, ranging from Italian to Korean. Based on a glowing letter of recommendation from a previous employer in Malaysia, William landed a job at a popular Mexican eatery in downtown Louisville, helping in all facets of food preparation. Recently, in an effort to enhance his skills and increase his marketability, William has started learning the art of sushi making.

Although much of his cooking experience has come from on-the-job

"I am very proud of my cooking." —William Thang (with his wife Rin and their two children) (Photo by Julie Johnston)

training, William inherited his passion for cooking and his appreciation of good food from his mother. In fact, he loved his mother's cooking so much that, as a child, he would never eat at anyone else's house. While walking through the streets of Malaysia after first leaving Burma, William sometimes encountered overpowering scents that instantly transported him back home to his mother's kitchen. With a little experimentation, he was soon duplicating from memory the recipes he'd learned by watching his mother.

Knowing that we will be in excellent hands for our first sampling of exotic and elusive Burmese food, my friend Julie and I visit William and Rin on a balmy summer afternoon. William is already in the kitchen, opening and closing cupboards, pulling out the ingredients he will need for the dishes he is making today: fish sauce, chili peppers (whole, flakes, and powder), turmeric, garlic, onions, shallots, paprika, ginger—all staples in a Burmese kitchen.

Zaw, a native of Mandalay in central Burma, is also present, acting as our volunteer interpreter. As William multitasks in the kitchen and Rin chases their toddler around the two-bedroom apartment, Zaw describes the appetizer laid out on the dining room table: a Burmese delicacy and a traditional and popular Burmese snack, *lahpet thoke* (tea leaves salad). The salad is a mix of pickled tea leaves, dry prawns, beans, green chilies, garlic, and tomatoes. Lahpet thoke can be served either on a plate with the ingredients divided into sections, so diners can choose their own combinations (this is a common presentation for special occasions, and it is how William prepared our appetizer today), or with the ingredients already mixed together (for more informal occasions). "If you want to know about Burmese culture," Zaw says, "then look to the food."

If this appetizer—with its sour tea leaves, crunchy fried beans, and dry prawns—is any indication, I can safely say that Burmese cuisine is unlike any I've ever had. Indeed, of all the cuisines I've sampled for this book, Burmese might be the most "foreign." It has a look, taste, and smell all its own.

Did I mention the smells? They are not for the faint of heart. When William begins cooking a hot chili paste over the stove, the aromas of garlic, onion, and chili powder become so pungent that Julie looks at me, her face pale, and says, "I think I'm going to step outside." It takes me a little

Shoes left outside the door of a refugee's home. (Photo by Julie Johnston)

longer, but soon my eyes start to water, and I feel a light burning deep in my throat. Rin, the ever-attentive hostess, immediately opens the windows and the front door to dissipate the accumulating odors. If the smell of the food is setting my nose on fire, I wonder what in the world it will do to my mouth!

The flavor profiles in many Southeast Asian cuisines are similar—hot, sour, sweet, and salty. But Burmese cuisine, my hosts tell me, is probably most similar to Thai. (I should note that Burmese cuisine varies across ethnic groups, from region to region, and even from village to village. For instance, Win Khine, featured in chapter 10, believes that Burmese cuisine is most similar to Indian, due to his Indian heritage and the region where he grew up.)

Burma was occupied by British India for a good portion of the nineteenth and early twentieth centuries, and although Burmese food definitely has Indian influences, the dishes tend to use fewer spices and more garlic and ginger. China, bordering Burma to the north, has also influenced Burmese cuisine. For example, the tart vegetables and dried shrimp

Kick off Your Shoes and Stay a While

Have you ever wondered about the proper etiquette when entering some-one's home? If family members leave their shoes at the door, are you expected to do the same? The custom of removing one's shoes is commonly practiced in Middle Eastern, Asian, and Scandinavian countries.

In many places, such as Japan, taking one's shoes off at the door is large-ly based on tradition and stems from practicalities. Places that experience heavy precipitation or hot and dry conditions have to contend with a lot of mud or dust, respectively. Homes would have to be cleaned several times a day just to keep up with all the dirt from shoe traffic. And traditional floor coverings, such as the Japanese *tatami* mat, are fragile and difficult to clean.

For some, home is a sanctuary, a sacred place. As such, it should be kept as clean and pure as possible. Many Hindus, for example, believe that gods reside in one's house, which often contains a prayer room; thus, the house is like a temple.

Additionally, health arguments abound for leaving one's shoes at the door. Research has shown that high levels of bacteria, including *E. coli*, and pollutants such as lead and pesticides can be tracked indoors on shoes.

Personally, I take my shoes off at the door if I see that my hosts have removed theirs. It has been my experience that resettled refugees don't expect Americans to conform to this custom, but as one of my Iraqi friends told me, "We appreciate it when you do."

So, even though no one is going to wrestle you to the floor if you keep your shoes on, why not slip them off, get comfortable, and leave the world and its debris at the door?

prevalent in the dishes of Yunnan, a region of China bordering Burma to the northeast, have been incorporated into Burmese salads.

As William meticulously garnishes our dishes with cilantro, he says with a smile, "I am very proud of my cooking." As well he should be. The predominant flavors in William's chicken curry are garlic and chilies, but his side dish of sweet, creamy coconut rice helps cool the palate. Unlike other cuisines that use a subtle mix of herbs and spices (Persian comes to mind), Burmese cuisine is bold and a bit schizophrenic, taking your taste buds on a circuitous joyride. Yet it's surprisingly balanced, and the many contrasting tastes work with, rather than against, one another. The stand-out dish on my plate is the Burmese tomato salad with peanuts, onions, and cilantro in a garlic-infused oil. I can imagine serving it to guests in my own home with grilled fish and coconut rice.

Speaking of rice, it is the most common food in Burmese (and Asian) kitchens and is served at almost every meal. "Don't you ever get sick of rice?" I ask. My friends look at me as if I'm the one living in a foreign land. They explain that in both Burma and America, where they still cook only Burmese food, they never feel full unless they've eaten rice.

According to my hosts, women generally do the cooking in Burmese households, working in the kitchen almost all day to prepare food for three meals. If cooking is traditionally a woman's role in Burma, then how did William get into the restaurant business? He explains that there are actually more male chefs from their region, partly because they have the physical strength to lift the huge pots and other traditional cooking equipment, and partly because men are generally the ones out in the workforce. However, times are changing, they tell me, and household duties like cooking that used to be divided between the sexes are now becoming a shared domain.

Rin and William have been in the States for two years and have two toddlers. They have no extended family in Kentucky, but they are active in their Baptist church. The friends they have made here are now their extended family. Zaw, who is also without family in the United States, adds, "Since I don't have a family, everyone is my family."

I ask William to tell me more about his idea to open a restaurant. He laughs bashfully. "It is a high expectation." Maybe so, but as Walt Disney said and proved, "If you can dream it, you can do it."

William's Khyan-Gyin Thee Thoke
(Green Tomato Salad)

Are you tired of the typical garden, Cobb, seasonal, and Greek salads? Do you like a little spicy heat? If so, this might become your new favorite salad.

Some of the most interesting Burmese dishes are the salads. William learned this recipe from his mother. With its garlic-infused oil, peanuts, citrus juice, and cilantro, this salad is bursting with flavor. It's also a good representative of some of the most common ingredients in traditional Burmese cuisine.

Chickpea flour (also known as gram, garbanzo, chana, and besan flour) is used in Burmese cuisine as a thickener and a flavoring agent. It can be found in Asian, Indian, Persian, or specialty markets, and even in some American groceries with well-stocked ethnic sections. Chickpea flour can be used as a substitute for eggs in vegan baking and for flour in gluten-free cooking. All-purpose flour can be used in a pinch in this recipe; it will act as a thickening agent, but it won't impart the nutty flavor of chickpea flour.

Safety note: Take care when storing garlic-infused oil. To avoid the potential growth of *C. botulinum* bacteria and its toxins, the US Food and Drug Administration recommends that home-prepared mixtures of garlic in oil be made fresh, just prior to consumption, and should not be stored at room temperature. Leftovers should be refrigerated and used within 3 days.

Serves 4
Ready in about 30 minutes

Garlic-Infused Oil
1 cup peanut or vegetable oil
2 small onions (a mix of sliced and diced segments)
10 cloves garlic, diced (small cloves can be left whole)

Salad
½ cup dry roasted peanuts
2 medium sour green tomatoes or 3 Roma tomatoes (about 3 cups total), cut into bite-size wedges
2 to 5 small green cayenne (hot) chili peppers, finely chopped
2 tablespoons garlic-infused oil

1 teaspoon chili pepper flakes

Juice from ½ large lime

1 tablespoon fish sauce

1 teaspoon salt

1 tablespoon chickpea flour

1 teaspoon chicken-flavored broth mix or 1 crumbled chicken stock cube

2 tablespoons fresh cilantro leaves, chopped

½ cucumber, cut into ⅛-inch round slices, then halved (optional for garnish)

To Prepare the Garlic-Infused Oil

Heat oil in a small skillet on medium-high heat. Add onions and cook for about 10 minutes, or until onions begin to lightly brown, stirring often. Add garlic and cook for another 5 minutes, continuing to stir. Cook until onions and garlic are medium to dark brown but not burned. Remove from heat, set aside, and cool. Do not drain off the oil. (After using the oil in this recipe, store the remainder in the refrigerator for up to 3 days [see the safety note above] and use in salads, stir-fries, or other dishes.)

To Prepare the Salad

With a mortar and pestle, blender, food processor, or nut chopper, finely grind the peanuts, leaving a few small chunky pieces for texture. Set aside.

Put tomatoes in a large bowl. Add peanuts, green chili peppers, garlic-infused oil, chili pepper flakes, lime juice, fish sauce, salt, chickpea flour, chicken-flavored broth mix, and cilantro. Stir until well combined.

Transfer to a medium serving platter with a shallow lip. Mound salad in the middle of the platter and surround with cucumber halves, round side facing out. Serve at room temperature or chilled.

Mein mein saa
(informal Burmese expression for "Enjoy a delicious meal")

21

Iraq

Zainab Kadhim Alradhee and Barrak Aljabbari,
January 5, 2012

"The eggs saved us," Zainab (ZANE-ahb) Kadhim Alradhee jokes, telling the story of how she and her husband, Barrak (Bah-ROCK) Aljabbari, first learned that their lives were in danger in Iraq. A neighbor had gone shopping for eggs at the market one day and happened to run into Barrak's mother. The neighbor informed her that Barrak had been blacklisted—targeted for assassination.

The news did not come as a complete shock to the young newlyweds. Barrak had been working for a security company as part of a private security detail. "I was like the Iraqi GPS," Barrak says. Because of his intimate knowledge of the land, he was able to safely guide his clients to their destinations. The work was extremely dangerous. Once, Barrak received a death threat from a militia group through the mail. The envelope contained a small bullet and an accompanying note describing in graphic detail how Barrak would be killed if he didn't stop working with the Americans.

Barrak stayed with the security company, but he became more vigilant. His employer provided him with weapons for his personal protection. However, after he and Zainab discovered that he had been blacklisted, they decided not to take any chances, especially since they had a young child to think about. Barrak and Zainab left their hometown of Baghdad with their daughter, Danya, and made their way to Syria in July 2007. A few months later, Syria tightened the restrictions on what used to be an "open-door" policy for Iraqi refugees. In 2007 the United Nations High

Educated refugees like Zainab Kadhim Alradhee and her husband Barrak Aljabbari often face employment challenges in the United States.

Commissioner for Refugees reported that about 4.4 million Iraqis had been displaced, about half within Iraq (called internally displaced persons, or IDPs) and the other half in neighboring countries, especially Syria and Jordan.

The family stayed in Syria for a few months. Barrak found work as a supervisor at a ceramic tile production factory. But Syria was overcrowded with Iraqis who had fled their own war-torn country, and the economy was poor. One day, Barrak's previous employer called to say that work was available in Karrada, a district in Baghdad, and that he could provide Barrak and his family with secure lodging near the Green (International) Zone. Barrak and Zainab seized the opportunity.

Shortly after their move back to Iraq in 2008, Zainab began to work for the Iraqi office of International Relief and Development, an American nonprofit organization headquartered in Virginia. She was third in command and performed a variety of duties, including organizing humanitarian programs for displaced families. The nature of Zainab's job, however, put her life in as much danger as her husband's. They decided to apply for refugee status with the International Organization for Migration (IOM). The couple had done so years before but had never received a response. This time, they were called in for an interview. A year later, they learned that the United States had accepted them and that they would be resettled in Louisville, where Barrak's brother lived. Zainab's American supervisor gave her a farewell care package filled with gift cards, money, and toys, along with a friendly warning that, at least for a while, life in the States would be difficult for Zainab's family, which now included another child, son Ali.

The IOM crash courses Zainab and Barrak took on how to pack for the move and what to expect in America reiterated the message that they should expect a rough road on the other side of the Atlantic. They were told, for example, that in the first year or so, they would probably have to accept whatever jobs came along, regardless of their skills or education. Then maybe, with a little luck and lots of hard work, they could climb their way up.

The family was given only two weeks' notice before their departure for the States. They were allowed only one suitcase per person. "I could have filled one whole suitcase with just diapers," Zainab says with a laugh. But the trip was no laughing matter. It took them three days to get to Kentucky, including plane changes in Jordan, Egypt, New York, and Chicago and an overnight layover that found them sleeping on the airport floor—with their two small children.

"I was brave, wasn't I?" Zainab says, answering her own question with a private smile.

I first met Zainab and Barrak for lunch at a small Indian restaurant in Louisville's Highlands neighborhood in early January 2013—almost one year to the day of their arrival in Kentucky. I asked them how life had treated them so far in the States.

"A nightmare," Zainab said without pause. Unlike Barrak, with his blue eyes and fair skin, Zainab fits the Western stereotype of the Middle Eastern "look": dark eyes and hair and olive skin. She has a hard strength about her—the mark of a survivor.

Back in Iraq, Zainab's mother died unexpectedly a few months after they arrived. Because she lacked the necessary legal documents, Zainab was unable to travel home to be with her family. The couple also had trouble making friends in town—even with people from their own country.

Although they both have good English-speaking skills, they feel that people don't take them seriously. They tell me there is a preconceived notion that refugees are uneducated and uncultured, especially when people hear their accents. Americans ask them irritating questions: Are there any restaurants in Iraq? Did Barrak have many wives? A camel?

During my many meetings with Zainab and Barrak, our conversations inevitably turn to their frustrations over their limited finances and the lack of employment opportunities in America. "My daughter keeps asking when she can have this toy she saw in Walmart," Zainab says. "When we have money," Zainab tells her. They were a double-income family in Iraq, and being unable to buy things for their children is difficult to accept. They want to have a better life. They eventually want to buy a home.

"It is hard to be believed," Zainab says, referring to the treatment she and Barrak have received from some potential employers. They don't seem to appreciate the extensive professional experience they have in their respective fields. Barrak is a trained mechanical engineer with broad experience working on all types of machines. Yet, at the time of this writing, he is working as a general technician at a car dealership. Zainab has an impressive résumé and a binder full of certifications and honors from her previous jobs in Iraq, including a public relations job with the Ministry of Trade. She gets bored at home and would like to go back to work. She also loves to cook and dreams of one day opening her own catering company featuring Iraqi cuisine. The majority of refugees I know learned to cook from their mothers, but Zainab is self-taught. She began cooking when she was about fifteen years old. Zainab's mother worked full time, and on summer vacations, Zainab would surprise her with home-cooked meals. Sometimes Zainab would throw her unsuccessful dishes straight into the garbage, her family none the wiser.

Though money is tight and job opportunities are limited, Zainab and Barrak realize that America has many advantages over Iraq. The most obvious and important advantage is that they don't have to worry about direct attacks on their lives or witness human atrocities on a daily basis. "We saw everything," Zainab says. One day, while on security detail, Barrak came across a pile of dead bodies in a truck. One morning Zainab watched a man get shot in the middle of the street as he was on his way to his sister's house. The sister, like the other onlookers, watched helplessly, afraid of meeting the same violent fate.

One afternoon, Zainab invites me over to cook biryani—a common rice dish with endless variations in the Middle East, India, and nearby countries. It is one of Zainab and Barrak's favorites. Zainab moves with admirable ease and confidence in the kitchen. She boasts that she is a good cook—and she is right.

Zainab's version of biryani, served with a tangy tomato-based sauce on the side, is comparable to an exceptional batch of fried rice with all the trimmings, including shredded chicken, peas, fried potato chunks, toasted almonds, and hard-boiled eggs. She made this dish for sixty guests at her sister's wedding reception. This evening, to accompany our biryani, Zainab prepares a salad made with lettuce, corn, beets, and pickles and topped with freshly grated Parmesan. It looks as pretty as any dish featured in *Southern Living*.

After dinner, we watch a video of the couple's wedding day. In one clip, Zainab and Barrak are riding in a car down a rain-slicked highway.

But the rain doesn't seem to dampen the wedding party's spirits. In another clip, at the wedding reception at Zainab's mother's house, the bride and groom seem to be aglow in the security of their young love. My two friends point out family relations on the TV screen: Zainab's mother and sisters and Barrak's brothers. How bittersweet it must be for them to revisit that day, to see people and places now relegated to memory. Who would have guessed then that, years later and thousands of miles away, they would be building a new life together, once again.

Zainab's Chicken Biryani

Biryani comes from the Persian word berya, meaning "fried" or "roasted." It is believed that this rice-based dish originated in Persia or Turkey and was brought to India by Muslim travelers. It is most closely associated with Indian cuisine but is also popular in Iraq, Iran, Pakistan, and many other Asian countries. Common additions are meat, fish, eggs, spices, and vegetables. In Zainab's version, I particularly like the toasted almonds, which are often omitted in other biryani recipes, as well as the extra texture provided by the addition of pasta. It makes a great one-dish meal.

Because the recipe involves multiple steps and is usually doubled to feed many people, biryani is generally served on weekends and special occasions. This recipe should serve approximately 6 people, but as Zainab likes to joke, it all depends on who you're feeding (Iraqi males, for example, are well known for their hearty appetites).

Biryani spice mix can be found in Indian or Arabic stores or online. It commonly includes a mix of cardamom, cinnamon, cumin, cilantro, black pepper, and bay leaf.

Serves 6
Ready in about 1¾ hours

> 3 chicken breasts, skinless and boneless
> 3½ teaspoons salt (divided)
> 2 teaspoons ground black pepper (divided)

¼ teaspoon curry powder

3 cups basmati rice

Extra virgin olive oil or vegetable oil for frying

1 cup Fideo Cortado (Fino) pasta (or vermicelli, broken into
    ½-inch pieces)

3 tablespoons biryani spice blend

4 medium gold potatoes, peeled and diced

1 (10-ounce) bag frozen green peas

½ cup (2.25-ounce bag) sliced almonds

3 to 4 large eggs, hard-boiled and sliced

To Prepare the Chicken

In a large saucepan, add 5 cups water, chicken, ½ teaspoon salt, 1 teaspoon black pepper, and curry powder. (Zainab recommends that you don't boil the water before adding the chicken; she believes it makes the meat moister.) Boil the chicken for about 20 minutes, or until cooked through. Reserve the chicken broth and set aside. After the chicken cools, shred it and set it aside.

To Prepare the Rice-Pasta Mixture

Pour rice in a medium bowl and add just enough warm water to cover the rice. Soak for 20 to 30 minutes.

Meanwhile, pour about 5 tablespoons oil in a large saucepan and heat over medium-high heat. Add Fideo Cortado pasta and cook until golden brown, about 10 minutes, stirring often to avoid burning. Remove pan from heat and let the pasta cool.

Ladle out 3½ cups reserved chicken broth and add to the cooling pasta. Return pasta to the burner and cook over medium heat. Add 3 teaspoons salt (1 teaspoon for each cup of chicken broth). Add biryani spice blend and 1 teaspoon ground black pepper. Stir well.

After the rice has been soaked, drain it well and add it to the pasta mixture. Stir all ingredients until combined. Cover and cook over medium-low heat about 10 minutes, or until most of the water has evaporated, stirring occasionally to keep the rice from sticking to the bottom of the pan. Test the rice to make sure it is tender. Fluff. Lower the heat and keep the mixture warm and covered, stirring occasionally.

To Prepare the Vegetables

Fully coat a large frying pan with oil, about ¼ inch deep. Add diced potatoes to form one layer and fry them in the oil (divide into several batches, if necessary). When the potatoes are golden brown, remove them with a slotted spoon and drain on a plate lined with paper towels. Transfer to a medium bowl.

Cook the peas, following either stovetop or microwave directions, until soft. Drain the peas and add them to the potatoes in the medium bowl.

To Prepare the Almonds

In a small frying pan, heat 1 tablespoon vegetable oil over medium-high heat. Add sliced almonds and toast them until golden brown, stirring often to avoid overbrowning. Remove with a slotted spoon and drain on paper towels. Add to the potatoes and peas.

To Combine the Ingredients

In a large serving bowl, add the shredded chicken to the potatoes, peas, and almonds. Add the rice-pasta mixture and stir well. Top with sliced hard-boiled eggs. Serve warm with Zainab's Spicy Tomato Sauce.

Zainab's Spicy Tomato Sauce

This zesty tomato sauce can be used with a variety of dishes. Zainab tells me Iraqis sometimes serve it with white rice and white beans as a side dish or a light lunch. When serving the sauce with her biryani, Zainab prefers to keep it on the side, although it could be mixed into the dish before serving. I've tried it both ways and prefer it on the side as well.

Serves 6

3 tablespoons extra virgin olive oil or vegetable oil
1 (15-ounce) can tomato sauce

3 to 5 tablespoons hot pepper sauce (adjust amount according to
    taste)
2 garlic cloves, minced
½ teaspoon salt
Ground black pepper (to taste)
2 tablespoons dried parsley flakes

Coat the bottom of a small saucepan with oil and heat. Add tomato
sauce and hot pepper sauce. Cook over medium-high heat. Add minced
garlic, salt, black pepper, and parsley flakes. Stir well. Remove from heat
and pour into a serving dish or gravy bowl. Serve with Zainab's Biryani.

Belafia
(Iraqi-Arabic for bon appétit)

22

Democratic Republic of the Congo

Sarah Mbombo, August 3, 2012

"They don't have these where I'm from," Sarah Mbombo calls over the whirring of the food processor blades in her Lexington kitchen. It is a narrow, windowless room with bright artificial light and white unadorned walls, but Sarah's energetic personality fills the space with more warmth than any furnishing or decoration ever could. On this first official day of summer, Sarah is using her food processor—a gift from a Kentucky Refugee Ministries (KRM) volunteer—to puree bell peppers, hot peppers, garlic cloves, eggplant, and onions for cassava leaves, a popular stew from her part of Africa.

The women in Africa have to do everything manually, Sarah explains, and the work can be strenuous. To demonstrate this, she sits on an end table she has hauled into the kitchen from the living room and pretends to cook as African women and children do: hunched over huge pots and using all their might to stir. *Fufu*—another dish we are making today, and similar in appearance to mashed potatoes—is extremely difficult to stir in its final stages, particularly when making large batches. This is why the women in Africa are so physically strong, according to Sarah—because of all the cooking, cleaning, and other manual labor they do.

When we first met earlier in the day, Sarah, a beautiful young fashionista with high cheekbones and large eyes, told me her name means "mother of the nations." I said it was a name with power behind it. She smiled and flexed her arm muscles. I thought of the iconic "We Can Do It!" poster from the early 1940s, featuring a female factory worker in a red

"I want to be a nurse, and I want to work for the United Nations and help refugees."
—Sarah Mbombo

bandanna with rolled-up sleeves—an image long associated with female empowerment. The more I get to know Sarah, the more I realize just how fitting this image is.

Sarah was born in the Democratic Republic of the Congo (DRC), the largest country in sub-Saharan Africa and host to the bloodiest conflict since World War II, including more than 5 million estimated dead, according to the International Rescue Committee. Though one of the poorest countries in the world based on per capita gross domestic product, the DRC is one of the richest in natural resources: gold, copper, silver, diamonds, coal, timber, fertile farmland, and hydropower, to name a few. Sarah spent most of her life, however, in the relatively peaceful country of Zambia, the DRC's southern neighbor and home to the famous Victoria Falls (known locally as the "Smoke that Thunders").

Sarah takes a break from her story to add the pureed vegetables to the cassava leaves already boiling in a pot on the stove. She feels fortunate that she can find some of her native foods, such as cassava leaves, in a local African grocery store; however, she can't get them fresh, only frozen. In this form, they remind me of chopped frozen spinach. In fact, spinach can be used as a substitute if cassava leaves aren't available. The cassava root is more commonly consumed in Africa than its leaves, but in the DRC and Zambia, according to Sarah, the roots, stems, and leaves are all eaten, so none of the plant is wasted.

Sarah grabs another ingredient for the cassava leaves recipe—a can of sardines, which she struggles to open with a butcher knife. "Don't you have a can opener?" I ask, worried that she might slice her hand open. She laughs and says no, and I make a mental note to buy her one, maybe even an electric one, since she loves kitchen gadgets. The sardines, in a spicy tomato sauce, are added to the pot, along with peanut powder and palm oil—none of which I've ever cooked with. I can't wait to discover what this curious conglomeration of ingredients is going to taste like.

While the simmering cassava leaves fill the warm kitchen with a sweet-bitter aroma, Sarah continues to tell me what life is like for women in her part of the world. "Pretend you're the man," she says, and motions

Palm Oil

One thing I learned from cooking with Africans: they love their palm oil. It is made from the fruits of several types of palms. Indonesia and Malaysia are two of the largest producers.

The oil, which is reddish in color and semisolid at room temperature, can be found in many manufactured products—from packaged sweets such as chocolate bars to cleaning agents and cosmetics. Palm oil is high in saturated fats and presents some social and environmental concerns. It has been related to irresponsible cultivation practices, such as widespread deforestation that has threatened valuable plant and animal species, most notably the critically endangered orangutan. It should be noted, however, that some palm oil is produced from sustainable plantations.

On the plus side, the cheap and efficient production of palm oil is the main source of income and employment for many Southeast Asian, Central American, and Central and West African farmers. Additionally, the demand for palm oil is on the rise, partly because of its biodiesel and renewable energy possibilities.

Sarah used to cook with a lot of palm oil in Africa, where it was more affordable than other cooking oils. The reverse is true here in the United States, so Sarah has begun to use other cooking oils; however, she still uses palm oil in her cassava leaves recipe because she believes it enhances the flavor of the dish.

for me to sit on the end table. "Okay, now say, 'Bring me something to drink.'" I repeat the words, using the same commanding tone. She scrambles to the sink, her hands shaking with feigned nervousness, and fills a cup with water. She scurries over to me, head bowed in submission, and holds out the cup, curtsying. She straightens and laughs, slipping out of her obsequious role and returning to Sarah the strong, the mother of nations. "That's how it is in Africa," she says.

One of the things Sarah loves about America is that women and men are equal. "Here it's fifty-fifty," she says. However, she concedes that things are slowly starting to improve in Africa. For instance, women now have more opportunities to pursue a formal education. Even so, Sarah would take her independence in America over life in Africa any day. She loves being able to pay her own rent and provide for her own basic needs, thanks to a job she landed all by herself a few months after arriving in Lexington. She works in food services at the Campus Group at UK Hospital—a fitting job, since she loves to cook. She's also studying for her driver's license and wants to save enough money to buy a car. Those are just her short-term goals. Sarah has big dreams for her future. "I want to be a nurse, and I want to work for the United Nations and help refugees." And when she becomes a US citizen in a few years (another goal), she hopes her mother and father will be able to join her in America.

Sarah prefers that I not disclose why she went to a refugee camp in 2006 without her mother and father. But she willingly describes the conditions in the camp: no electricity, limited food with low nutritional value, and smelly water that damaged her skin and hair. She even contracted malaria. Periodically, she was able to visit her family, who lived in the town of Lusaka. But whenever she did, her mother wept over Sarah's appearance.

Sarah, an only child, and her parents used to pray every day that she would be allowed to immigrate to America. It was such a painfully slow process, however, that when she finally got the good news—seven years later—she had almost forgotten she had applied. How Sarah ended up alone in Kentucky, with only KRM as a support system, is another off-limits topic. Suffice it to say, she misses her parents very much and keeps in touch with them regularly via phone and Skype, using her new laptop—her first major purchase. She also uses her computer to stay updated on breaking news from her homeland. "People are dying every day," she says with disgust. "And for what?"

Perhaps it's noteworthy that almost every resettled refugee I've met in America has a computer, a cell phone, and a TV, even if they lived without these modern luxuries in their native countries. But in the States, these aren't luxuries; they're necessities—a vital way to stay connected to the larger world and to friends and family both here and abroad.

The cassava leaves are almost done cooking, and Sarah begins to prepare the fufu, our side dish. Fufu is the first dish she ever learned to cook from her mother. Sarah used to eat it every day in Africa and still has it several times a week in America. In a small pan, she blends the only two ingredients in the recipe—water and cornmeal. She lets me taste it in its porridge state. Hmm, it's a little like Cream of Wheat. Then she begins stirring nonstop, to avoid lumps, and she continually scrapes the sides of the pan so the fufu, which is turning gummy, doesn't stick. She makes it look effortless, but I can tell this is a recipe that might require some trial and error. As if reading my mind, Sarah tells me that the first batch of fufu she ever made, when she was only nine years old, didn't turn out well at all, but by batch number two, she had fufu down pat.

When we finally sit down at a small table in the dining area, I'm a little leery of the pea-green pile of mush on my plate. Sarah shows me the proper way to eat the cassava leaves—with the hands, by way of fufu. She tears off a small piece from the mound of fufu on her plate, rolls it into a ball between thumb and forefinger, and makes an indentation with her thumb, creating a hollow in which to scoop up the stew. She's a good teacher, and before long, I'm eating like the natives, as they say.

Cassava leaves might not win any "prettiest dish" awards, but what it lacks in appearance it makes up for in personality. What I love about this dish is the complexity of flavors. It's unlike anything I've ever tasted, with its slightly bitter, nutty, spicy hot, and salty flavor combination. Fufu, in contrast, is as bland as you might imagine, with its lack of seasonings. But this is as it should be. Fufu's purpose is more or less functional—not just as a type of utensil but also as a supporting player to the entree, similar to rice and bread in other cultures' cuisines.

After lunch, Sarah asks me to review her résumé. I'm impressed with how polished it is. I see that she speaks not only her native Lingala (a Bantu language spoken primarily in parts of Central Africa) but also French and three other languages. Even though she learned some English in high school, she took over 100 hours of ESL classes through KRM when she arrived in Lexington.

KRM, headquartered in Louisville, officially opened its Lexington suboffice in 1999, and Congolese have been resettling in the area since 2000. Today, Lexington is one of the largest resettlement sites for Congo-

The Curious Cassava Plant

Cassava (also known as yucca, manioc, and tapioca) is a staple in India and in some developing countries of Africa, South and Central America, and Southeast Asia. After rice and corn, it is the third largest source of carbohydrates in the tropics. Cassava constitutes the basic diet for more than half a billion people. It is also used for a variety of ailments in herbal medicine.

A woody shrub native to South America, cassava is drought-tolerant, making it a critical crop in times of famine. The cassava root can be eaten much like a potato: peeled and boiled, fried, or baked. Cassava flour, made from the cassava root, is gluten-free and is a good substitute for wheat flour. It is also used to make fufu, which many Africans eat on a daily basis. Although the cassava root is eaten in many parts of Africa, consumption of the cassava leaves, which are cooked like greens, is specific to certain regions, such as Central Africa. The leaves are boiled and cooked until tender. Frozen cassava leaves are available in many African, Asian, and even some American groceries and health-food stores or online. Spinach, kale, collards, and turnip greens make decent substitutes.

No part of the cassava should ever be eaten raw, as it contains small amounts of cyanogenic glucosides. It must be properly processed and cooked before consumption.

lese in the United States. KRM director Barbara Kleine tells me that the Lexington office resettles an average of 250 refugees per year from across the world. Other significant refugee populations in the area include those from Congo Brazzaville (Republic of the Congo), Bhutan, Burma, Bosnia, and Iraq.

Sarah goes to the back bedroom to fetch her ESL completion certificates to show me. From my own teaching experience, I know that earning a certificate is a huge confidence booster for students of English—tangible proof that they are making strides. I hear music playing down the hall. I can't place the melody, but it doesn't sound African or American or of any particular ethnic or national persuasion. It sounds peaceful, universal. "Aimee," Sarah says when she returns, becoming serious. "I want to one day stand up in front of people and give the testimony of my life." She pauses to collect her thoughts, then an all-knowing smile spreads across her face. "Here [in America], I can . . . I can *feel* it," she says. "I can make my dreams come true."

Sarah's Pondu (Cassava Leaves)

Pondu (also known as *saka-saka* and *mpondou*) is a popular dish in certain parts of the world, especially Central Africa. The stew generally consists of cassava leaves, eggplant, onions, galic, and hot peppers in a palm oil– and peanut butter–based sauce.

I had never heard of cassava leaves before cooking with Sarah, and I imagine I'm not the only one. When I went into an African grocery to purchase cassava leaves, an African customer at the counter said in astonishment, "How do you know about cassava leaves? Are you married to an African?" Though cassava leaves are always eaten fresh in Africa, in the United States they are usually available only frozen. You can find them at African, Asian, and some American markets, as well as at some health-food stores and online. Sarah uses the Kabeya brand.

This dish might not be much to look at, but don't be fooled by appearances. Take one bite, and you'll be hooked. Pondu has become a true comfort dish for me. I usually use a mix of spinach and kale or turnip greens and serve it over plain rice. I've also discovered that it makes a great appetizer dip, served warm with blue sesame chips.

Sarah uses peanut powder in her recipe, as she doesn't care for the full flavor of peanut butter. I had trouble finding the powder, however. What you want is a nutty flavor and a slight thickening agent for the sauce. Once I started experimenting with creamy and crunchy peanut butter combinations, the dish began to sing.

In Africa, pondu is often served without fish because of the cost, but a minnow-like fish called *ndakala*, sardines, or smoked fish are commonly added for special occasions. The fish adds a salty note and textural contrast to the dish, and I must say, I like it much more with the fish. You can find canned sardines or mackerel in spicy or plain tomato sauce (I prefer the spicy) in African and many American groceries. If you're using a fresh smoked fish, I suggest cutting it into bite-size pieces and adding a 15-ounce can of diced plain or spicy tomatoes. The acidity complements the dish.

Palm oil contributes more flavor to the dish, but canola and vegetable oil are fine substitutes. For extra heat, add another hot chili pepper or even cayenne or crushed red pepper.

Sarah uses a food processor to blend many of the ingredients in this recipe. You can save time by adding the chopped ingredients directly to the pot with the boiled cassava leaves. I find this version just as tasty, and I like the additional texture.

Serves 2 to 4
Ready in about 1 hour

> 2 (8-ounce) packages frozen cassava leaves or frozen chopped spinach, thawed, or 2 (6-ounce) bags fresh spinach leaves, kale, collard or turnip greens, or a mix of these
> ½ green bell pepper, chopped
> ½ large eggplant, skinned (optional), cut into small chunks
> 2 cloves garlic, minced
> 2 green (spring) onions, chopped
> ⅔ cup creamy and/or crunchy peanut butter
> 1 to 2 tablespoons palm oil (or vegetable or canola oil)
> 1 to 2 teaspoons salt
> 1 hot chili pepper, chopped
> 1 (15-ounce) can sardines in spicy (or regular) tomato sauce

In a medium saucepan, combine 1 to 1½ cups water with thawed cassava leaves (or other greens). Bring to a low boil over medium-high heat and cook for 10 to 15 minutes.

Add bell pepper, eggplant, garlic, and green onions to the pot. (Or puree them in a food processor and then add to the pot.) Stir to combine, and cook for about 10 minutes on medium-low heat. Add peanut butter and oil and stir until well combined with the other ingredients. Add salt and hot chili pepper to taste. Stir. Add sardines in tomato sauce.

Continue cooking on a low boil, partially covered with a tilted lid, for 30 to 45 minutes. (If you're using cassava leaves, cook for 45 minutes to 1 hour.) Check the stew periodically, stirring to keep the mixture from sticking to the bottom of the pan and adding small amounts of water as necessary so the sauce maintains a gravy-like consistency. (When the heavy vegetative smell burns off, the dish is usually ready, according to Sarah.) Serve with fufu, rice, or bread. This dish reheats well in the microwave.

Sarah's Fufu

This recipe might win an award for the fewest ingredients—and the best arm workout. Fufu by itself is bland and looks like mashed potatoes, but it has a thicker, stickier texture. Fufu and dishes like it are Africa's equivalent to rice and bread.

Fufu is a sticky dough-like dish made by pounding or mashing a starchy food (such as cassava or corn) and mixing the processed starchy food (flour) in hot water. In Sarah's region of Africa, cassava flour, corn flour, or a combination of the two is traditionally used to make fufu. Since cassava flour isn't readily available in the United States (and is harder to work with, according to several Africans I know), Sarah uses a finely ground (not coarse) white or yellow cornmeal.

This traditional African dish is eaten daily, or sometimes even multiple times a day. Similar dishes go by different names in different parts of the world and might be made with other types of starch (plantains, yams, cocoyam). Like *ugali*, served in the African Great Lakes region and southern parts of Africa, fufu is almost always eaten with the hands. A small piece is torn off from the fufu mound and rolled into a small ball, which is used to scoop up the main dish it accompanies, such as a stew or a soup.

Of all my cooking adventures for this book, fufu turned out to be my nemesis—which is fairly embarrassing, considering it has only two ingredients and takes just 15 minutes to make. The key, they say, is to stir, stir, stir as you're adding the flour (cornmeal) to the water. Actually, you need to stir until your arm muscle burns. Lumps commonly form during the stirring process, but the key is to break them apart with a large wooden spoon, mashing them against the bottom and sides of the pan with a scooping rather than a stirring motion, before adding more cornmeal.

It seems that everyone has a different method of making fufu: add flour to boiling water; make a paste of water and flour first, then add the paste to boiling water; cook over low heat; cook over high heat. And don't get me started on types of flour and flour-to-water ratios.

Like any good nemesis, fufu has my full respect, as do the Africans who make it without batting an eye (or straining a muscle). If you're not up to the challenge of making fufu from scratch, there are some popular premade fufu flour mixes (often made from plantains or yams) available in African and some specialty markets.

Serves 1 to 2
Ready in about 15 minutes

> 2⅔ cups water (more as needed)
> 1 to 1⅓ cups fine white or yellow cornmeal or cassava flour (more or less as needed)

In a medium saucepan, bring water to a low boil. Add cornmeal *very slowly* in small increments, stirring continuously with a large wooden spoon and mashing any lumps that form, until a porridge or polenta consistency is achieved. Slowly add more cornmeal until the fufu becomes a bit thicker than mashed potatoes. Cook for 3 to 4 minutes, adding more flour or water as needed, stirring nonstop to avoid lumps and to prevent the fufu from sticking to the pan. The finished consistency should be thick, slightly gummy or tacky, and difficult to stir.

Remove the pan from the heat (the fufu will continue to thicken as it cools). Stir some more, scraping the sides of the pan and making sure the fufu is well combined and has achieved the desired consistency.

Scoop out the fufu with a ½-cup round measuring cup, level it off, and then turn it over onto a serving platter or individual plate. Serve as a side dish to stew, soup, or anything with a gravy or a sauce, such as Sarah's Pondu (Cassava Leaves) or Aline and Genevieve's Matoke (Banana Stew) (see chapter 13).

Bon appétit
(this French expression for "Enjoy your meal" is also used in the DRC)

23

Cuba

Omar Pernet Hernández, September 1, 2012

After class is dismissed and the other students have left the room, Omar Pernet Hernández calls me over to his chair. He pulls a Cuban flag out of his book bag, unwraps it slowly and respectfully, and retrieves from its folds several old letters, photographs, and a medal. In one of the photographs, a group of people is assembled around a large oval table.

"Wait," I say, "is that President George W. Bush, Omar?"

"*Sí.*"

"And is that *you* at the head of the table, Omar?"

"*Sí, sí.*"

In another picture, Omar is with the same group of people, and the Statue of Liberty is in the background. And there he is again, this time posing with President and Mrs. Bush.

"Omar, explain this, *por favor!*"

The pictures had been taken on September 23, 2008, when Omar was still living in Spain. A small group of activists from countries with repressive governments had been invited to a Freedom Agenda lunch on Governors Island in New York during meetings of the UN General Assembly. They had been asked to share their heroic tales and discuss how to better promote liberty. But how had Omar been selected to participate in this event? He looks at me, smiles smugly, and says, "I am universal."

Omar grew up in a poor household in Las Villas (now Villa Clara) in central Cuba. At a young age, to help put food on the table, he performed odd

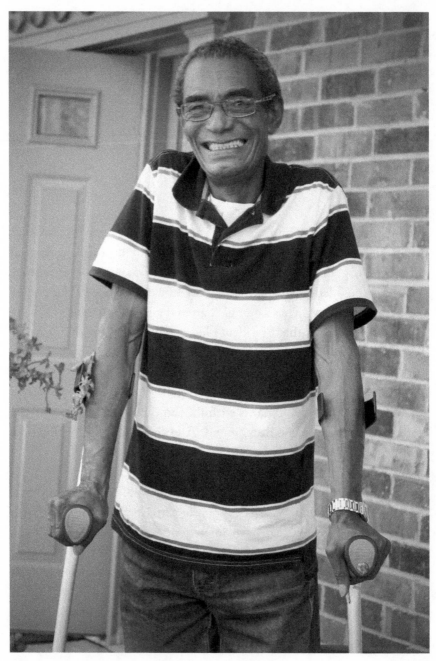

"Castro called me a counterrevolutionary. But I represent the new revolution." —Omar Pernet Hernández (Photo by Julie Johnston)

jobs, including shoe repair and door-to-door sales. He went to a Catholic school and received a high school education. When he turned eighteen, he refused to fulfill his obligatory military service and was sent to jail. Thus, Omar the activist was born.

Throughout his lifetime, Omar has served four separate prison sentences—a total of twenty-two years. If you ask him why he went to prison, he says, "Always to defend human rights." Once, teasing, I asked Omar, who has three grown children, how he had time to make babies when he spent so much time in jail. He chuckled and said, "I married young."

Even in jail, Omar's voice couldn't be silenced. He occasionally went on hunger strikes and refused to wear the prison uniform for criminals because, to his mind, he had committed no crime. Instead, he wore the yellow uniform for political prisoners. He wrote political statements on scraps of paper and handed them off to trusted visitors, and some of these statements were apparently printed in European and American publications.

When Omar wasn't serving time in jail, he worked as a welder and operated an independent "library" called May 20, named after the day Cuba gained independence from the United States in 1902. Independent libraries like Omar's, my Cuban sources tell me, are usually small underground operations dedicated to disseminating censored works. One of Omar's favorite authors is José Martí, a Cuban poet and leader of the Cuban independence movement of the late 1800s. Although Cuba has an impressive adult literacy rate of almost 100 percent, Cubans lack access to the Internet, cell phones, and any material or literature that is considered antigovernment.

Omar founded and is still considered the international representative of Cuba's unofficial national human rights movement, created in honor of Mario Manuel de la Peña. Peña, an American pilot born to Cuban parents, voluntarily flew search-and-rescue missions to save Cuban rafters. He died when Cuban MiGs shot down his plane. When I ask Omar what year Peña died (1996), his activist spirit flares. He raises his voice and pumps his fist in the air: "He didn't die. He was *assassinated*."

Omar's independent library and his involvement with his human rights organization eventually led to another imprisonment in early 2003—part of the "Black Spring" roundup of Cuban dissidents that sent about seventy-five journalists and grassroots democracy and human rights activists to prison. Omar was sentenced to an astounding twenty-five-year prison term.

In 2004 Omar was hurt in a terrible automobile accident while being transported from one prison to another. The details surrounding the accident are sketchy, but Omar was in intensive care for many days and had to undergo more than a year of rehabilitation. As a result of the accident, he still requires crutches to get around today.

One day Omar entered my classroom and said, "Today, teacher, I am sad."

"Why, Omar?"

He ran his fingers under his eyes and down his cheeks, mimicking tears. In his limited English, he communicated that he missed his family and friends back in Cuba.

Another day Omar came into the classroom smiling from ear to ear. "Teacher, today, I am happy."

"Why, Omar?"

Laying aside his crutches, he pointed to his bad leg and gave an "okay" sign, indicating he was pain free.

"The things we take for granted," I said to my teaching assistant.

On February 16, 2008, Omar finally caught one of the biggest breaks of his life when he and some of the other Black Spring dissidents, whom Amnesty International had designated "prisoners of conscience," were released from jail and exiled to Spain. Omar liked Spain, but it had always been his hope to live in the United States because, at his core, he identified himself as an American. He now enjoys the basic freedoms that were denied him for so long.

But Omar's situation raises an interesting philosophical question: What *is* true freedom? What is the point of the pursuit of happiness when happiness is dependent, at least for Omar, on family and loved ones? "I don't know when I can see my family again," he says. "It is very hard for me. Some days I come into the house and close the door and cry."

Omar sets the table for a traditional Cuban meal with his new family in the United States.

Omar, like other refugees and immigrants, has had to build a new network of friends, a surrogate family, here in America. I have the privilege of meeting some of Omar's chosen family when I visit his apartment one Sunday afternoon to cook with him. Omar's Cuban friend Lazaro, a stocky and amiable man, is helping Omar prepare several dishes simultaneously in the kitchen. At one point, there is so much heat from a steaming pressure cooker, a rice cooker, and a simmering *sofrito* (sauce) on the stovetop that my interpreter Robin and I slip outside to get some air. As we sip on cold *cervezas*, we decide we could get used to a couple of gentlemen cooking for us while we relax on the sidelines.

Omar claims he isn't a cook, but after seeing him in action, I beg to differ. He peels, chops, sautés, and serves like an entertainment guru. He seems to get pleasure from cooking, or at least from the companionship of cooking and sharing a meal with others. The men don't just cook for us, however. They provide a feast: fried plantain slices to tide us over, followed by a meal of perfectly seasoned rice and beans, slow-cooked pork, mixed salad topped with Florida avocados and juicy tomatoes, and, to top it all off, a syrupy sweet mango dessert balanced with a mild, soft white cheese.

Omar plays some Spanish music on his cell phone, puts aside his crutches, and shows me some salsa moves in slow motion. He closes his eyes, lost in the music and the rhythm. For a moment in time, I see a look of carefree abandon and peace wash over Omar's face, revealing the man he could have been, or perhaps the man he once was, in another time and place.

Although his brave fight to defend human rights and end oppression has cost him a lot—his health, his family, his homeland—Omar has no regrets. Nor has he lost any love for his native Cuba. However, he feels repugnance for the government. "Castro called me a counterrevolutionary," Omar once said. "But I represent the new revolution."

Omar's Tostones (Twice-Fried Green Plantains)

Tostones (toes-TOE-nays) are a popular side dish in Cuba, Latin American countries, and the Caribbean. It is believed that the tostone tradition originated with African slaves. Tostones (from the Spanish *tostar*, "to toast") are fried twice, salted, and eaten like french fries or potato chips.

I found some recipes that said tostones are often served with a garlic dipping sauce (*mojo*), but three Cubans I spoke to said tostones are traditionally served plain, just as Omar made them for me. Nevertheless, feel free to serve them with a dipping sauce of your choice.

To peel a green plantain, cut off the top and bottom and score a line along the length of the plantain. Lifting up from this line, remove the peel (use a knife to help if necessary).

Serves 4 (makes about 20 to 25 pieces)
Ready in about 30 minutes

> Vegetable or canola oil for deep-frying
> 3 green (unripe) plantains, peeled and sliced into ¾- to 1-inch
>   rounds
> Salt or sea salt
> Fresh ground pepper (optional)

Fill a large skillet about ¼ full with oil and heat over medium-high heat. When the oil is hot enough to pop, carefully add plantains in a single layer (this will take a couple of batches). Fry the plantains until they're cooked halfway through and slightly brown (5 to 6 minutes), turning once with a slotted spatula.

Transfer the plantains to a plate lined with paper towels. Keep the oil in the skillet heated. With the bottom of a glass or a can, smash the plantains to about half their thickness.

Carefully return the plantains to the oil and fry again, turning occasionally, until golden brown on both sides.

Transfer back to the paper towel–lined plate. Sprinkle with salt and pepper to taste. Serve warm as an appetizer or as a side dish. Tostones are best when eaten warm and fresh.

Omar's Ensalada Mixta (Mixed Salad)

This is a very easy, traditional Cuban salad. Omar punctures the skin of the cucumber down all sides with the tines of a fork before slicing, which adds a decorative flourish. Other toppings can include olives, green beans, asparagus tips, sliced hard-boiled eggs, artichoke hearts, corn, and sliced red onion.

Another common (and yummy) dressing for *ensalada mixta* is a fresh cilantro-lime vinaigrette. To make it, mix ¼ cup olive oil, ¼ cup lime juice (from 1 medium lime), ⅛ cup chopped fresh cilantro, and salt and pepper to taste.

Serves 6

Salad

1 head iceberg lettuce, chopped

1 cucumber, thinly sliced

2 ripe medium tomatoes, thinly sliced

1 large avocado (preferably Florida), peeled and sliced into 2-inch
   segments

Dressing

⅛ to ¼ cup white distilled or apple cider vinegar

⅛ to ¼ cup olive oil

Salt and pepper to taste

Place the chopped lettuce on a large serving platter. Top with cucumbers, tomatoes, avocados, and any other toppings you like. Combine the dressing ingredients in a small bowl and drizzle over the salad just before serving. Serve at room temperature or chilled.

Omar's Dulce de Mango (Mango Dessert)

Knowing that I love mangoes, Omar made this dessert especially for me when I visited. His version of this common dish, found throughout Latin America, is served in a bowl and has a consistency similar to stewed apples. However, *dulce de mango* (DOOL-say day MANG-go) can also be made with pureed mangoes placed in a mold and refrigerated to produce a firm paste. Either version is wonderful paired with a slice of semisoft white cheese. Cubans also serve dulce de mango on crackers, breads, or cookies.

In Omar's easy recipe, the mango pits are not wasted. It is considered perfectly acceptable for the lucky guests who find the pits to pick them up with their fingers and suck off the fruit.

I think 1 cup sugar (or even less) is sufficient for this recipe, although Omar uses a full 2 cups.

I love this dish served warm with a scoop of caramel ice cream and topped with an extra dash of cinnamon. It could also be modified into a fruit crisp or cobbler.

Serves 4
Ready in about 1 to 1½ hours

4 ripe mangoes (including pits), peeled, washed, and sliced into
    long segments
1 cinnamon stick
1 to 2 cups sugar

Place mango segments and pits in a medium saucepan. (Discard any brown, rotten sections.) Add enough water to almost cover the mangoes. Heat over medium-high heat until boiling. Simmer for 10 to 15 minutes. Add cinnamon stick. Stir, lower heat to medium, and cook, covered, for 30 to 35 minutes, or until mangoes have softened.

Add 1 cup sugar, stir, and taste. If desired, add more sugar. Stir and cook on medium heat, uncovered, for an additional 20 minutes, or until the mixture has thickened. (You can drain off excess liquid to achieve a thicker syrup consistency.)

Transfer to a serving bowl and serve slightly warm, at room temperature, or chilled. Serve plain or with ice cream, cheese, or an accompaniment of your choice. Refrigerate leftovers.

¡Que le aproveche!
(Spanish for "Enjoy your meal!")

Afterword

When I look around my kitchen today, more than two years after I began this journey, I hardly recognize it: a double-stacked Turkish teapot sits on my stove, there's a rice cooker on my storage shelf, and my refrigerator and pantry are full of ingredients I had never heard of before, let alone cooked with. My tastes have changed too. I knew, going into this project, that I would encounter dishes I liked—perhaps even loved. Little did I know that I would actually *crave* many of them, my friends' comfort foods becoming my own. (Even as I'm writing this, I'm craving CoCo Tran's green curry soup.) Not only have I discovered flavors, dishes, and culinary techniques and traditions that were previously "foreign" to me, but I have also witnessed firsthand how the offering and sharing of food can transcend language and other boundaries and ultimately remind us of the rich cultural heritage we each bring to the table.

Someone recently asked me a difficult question: "What will you take away from writing this book?" I have learned countless lessons from my time spent with refugees. For starters, I've learned the importance of slowing down and simplifying, of embracing the unknown, of maintaining a hopeful and resilient spirit in times of adversity, of doing more and complaining less, and of always being grateful—especially for my most basic freedoms. But even more than these life lessons, more than the food and the fellowship, refugees have taught me about hospitality. No one does hospitality like refugees, perhaps because so many of them know what it's like to be without a home, to live under the most wretched conditions and in the most inhospitable of environments. If you enter a refugee's home, be prepared to be greeted with open arms and to eat well.

Refugees' hospitality, however, extends far beyond the role of host in their own homes. Refugees tend to be very generous (and loyal) to the communities that have embraced them. This might involve speaking to groups and sharing their stories of faith and survival, contributing to the local economy and workforce, volunteering their time, donating their hard-earned dollars, or, as this book illustrates, leaving their distinctive marks on the foodways of the communities they now call home.

I hope opportunities like the one that prompted this book—potlucks where people from radically different cultures and backgrounds share their native foods—will continue and spread throughout Kentucky and this country. (Many communities, organizations, and churches already host international events honoring immigrants and their cultures.) I hope people will discover for themselves how the simple act of breaking bread can serve as an entry point, a catalyst for further communion and a deeper understanding among people of every race, creed, color, and nationality.

I also hope that *Flavors from Home* has captured the brave, pioneering spirit on which this great nation was—and continues to be—built and will in some way add to the evolving definition of American cuisine and what it means to be an American.

Acknowledgments

It has been my pleasure, my joy, and often my saving grace to work with the fascinating people featured in this book. To be able to share their brave and inspiring journeys and the foods that nourish them physically, emotionally, and spiritually has been an honor. To these refugees and all the refugees and immigrants I have worked with over the years who helped shape my ideas, influenced *Flavors from Home*, and made me a better, stronger person, I owe so much more than mere thanks.

How this book came into being, I once told someone, was like driving down a long, heavily traveled road and hitting every green light. That's not to say I didn't encounter a fair share of speed bumps and potholes, but my path was routinely made easier thanks to the helping, guiding hands of so many:

Kentucky Foundation for Women, which provided a generous grant to get me on my way; the staff of the University Press of Kentucky, particularly David Cobb and my editor extraordinaire Ashley Runyon, who believed in this project from the get-go, and the press's peer reviewers; Catholic Charities Migration and Refugee Services (especially Darko Mihaylovich, Chris Clements, Lauren Goldberg, Robbie Adelberg, Laura Peot, Sara Renn, and Adam Clark); Kentucky Refugee Ministries (especially Elizabeth Kaznak, Barbara Kleine, Staci Kottkamp, Allison Schumacher, Lee Welsh, Abby Webb, Jenny Johnson, and all my coworkers and students at the Refugee Elder Program); International Center of Kentucky (especially Albert Mbanfu and Martha Little); the staff and my mentors from Spalding University's MFA program, including Julie Brickman, Kathleen Driskell, Kirby Gann, Silas House, Robin Lippincott, Karen Mann, Sena Jeter Naslund, Neela Vaswani, and Katy Yocom; St. Francis of Assisi School (especially Fred Whittaker); and *Edible Louisville* for first publishing a version of Amina Osman's story.

All the manuscript reviewers, recipe testers, and other project supporters and consultants: Tricia Barry Biagi, Kathleen and Jim Blevins, Olga Bocharova, Julie Borders, the Boyd family, Lisa and Lilly Crawford, Kim Crum, David Dominé, Pat and Sally Galla, Jud Hendrix, Jason Howard, Bonnie Omer Johnson, Linda Korfhage, Surekha Kulkarni, Judy Lippman, Carmen Marti, Janna McMahan, Frank Miller, Michelle Miller, Peggy Miller, Jayne Myers, Bob and Dee Orendorf, Cesar Perez-Ribas, Karen Portelli, Terry Price, Conchita Recio, Bev Rohmann, Dave Ronning, Mark and Brooklynn Rose, Jane and Ralph Ross, Clarissa Umuhoza, Ashley Urjil-Mills, Maurine Waterhouse, Anna Weldy, Sue McNally Wray, and Rob Zaring.

To those who saved my hide on a continual basis, particularly in the final stages of manuscript preparation, I owe you big time: Verna Austen, Shelley Bales, Paul Hiers, Matt Jaeger, and Paula Matthews.

I thank Mirzet Mustafić, Abdulah Rastoder, Lamia Shnawa, and Hiba Shnawa for providing individual photos. And I am grateful to my indispensable interpreters: Robin Bensinger, Oma Kafley, Mukhtar Ahmed, Marcel Nkwiyinka, Sylvian Mulinda, Mya Zaw, Teresa Pacheco, and the featured cooks' family members who assisted in interpreting or translating.

To Julie Johnston, my copilot and biggest "fan," who gave me the courage to take the leap of faith to write this book and who snapped almost half the pictures in these pages—you get a line all to yourself.

To these and all the people who cheered me on at critical points along my journey and without whom I would never have crossed the finish line, I love and appreciate every one of you.

Appendix

Fast Facts about Refugees

- The Refugee Act, passed by Congress in 1980, defines a refugee as any person who is outside their country of residence or nationality, or without nationality, and who is unable or unwilling to return to that country because of persecution or a well-founded fear of persecution based on race, religion, nationality, membership in a particular social group, or political opinion.

- At the time of this writing, there are about 15.4 million refugees in the world, according to the United Nations High Commissioner for Refugees (UNHCR).

- Only about 1 percent of the world's refugees are resettled in a third country (the second country being the first country of asylum). According to the US Department of State, the United States resettles over half of these refugees, more than all the other resettlement countries combined.

- Each year the president authorizes the admission of a set number of refugees into the United States, based on consultations with Congress and several federal agencies. Since 1975, the United States has resettled about 3 million refugees, approximately 77 percent of them from Indochina or the former Soviet Union. Annual admissions have ranged from a high of approximately 207,100 in 1980 to a low of 27,100 in 2002, according to the Office of Refugee Resettlement.

- The process for obtaining refugee status and applying for relocation usually begins with an individual applying to the UNHCR in the country to which he or she has fled. The UNHCR determines whether the person qualifies as a refugee, then works toward the best durable solution: safe return to the home country, local integration, or third-country resettlement.

• Refugees must undergo a thorough interview, medical screening, and security clearance process before they are allowed into the United States.

• The goal of the United States' Refugee Resettlement Program is early financial self-sufficiency in every refugee household (provided the household has at least one employable person).

• Resettlement agencies must provide certain core services to refugees, including assistance in the following areas: temporary housing, job placement, health screenings and immunizations, access to social services and community resources, applying for Social Security cards, school enrollment, and English language training.

• Refugees must be met at the airport by a representative of the sponsoring agency and taken to their new residence, which must be equipped with basic furnishings, culturally appropriate and ready-to-eat food (or a food allowance), suitable clothing for the season, cooking and eating utensils, toiletries, and cleaning supplies.

• The cost of each refugee's transportation to the United States is covered by a loan. Refugees are required to start paying off this loan after they establish themselves.

• One year after arriving in the United States, refugees must apply for a green card (permanent residence status). After five full years of living in the United States, refugees are eligible to apply for US citizenship.

• Kentucky officially began resettling refugees in 1975 when the Archdiocese of Louisville, which had been informally assisting refugees through individual parishes, assigned resettlement duties to Catholic Charities. In 1992 Kentucky terminated its state Office of Refugee Resettlement, and Catholic Charities took its place as the state refugee coordinator. The Kentucky Office for Refugees (KOR) was established in 2006 as a department of Catholic Charities. It administers and awards federal funds from the Office of Refugee Resettlement. Catholic Charities also represents the US Conference of Catholic Bishops in Kentucky.

• Kentucky Refugee Ministries (KRM) officially opened in 1990 and is headquartered in Louisville; it has a suboffice in Lexington. It is the refugee resettlement office in Kentucky for two national church-based programs: Episcopal Migration Ministries and Church World Service.

• The International Center of Kentucky, a nonprofit organization assisting immigrants and refugees primarily in western Kentucky, opened in 1979. It is headquartered in Bowling Green and has a satellite office in Owensboro.

• Other organizations that provide support for international families include the Louisville Metro Government's Office for Globalization, Louisville's Americana Community Center, and many other groups and churches throughout Kentucky.

To learn more about refugees or how you can become a volunteer or make a donation, please contact a refugee resettlement agency in your area. Resettlement agencies in Kentucky include the following:

Catholic Charities Migration and Refugee Services
    2220 West Market Street
    Louisville, KY 40212
    (502) 636-9263

Kentucky Refugee Ministries
Louisville office:
    969B Cherokee Road
    Louisville, KY 40204
    (502) 479-9180

Appendix

Lexington office:
    1206 North Limestone
    Lexington, KY 40505
    (859) 226-5661

International Center of Kentucky
Bowling Green office:
    806 Kenton Street
    Bowling Green, KY 42101
    (270) 781-8336
Owensboro office:
    233 West 9th Street
    Owensboro, KY 42303
    (270) 683-3423

Selected Bibliography

Alford, Jeffrey, and Naomi Duguid. *Flatbreads and Flavors: A Baker's Atlas*. New York: William Morrow, 1995.

Asia Institute—Crane House. *Bhutan: The Cloud Kingdom*. Louisville, KY: Asia Institute—Crane House, 2012.

Barsness, Sarah, ed. *Making West Home in Idaho: Stories and Recipes from Boise's Refugee Community*. Elko, NV: Western Folklife Center, 2010.

Duguid, Naomi. *Burma: Rivers of Flavor*. New York: Artisan, 2012.

Hemphill, Ian. *The Spice and Herb Bible*, 2nd ed. Toronto: Robert Rose, 2006.

Jaffrey, Madhur. *From Curries to Kebabs: Recipes from the Indian Spice Trail*. New York: Clarkson Potter/Publishers, 2003.

Knipple, Paul, and Angela Knipple. *The World in a Skillet: A Food Lover's Tour of the New American South*. Chapel Hill: University of North Carolina Press, 2012.

Lee, Edward. *Smoke and Pickles: Recipes and Stories from a New Southern Kitchen*. New York: Artisan, 2013.

Lee Kong, Aliya. *Exotic Table: Flavors, Inspiration, and Recipes from around the World—To Your Kitchen*. Avon, MA: Adams Media, 2013.

Index of Recipes by Country

Index of Recipes by Country

General Index

CPSIA information can be obtained
at www.ICGtesting.com
Printed in the USA
BVHW01s1142161217
502764BV00002B/3/P